PRICED OUT

# Priced Out

*Stuyvesant Town and the Loss of*
*Middle-Class Neighborhoods*

Rachael A. Woldoff
Lisa M. Morrison
Michael R. Glass

NEW YORK UNIVERSITY PRESS
*New York and London*

NEW YORK UNIVERSITY PRESS
New York and London
www.nyupress.org

The views expressed are those of the authors and are not necessarily those of the United Nations.

References to Internet websites (URLs) were accurate at the time of writing. Neither the author nor New York University Press is responsible for URLs that may have expired or changed since the manuscript was prepared.

Library of Congress Cataloging-in-Publication Data
Names: Woldoff, Rachael, author. | Morrison, Lisa M., author. | Glass, Michael R., author.
Title: Priced out : Stuyvesant Town and the loss of middle-class neighborhoods / Rachael A. Woldoff, Lisa M. Morrison, and Michael R. Glass.
Description: New York : New York University Press, [2016] | Includes bibliographical references and index.
Identifiers: LCCN 2015043169 | ISBN 9781479812462 (cl : alk. paper) |
ISBN 9781479818631 (pb : alk. paper)
Subjects: LCSH: Housing—New York (State)—New York—Case studies. | Rent control—New York (State)—New York—Case studies. | Mixed-income housing—New York (State)—New York—Case studies. | Housing development—New York (State)—New York—Case studies. | Neighborhoods—New York (State)—New York—Case studies. | Middle class—New York (State)—New York—Case studies.
Classification: LCC HD7304.N5 W65 2016 | DDC 307.3/36097471—dc23
LC record available at http://lccn.loc.gov/2015043169

New York University Press books are printed on acid-free paper, and their binding materials are chosen for strength and durability. We strive to use environmentally responsible suppliers and materials to the greatest extent possible in publishing our books.

Manufactured in the United States of America

10 9 8 7 6 5 4 3 2 1

Also available as an ebook

# CONTENTS

# ACKNOWLEDGMENTS

We would like to thank our families for their support. This research project would not have been possible without the encouragement and assistance of Rob Litchfield. We are grateful for your honesty, encouragement, insights, and your critical mind. You have been our trusted listener, reader, and editor, and have graciously been the sounding board for every idea, debate, and revision. We have been fortunate to have you nurturing and pushing us.

We are also grateful for the effort and interest of our research assistants, Kent Hastings, Megan Nicholson, Miranda Riffle, Amira Samuel, Jordan Steinfeld, and Alixandra Tate. We thank Daniel May of the MetLife Archives for his assistance with historical documents and images pertaining to Stuyvesant Town. We also appreciate the assistance of the curators at the New York University Public Library's Archives and Manuscripts collection and for their help with accessing the Robert Moses papers.

We extend thanks to the community of colleagues who were very helpful throughout the research and writing process, offering encouragement, providing feedback, engaging in insightful discussions, and sharing their support. We thank Manuel Aalbers, Charles Bagli, and Desiree Fields for their helpful comments on aspects of this research. We are especially grateful to Katrin Anacker, Ylana Beller, and Jerry Krase, whose careful reading and advice greatly improved the manuscript. We are so fortunate to have generous colleagues who share our passion for neighborhoods and cities and who cheer us on so we may improve our work.

We want to thank our editor from New York University Press. Ilene Kalish was enthusiastic about this study at an early stage in the process, and provided practical guidance toward the end. Karen Verde copyedited the book, and Robert Swanson indexed the content. We also thank the anonymous reviewers, as well as Sharon Zukin, who conducted an early and enthusiastic review of the book and offered useful suggestions.

Above all, we wish to express our deepest gratitude to the residents of Stuy Town, past and present, for sharing their time and stories.

# ABBREVIATIONS

ANCHOR  Alliance for Neighborhood Commerce, Homeownership, and Revitalization

EPCA  Emergency Price Control Act

ETPA  Emergency Tenant Protection Act

HCR  (New York) Homes and Community Renewal

IAI  Individual Apartment Improvement

MCI  Major Capital Improvements

MHP  MacCracken Housing Program

NORC  Naturally Occurring Retirement Communities

NYCHA  New York City Housing Authority

NYU  New York University

PAR  Petition for Administrative Review

RCL  Redevelopment Companies Law

SCRIE  Senior Citizen Rent Increase Exemption

# Introduction

## *The Transformation of Stuyvesant Town*

When the war was over there was absolutely no housing for the veterans. Most of my friends either lived with parents or in-laws, and Herschel and I lived in an unfurnished room with one of my mother's neighbors who had a two-bedroom apartment, and one of the rooms was empty. We had a bed, a hamper, and a chest. That was it. My mother lived on the second floor. I ate there, showered there, and did everything there for just one room to sleep in. Then they built Stuy Town, and you had to apply for it. You could only be a veteran to move in. One of my neighbors moved in with her son. He was in the Navy, so he got the apartment, and his parents were able to live with him. Now, they take *anybody*. Kids from college? They take this room, and they divide it.
—Ruthie Goldblum, longtime resident, aged eighty-five[1]

I think my rent is going to keep going up. We tried to negotiate the rent and were told that they *don't* negotiate. Probably about two to three weeks ago [in June 2011], I was walking past the leasing office on First Avenue, and I noticed that it was packed full of people. There were so many people there that people were standing, and it was a Saturday, which I just thought was strange because I'd never seen it that full. So I think demand is up for Stuy Town, and I think a lot of people are interested in moving in. It obviously helps that every single apartment has, or most apartments have, marble countertops, and there's dishwashers, and everything just looks a lot more suburban than other typical New York City apartments. So I think, if anything, these people moving in is just going to make the prices go up, because they know that if you're not willing to pay, someone else is going to move right in. And if it's two people sharing it—which a lot of times they have parents helping them out—it's not going to be a problem to split $2,500 in rent.
—Jackie Sabatino, market-rate resident, aged twenty-eight

The first thing you see when you walk out of Stuyvesant Town's red brick tower apartment buildings on a Sunday morning is the odd mix of people who share this community. Wait a bit longer, and the clash of cultures that now characterize modern Stuyvesant Town become apparent. Walking along the landscaped paths and taking in the quiet, park-like setting, birds chirp as the early risers—typically, white professionals in their 20s, 30s, and 40s—walk their dogs or take a run, and on weekdays, they rush off to work. Weekday mornings are far busier, as a cluster of parents hurry to get their children to school on time, and then hurry to their jobs.

But on this Sunday, it is quiet as a mother of two quickly pushes a bright orange, sporty double-stroller toward a sprinkler-filled playground, offering her children some relief from the oppressive heat and a chance to play before the shade recedes behind the surrounding buildings. Continuing along the winding paths, you see merchants from the farmers' market unpacking boxes of produce on the walkway between two of Stuyvesant Town's community focal points: the large central lawn called "the Oval," and the "clock playground," which has a prominent clock feature on the jungle gym, as well as a swing set, a fire truck, and play houses. Three other playgrounds circle the Oval, one with Astroturf that converts to an ice rink in the winter, and two asphalt playgrounds. The Oval also has a large fountain and includes upscale amenities that cater to newer residents, such as a café, a lounge, and an indoor kids' play space. At one time this area also held a film screening room, but it closed after flood damage caused by Hurricane Sandy. It has since reopened as a membership-based location for children's events and fitness classes.

A tall lamppost is covered with a collage of advertisements. Upon closer look, the bright posts are not ads of the variety commonly seen in New York City, such as those advertising sales, arts events, or activist messages; instead, they recall the bulletin boards found on college campuses. In one, a tenant is trying to sell a futon and some used IKEA furniture—items unlikely to belong to, or garner interest from, the more stable, longer-term residents of Stuyvesant Town. The other flyers publicize a free outdoor screening of a comedy entitled *Mall Cop* at an event called "Movies on the Oval," a call for participation in various sports teams (for a $250 sign-up fee), and a free DJ concert at "Music on the Oval"—all to be held on Stuyvesant Town's quad-like outdoor field.

Walking along the path that encircles the Oval lawn, a different group of Stuyvesant Town residents appears. It is obvious that these tenants are not the intended audience for a slapstick comedy, a volleyball team, or a bass-heavy hip-hop concert. Three elderly white people are sitting on the park benches next to their two home health aides, one Latina and one African American, both dressed in pastel-colored hospital scrubs. Parked nearby are the elderly tenants' chrome mobility walkers, modified with tennis balls on the "feet" to prevent users from slipping and falling. One of the elderly tenants is a man with oxygen tubing taped to the side of his face; he smiles and says hello to a little boy who walks by with his father.

Stuyvesant Town is *iconic*. It is an overused word, but one that has been widely applied to the dialogue about Stuyvesant Town/Peter Cooper Village.[2] Usually referred to as simply "Stuyvesant Town" or "Stuy Town," this sprawling, eighty-acre New York City residential community containing ninety-one uniform buildings was once known for its affordable, rent-controlled apartments. However, since 2001, management has converted many units to so-called luxury market-rate apartments, significantly transforming the demographic profile, culture, and ultimately, the sense of place that is associated with this famous community. Though today the notorious waiting list is gone, depending on location, amenities, square footage, and the length of the lease (one or two years), one-bedrooms range from $3,212 to $3,941 a month and two-bedrooms (with two bathrooms) range from $4,859 to $5,847, as of July 2015. As of this writing, studios, units with patios, and three-bedrooms are also available for rent; some of these are marketed as "platinum" apartments. College students, single professionals, young families, and elderly people: how did this curious menagerie of people come to live here? What is it like for such different groups to live in Stuyvesant Town together? Are all of these residents happy here? How long do they plan to stay? What does the future hold for them now that the apartment complex is again being sold in one of the largest residential real estate transaction in U.S. history?

Over the course of the 2000s, Stuyvesant Town's owners have leveraged their financial holdings in an effort to realize their ultimate goal of converting an established, rent-stabilized, affordable community into market-rate luxury housing that caters to a class of renters who are willing and able to afford the higher prices for this Manhattan address. For the more than 25,000 tenants residing in Stuyvesant Town's 11,250 apartments, the property owners' implicit and explicit efforts to expel longtime, rent-stabilized residents in favor of younger, more affluent market-rate tenants has disrupted the community, residents' sense of place, and their perceived quality of life. The changes have also triggered a stream of conflict between the management and tenants and have altered relationships among residents in unexpected ways. Now, a well-known and formerly stable community has become a contested site in the battle for renters' rights.

In this book we present an ethnographic study of Stuyvesant Town, focusing on the changing social dynamics within a community at the mercy of New York's real estate actors.[3] To understand the changes under way in Stuyvesant Town, we explore the story during three key stages in its transformation. First, we describe the rent control era when predominantly middle-class New Yorkers, many of whom were families of veterans and civil servants, first moved into this newly built complex. Though many residents reported sentimental and fond memories of this time period, Stuyvesant Town's earliest years were also a shameful period in the history of fair housing as the community was initially established as a "whites-only" development.

We then describe the second stage when Stuyvesant Town's original owner, Metropolitan Life Insurance Company (hereafter called MetLife), made its goal to transition rent-stabilized apartments into market-rate housing during the early 2000s. This was a period when longtime residents on fixed incomes expressed alarm about their housing security and their growing feelings of exclusion from the community. Even as these residents coped with the universal challenges of aging in place (e.g., declining health, death of spouses, loss of friends, and financial constraints in the midst of a severe recession), longtime tenants also confronted specific sweeping changes to the residential environment that they had called home for decades—all as the economy was failing, and Manhattan housing was in short supply.

MetLife, by design, ensured a way for the development to better cater to a market of potential tenants who would differ from the longtime residents in age, appearance, budget, lifestyle, and housing demands. Soon, the community was rocked by an influx of younger neighbors, new policies and procedures, and nearly constant construction and continuous landscaping projects that would change the physical environment. Management introduced a more liberal tenant culture to accommodate younger people's more carefree, socially oriented lifestyles and amenity preferences, as well as the crowding of public spaces with small children and loud entertainment and sporting events. For some established residents, these changes triggered conflicts with the incoming tenants, but more importantly, they translated into widespread feelings of uncertainty about what else the future would hold.

This all led to a third phase—what we call the post-default years, and what others have called "Stuypocalypse Now,"[4] during which Stuyvesant Town's status became uncertain. Tishman-Speyer Properties bought the property from MetLife in 2006 and then in 2010 defaulted on the mortgage. As of the printing of this book, the management company CWCapital controls the complex on behalf of the bondholders, with poor reviews from residents, some of whom are long-term tenants who were awarded rent rebates totaling more than $68 million in order to reimburse them for rents that MetLife and Tishman-Speyer illegally raised. Notably, large sums have been deducted from former and current tenants' rebate payouts for legal fees, expenses, and retroactive charges for improvements to the property.[5]

On May 14, 2013, in what the Stuyvesant Town-Peter Cooper Village Tenants Association (hereafter referred to as "the tenants association") called a "blood boiling" and "predatory" action, at least one thousand households received notices under their apartment doors notifying them that CW would be imposing mid-lease rent increases, which translated into a rent hike of as much as thousands of dollars a month for some residents. Tenants organized a press conference in response to what they called a "crude and callous act" that was "just the latest assault on the affordability and stability of a community we all need to join in protecting." Rumors were swirling that after squeezing more rent money from tenants, CWCapital would sell the property to the highest bidder, leaving many residents agonizing about the prospect that rents would rise even further, and they would be left without an affordable housing option in the city.

The state's rent stabilization laws formally expired on June 15, 2015. After a five-day extension and many difficult sessions in Albany during which tenants' rights groups accused Governor Cuomo of siding too heavily with the landlord lobby, state lawmakers extended existing rent regulation for four more years.[6] The extension includes some protections for tenants as part of the Rent Act of 2015. For instance, the rent at which an apartment can be deregulated increased from $2,500 to $2,700, limits were placed on Major Capital Improvements charges, and penalties for landlords for harassing tenants were increased.[7] Also, the city's Rent Guidelines Board voted to freeze rents for stabilized tenants who hold one-year leases and to limit increases on two-year leases to just 2 percent.[8] The most recent development in Stuyvesant Town's history is the sale agreement announced in October 2015. The Blackstone Group and its investment partners have made a $5.3 billion deal to buy the property. Controversially, the terms of the sale include the provision that only 5,000 units of the 11,241 will remain "affordable" for twenty years, ensuring temporary stability to some residents. The story continues.

* * *

This book presents in-depth interviews with residents and a chronological narrative structure to tell the story of the demise of affordable housing in Stuyvesant Town and New York City. In so doing, we argue that one cannot fully understand the conversion of a neighborhood from rent stabilized to market rate without first coming to terms with the historical, social, and cultural dynamics of urban housing that accompany it. More generally, we argue that Stuyvesant Town is of interest because it exemplifies the intersection of changing community demographics and neoliberal housing policy. In Stuyvesant Town, the relatively fast and substantial turnover of units occupied by an aging cohort of residents came to be seen as a market opportunity in a hot real estate sector. The act of flipping houses—where speculators purchase houses, make superficial changes, and attempt to resell them at higher prices in tight markets— became a significant trend during the housing boom of the late 1990s and early 2000s. Though it increased curb appeal, flipping also damaged many neighborhoods nationwide by inflating prices and introducing residents who were less likely to remain stable community members. Stuyvesant Town is an example of what happens when an entire community is placed for sale at such a high price that a company can only afford to pay for it by flipping the whole neighborhood—in this case, changing its composition from long-term rentals mostly inhabited by families to short-term rentals mostly inhabited by affluent college students and other well-heeled transient populations seeking to get their first foothold in the city.

That flipping an entire neighborhood is even conceivable is, we suggest, a testimony to one major downside of neoliberal (or free-market) housing policy. When supply is scarce, as it is in New York City and many other major urban real estate markets, a "free market" serves only the wealthiest. Hence, policymakers' deliberate actions are necessary to counter these market forces and preserve the proportionate income diversity that is vital to city life. Ultimately, neoliberal housing policy risks a sort of tragedy of the commons, where the best interests of real estate actors eventually bring ruin to the vibrancy that attracted the wealthier tenants in the first place. Given recent data suggesting that 29 percent of Manhattan apartments are not primary residences,[9] this is no idle concern. This book serves as a call to action for all of those who care about cities and believe that neighborhoods, *real* neighborhoods given life by long-term residents, are fundamental to their success.

## Updating and Extending the Rent-Control Narrative

In general, when one thinks of affordable housing, middle-class New York City neighborhoods like Stuyvesant Town are not what come to mind. Instead, one imagines the run-down apartments and houses built for poor people, including residents of public housing projects and recipients of need-based rent subsidies from the government. However, the concept of affordable housing also includes residential properties catering to middle-class populations, where the high demand for real estate can lead to the exclusion of all but the wealthiest tenants, thus creating exclusionary property markets. In the United States, policies that regulate rent to expand middle-class access to housing markets (e.g., placing caps on rent increases or total rent costs) are sometimes generically called "rent controls," and they remain in only a handful of large cities, such as New York City and Los Angeles.

To the extent that people are even aware that rent-control policies exist, many misunderstand or vilify these laws, despite their intended purpose of alleviating exclusionary practices in local housing markets. When people *do* learn about rent control, it is often from acquaintances and media sources. The typical narrative includes outrageous tales about wealthy, undeserving tenants inheriting the rights to extremely inexpensive apartments where the gentry live lavishly even though they can well afford to rent market-rate units. Sometimes, these rent-control yarns feature regular people, but they are still deemed to be undeserving schemers who are living off of government benefits that unfairly provide them with far more spacious apartments than their life-cycle stage requires or than their income would purchase in the "free" housing market.

Some scholars, policymakers, and citizens view rent control as an unjust "entitlement," a market-distorting violation of the neoliberal rhetoric upon which the United States prides itself. It is true that some New Yorkers have been lucky enough to score affordable, or even inexpensive, rent-stabilized apartments, either through an inheritance or a lottery. However, this is a relatively small, and, arguably, privileged group. Still, friends and neighbors envy them, newspaper headlines vilify them, and their fellow New Yorkers scorn them. This all feeds into accounts that promote rent deregulation and housing privatization. Those who take this view hold that rent-control policies create market distortions that prevent, rather than enable, access to housing. Further, such neoliberal critiques of rent control tend to suggest that tenants who benefit from such policies are abusing outdated laws and ordinances in order to lease apartments at far lower prices than those to which the rest of the city's population is entitled. Indeed, critics have blamed rent control for a wide range of economic and social ills, from homelessness and the loss of affordable housing, to declining neighborhood property values, to the rise of socialism and the inability of independent landlords to make an honest living. The case of Stuyvesant Town provides a rare opportunity to explore these claims as they relate to the broader context of affordable housing and to bring the tenants' voices into the forefront of the debate.

## Gentrification, Community, and Market Forces

In addition to a case study about rent stabilization, Stuyvesant Town's transformation can be seen as a type of *gentrification*, a term that refers to the process whereby newcomers, who are often wealthier than existing residents, move into declining residential neighborhoods. The newcomers' arrival is accompanied by improvements to existing housing and common spaces in order to increase the community's appeal and value. This process often displaces the working-class, poor, and moderate-income residents, as well as racial and ethnic minorities.

Much of the extant sociological literature on gentrification focuses on the relationships between affluent professional residents who take on individual investment risk by buying homes in disadvantaged neighborhoods within a rising housing market and the poor, nonwhite families who are priced out and uprooted. However, in the face of tight markets for affordable rental housing in expensive cities, an emerging literature calls for a more structural examination of "free-market gentrification." Such a perspective examines neoliberal development policies and zoning laws that result in gentrification and suggests that government policies should balance free-market forces in order to level the playing field for average citizens and to protect public goods, such as quality local schools.[10] In contrast to conservatives who blame government-imposed rent-stabilization policies for real estate market failures and the loss of city tax revenues, critics of free-market gentrification assert that the neoliberal ideology that advocates for free enterprise, deregulation, and unfettered pro-development policies has transformed cities into global real estate development markets that reduce affordable housing options for families and make cities less democratic.[11]

Instead of examining the individual housing investments of the rich, this book shows the hazards of applying the free-market doctrine to the community sphere. The East Side of New York City, like the rest of the city, is rapidly gentrifying, but many people had assumed that Stuyvesant Town would remain the middle-class haven it always was. Robert Moses and MetLife built the community with public subsidies to house the middle class, but because of deregulation, Stuyvesant Town is becoming just another gentrified swath of New York real estate. Our research challenges the view that neoliberal policy results in an urban utopia where market forces take care of everyone's housing needs. It shows that free-market gentrification is not oriented to building communities, and it leads to both unintended outcomes and predictable negative pathways for citizens' residential outcomes. The case of Stuyvesant Town forces the question: "What kinds of communities do neoliberal policies create?"

## Plan of the Book

This is a contemporary story of a large-scale apartment complex's change from rent-stabilized to market-rate housing from the perspectives of the residents themselves, in real time as they are experiencing the rapid and distressing changes to their community. Longtime and newer tenants provide rich accounts that paint a portrait of the events that took place, while also going beyond historical time lines and journalistic summaries to better critique the impact that neoliberal, free-market policies have had on formerly affordable, cohesive, and stable communities. The sociological analysis provides a richer and more theoretical understanding of the importance of rent-stabilization policies for urban democracy and community-building.

Chapter 1 offers a history of Stuyvesant Town, beginning with New York City's LaGuardia administration and the "master builder" Robert Moses contracting with MetLife to build this now-famous housing complex. Stuyvesant Town's origins were fraught with controversy: the forcible clearing of the Gas House District's residents, the favorable terms of the city's partnership with MetLife, its stark design, and the racial discrimination against African Americans, all caused consternation. We describe these early years, the community-building efforts of residents and MetLife, and the devolution of rent-control policies that once made Stuyvesant Town an affordable community for middle-class families. We also introduce the two key groups we interviewed: the original rent-stabilized residents and the market-rate newcomers (who are treated as three distinct subgroups: single professionals, younger families, and college students). We review the setting for the study and outline the three periods of community change in Stuyvesant Town: (1) the dynamic but still regulated pre–market-rate era prior to 2006; (2) the market-rate years when MetLife began raising rents and converting apartments to market rate and when Tishman-Speyer Properties speculatively purchased the complex from MetLife; and (3) the era that followed Tishman-Speyer's 2010 mortgage default, the largest commercial mortgage default in U.S. history, a period of continuing instability, court settlements, and rent increases. Presumably, this era has closed with the 2015 sale deal. To remind readers that Stuyvesant Town is not just a historical case study about an anonymous piece of real estate, but rather a community with important human and cultural dimensions, we highlight residents' first-person accounts and provide readers with an opportunity to better understand the nuanced ways in which housing policy decisions shape people and places over time.

Chapter 2 shifts the focus to the longtime residents' experiences of Stuyvesant Town. This chapter provides readers with an understanding of older residents' perceptions of the joys and problems of community life through their accounts of their early years in Stuyvesant Town, as well as their current experiences there. Though residents describe the original Stuyvesant Town of their childhoods and younger adulthoods in generally positive terms, they also report the desperate circumstances that drove them to seek housing there, and they assert that the road to gaining access to a Stuyvesant Town apartment was littered with obstacles to overcome. This chapter also shows that today, older residents are ambivalent about the community, viewing it as an ideal environment for aging in place, but also a place where landlord policies and management practices have made life difficult. Sources of stress include the practice of subdividing apartments to attract college students, the implementation of costly and inconvenient upgrades, and the removal of valued amenities. With so much flux in Stuyvesant Town's rent fees, ownership, management, and population, many longtime residents feel alarmed about housing insecurity at this fragile stage of their life cycle.

Chapter 3 is the first of two vignette chapters that spotlight resident narratives and demonstrate how members of tenant subgroups interpret their respective places in Stuyvesant Town. Ruthie Goldblum has resided in Stuyvesant Town since 1948. Her chapter provides the groundwork for understanding long-term residents' perceptions of the changes in Stuyvesant Town and their decision to become activists in the fight to maintain quality of life and "stay put" in their homes at an affordable rent. Her account highlights the sense of place that longtime residents of a stable community have constructed over time, detailing their sentimental attachments to their home in the city, their investment in their community, and their vigilance about their right to stay.

Stuyvesant Town's story is tied to the broader currents of New York City's housing policy and economic development. Chapter 4 provides a context for understanding Stuyvesant Town's recent history in three ways. First, it provides a brief overview of neoliberal policies that affect housing, such as rent deregulation. Second, it explains the historical role of New York government interventions in subsidizing housing and regulating rents to preserve middle-class residency. Third, using housing market data, it provides readers with an understanding of the current state of housing in New York City, and the particular challenges for the middle class. Finally, we discuss the economic crisis of 2008–2009, which coincided with sweeping home foreclosures across the country, significantly affecting New York City's housing market as entire apartment complexes, some filled with tens of thousands of tenants, underwent foreclosure. It was in this fragile climate that Tishman-Speyer defaulted. Though many tenants viewed this as a case of "just desserts" for real estate moguls choosing to take speculative risks, residents were left in a state of limbo, worried that their lives in Stuyvesant Town were hanging by a thread and scared of what would come next. We assert that New York's global investment networks and urban development patterns are fueled by a neoliberal economic paradigm that values housing solely as an investment, rather than as a building block for neighborhoods, sense of community, and sustainable, vibrant urban life.

Chapter 5 explains the ways in which landlords in general, and specifically Stuyvesant Town's owners and tenants, have reacted to the real estate conditions and deregulation described in the previous chapter. It uses interviews with residents to show how the rising cost of living and the transition to market rate has affected the Stuyvesant Town residents who are most in need of affordable housing. Residents describe their concerns about declining quality of community life and share their fears about housing insecurity, which mostly stem from the bold imposition of costly "major capital improvements" that seem to have been designed to increase rents, to attract a different class of residents, and to push out older rent-stabilized tenants and residents who rely on only one income. Residents explained that life in Stuyvesant Town has become infused with worry and paranoia about aggressive eviction tactics and large, unexpected, and immediate rent increases, sometimes in the middle of a lease term. This chapter also highlights tenant activism as a meaningful response to increased rents.

The focus on Stuyvesant Town's social dynamics continues in chapter 6. We describe the market-rate tenants, outlining their diverse subgroupings and the ways in which they differ from longtime residents. Expecting to age in place in the city with stable rents, longtime residents simply want to remain in their homes and maintain their way of life. Many report a decline in their satisfaction with Stuyvesant Town since the in-migration of college-aged market-rate tenants, although some appreciate the younger residents' energy and liveliness. In contrast, the younger, market-rate tenants (many of whom are singles, college students, and single- or dual-income professional families with small children, some with nannies and housekeepers) have more resources and different life-styles. Some market-raters have embraced the fact that Stuyvesant Town is a community and continue to make an effort to become acquainted with their older neighbors, form friendships, and appreciate this new sense of stability and safety in the city. However, many others, especially those without children, feel detached from Stuyvesant Town's history and the longtime residents' concerns, and to varying degrees, they actively contribute to disorder and conflict. With no memory of another Stuyvesant Town and strained, or at best minimal, contact with elderly neighbors and families with children, many newcomers seem oblivious to and disinterested in the community, and many resent their neighbors who pay lower rents and whom they view as over-involved in community life in their apartment complex.

Chapter 7 is the second vignette chapter and showcases the most controversial category of newcomers: college students. The narrative of a New York University undergraduate named Kara provides a stark contrast to longtime residents' stories, but also highlights the diversity among Stuyvesant Town's market-raters and their role in neighbor conflict and decline in community quality of life. Kara's story provides a glimpse into the reasons that the growing population of college students is a major source of neighbor tension, especially to the longtime residents and families.

In the conclusion chapter, we review and discuss the book's key findings and implications. Stuyvesant Town residents have come to create a real home for themselves in a city where this is notoriously hard to do. Unfortunately, the rare combination of characteristics that make Stuyvesant Town an idyllic community for middle-class families and longtime aging residents—its use value—is of limited interest to Manhattan's powerful real estate actors; to them, anything other than high-rent apartments on this prime chunk of land is a wasted opportunity to increase profit. The changes that landlords and management imposed upon residents were not merely cosmetic, but were accompanied by dramatic shifts in the neighborhood's population composition, family structure, and community norms and values. In light of the tentative sale agreement (as of November 2015), we conclude by discussing Stuyvesant Town's future, highlighting the ways in which our study contributes to urban theories about the social and economic value of community stability—a facet of neighborhood vitality that is often overlooked in the ever-churning New York housing market. We conclude with our assertion that Stuyvesant Town provides an ideal case for investigating middle-class residents' right to the city, especially in an era of neoliberal urban policy that privileges the city's business elite—their development projects, their tax agendas, and their push for housing attributes that diminish affordability and community for other citizens.

1

# History

The Lower East Side of Manhattan in the early 1940s was in many ways a relic of a bygone era. Historic neighborhoods such as the Gas House District evoked the life and memories of the nineteenth-century city. Tenement blocks and ethnic neighborhoods housing first- and second-generation migrant communities held much in the way of social capital, or what some refer to as the invisible "ties that bind." However, the housing was functionally obsolete and ripe for renewal. Forces pushing for modernization could be found in former Mayor LaGuardia's policies and in plans for a new Manhattan that would house veterans returning from World War II battlefields. Stuyvesant Town merged these backward- and forward-looking characteristics in a unique fashion that has, perhaps, never been precisely repeated.

This chapter describes the formation of Stuyvesant Town as a new neighborhood, and it places particular emphasis on public works administrator Robert Moses and his collaboration with the private-sector developer, MetLife. We examine the sense of place that emerged in the new Stuyvesant Town superblock, a community created and shaped by rent-control policy. This chapter also outlines the significant events surrounding the disappearance of New York City's rent-controlled housing, a phenomenon that continues to affect the community more than fifty years later. We also begin to hear from members of two distinct communities within Stuyvesant Town: original tenants and newcomers, both of whose experiences are detailed throughout this book.

## The Master Builder Plans a Neighborhood

The story of Stuyvesant Town, as with New York City's broader twentieth-century urban history, is inexorably linked to the plans and philosophy of Robert Moses, an appointed city official with a definitive vision for his city. Moses was trained in political science at elite institutions—Yale,

Oxford, and Columbia—reflecting both his background and his attitudes toward social structure. He developed a strong belief in the power of public administration through his scholarship and early employment with the Bureau of Municipal Research; this attitude was very much in keeping with the guiding principles of his contemporaries.[1]

What came to distinguish Moses from other New York City public officials was his success at building upon his career ambitions. By the early 1940s Moses had accumulated considerable power through his participation on several New York City planning commissions, committees, and through his appointment as Mayor LaGuardia's housing coordinator.[2] The power that Moses wielded during the mid-twentieth century continues to be a polarizing topic in planning and community development circles, raising the ire of urban activists concerned with the rights and needs of all urban residents.[3] Adhering to the planning axiom "make no small plans," Moses' approach to city planning was informed by the modernist principles of urban designers, such as French architect Le Corbusier's preference for large-scale developments that often centered on high-rise residential structures and the use of the automobile. Moses' influence as a "public entrepreneur" wielding bureaucratic power led to the construction of Stuyvesant Town—a centerpiece of his broader objectives to reshape New York's social geography through large-scale, privately financed redevelopments of so-called slum areas throughout the city, including Harlem, Hell's Kitchen, and the Gas House District.

Stuyvesant Town was built, at least in part, as a response to the broad housing crisis that started during the Depression and was intensified by the Second World War. Tenement buildings known for being cramped, dark, unsanitary places with poor air circulation dominated the residential landscape of New York City's poor and working-class communities, and this form of housing persisted despite housing reform legislation and amendments. A housing inventory conducted in 1934 for the New York City Housing Authority (NYCHA) found seventeen square miles of slums and blight in the city; the report recommended that the city demolish the slums on the grounds that they were unfit for human dwellings, were economically unprofitable, and acted as "breeding places of crime and disease."[4] The deplorable conditions in the nineteenth-century tenements continued into the 1930s, as historian Jan Morris explained: "The most diligent housewife could hardly maintain a decent home in a place like this. Damp got into everything, you could keep nothing clean, roaches were inescapable and rats brown, black and Alexandrian defied extermination—the only cure for rats, it was said, was to 'build them out.'"[5]

Humanitarian rationales for slum clearance were only part of the equation for New York's leaders; as suburban developments created new residential options for city residents, Moses and the LaGuardia administration began to consider plans for modernizing the city's housing stock in order to better compete with the suburbs.[6] World War II hastened these plans when it became clear that postwar New York would need to provide safe, stable, and affordable housing to returning veterans. In his role as city housing coordinator, Moses was responsible for selecting the neighborhoods to redevelop in order to meet the city's postwar needs. By 1942 he had turned his attention to the Gas House District on the Lower East Side as a target for redevelopment.

The Gas House District, named for the placement of large gas storage tanks along the East River, was located between Fourteenth Street and Twenty-Seventh Street. From the late 1800s, poor immigrant communities populated this neighborhood, and it had a reputation for criminal activity arising from groups such as the Gas House Gang, who were known for street fighting and looting homes and stores. The combination of crime, poverty, and the foul odor emanating from the gas houses garnered this area an unsavory and turbulent reputation; a journalist in 1907 reported that the Gas House District "is not a pleasant place in the daytime, much less at night. But then you don't go there at night ordinarily. Having created these places, we leave them severely alone."[7]

According to period accounts, the area had improved somewhat by 1942, with most of the gas tanks removed and with better access through the newly constructed East River Drive. Yet the Gas House District remained blighted and was an obvious site for Robert Moses' redevelopment agenda. Moses had what many would refer to as an "opportunistic" approach to urban development. Writing about New York's Astoria neighborhood in 1942, Moses could have just as easily been describing the Gas House District when he explained that Astoria's current state of neighborhood decay provided "an opportunity to acquire a large tract at low cost, to build a bulkhead out into the river with a park and esplanade along the waterfront, to wipe out some pretty poor buildings, a few fairly good ones, and to build on native land."[8]

Moses' plans for New York's postwar redevelopment called for slum clearance on several sites simultaneously. Given the extent of his planned postwar housing program, Moses sought to involve private investors in the redevelopment projects in order to subsidize the costs of slum clearance and to minimize the public financial risk of new developments. Moses believed strongly that the private sector should take the lead in providing housing, and during 1942 he worked with City Corporation Counsel Paul Windels, Insurance Superintendent Louis Pink, and State Housing Commissioner Edward Weinfeld on a new law enabling the creation of limited-dividend redevelopment companies to spearhead slum clearance in New York.[9] Signed into law as the Redevelopment Companies Law (RCL) of 1942, this legislation created a groundbreaking partnership between the public and private sectors that other cities subsequently would replicate, and that would have significant implications for urban renewal projects over the next fifty years.[10]

The RCL leveraged the city's legal rights as a public corporation, and by authorizing the city to exercise eminent domain, it could assemble parcels of land on behalf of a private redevelopment company. Savings banks and life insurance companies could invest directly in these limited-dividend companies and gain tax exemptions from the increased value of the property after improvements for twenty years.[11] In return for these benefits, developers were required to comply with three conditions. First, they had to certify that tenants who were displaced from the development site would find adequate replacement housing; second, developers were required to build interior streets and parks within the site; and third, and perhaps most relevant to Stuyvesant Town's story, the developer had to agree to place rent controls on the new housing for the duration of the development's tax exemption.

The area above Fourteenth Street would be the first in New York to be redeveloped with a public-private partnership enabled by the RCL. Moses first approached the New York Life Insurance Company with plans for a middle-income housing development on the site, but the board proved too risk-averse to pioneer such a scheme. After several other companies also expressed a reluctance to lead the area's rehabilitation, Moses approached Frederick H. Ecker, chairman of the Metropolitan Life Insurance Company. MetLife had recent experience with a residential construction project on largely vacant land in the Bronx, and Moses wanted to convince the company to redevelop the blighted land in Manhattan. He was able to secure their cooperation by amending the Redevelopment Companies Law to loosen regulatory controls. The amendment extended the tax exemption to twenty-five years, dropped the stipulation to obtain replacement housing for displaced residents, and raised residents' income limits in order to attract a higher social class of tenants. With MetLife installed as a redevelopment partner, the plans for Stuyvesant Town were first made public on April 18, 1943.[12] These plans called for the construction of apartment buildings on an eighteen-block area that could house 11,250 middle-income World War II veterans and their families.

Moses considered it necessary to award MetLife considerable latitude to overcome corporation leaders' historic reluctance to invest in New York's housing market. However, many New York residents were vocal in their concerns that the local government was overreaching by encouraging private-sector investment in the city's medium-income housing. New York citizens and planners alike also worried that city officials and private investors would fail to include in their plan the needed public facilities and schools for such a large population of tenants. After all, despite its squalor and functional obsolescence, the Gas House District could at least lay claim to one public school and two parochial schools, which under the new plan, would be relocated outside of the Stuyvesant Town footprint. Further, many New Yorkers were critical of the fact that MetLife would have the power to deny unrestricted citizen access to the entire site, despite the purported "public" basis for the housing development.

Fear of displacement was an added concern felt by residents of the Gas House District and other neighborhoods facing urban renewal. At the time, 11,000 people were living in the area, and these residents worried about how and where the city would relocate them. In a letter to the editor published in the New York Times on June 3, 1943, Robert Moses indicated that MetLife and the Stuyvesant Town Corporation would relocate the residents at no cost to the city.[13] Local residents formed the Stuyvesant Tenants League, a branch of the United Tenants League, to advocate for residents, coordinate social services, and provide support for the soon-to-be-evicted tenants.[14] However, the seemingly inevitable destruction of the Gas House District meant that opposition to displacement was muted.

As the plans for Stuyvesant Town became more publicized, residents of the Gas House District and a variety of civic groups including the Citizens Housing Council and labor unions raised concerns over privatization, accessibility, and displacement,[15] but these social justice concerns were considered secondary issues when compared to the vocal criticisms of Stuyvesant Town's racial segregation policy. MetLife had made it clear from the start of the project that it did not intend to accept African American veterans' applications. This decision was in direct opposition to the growing public sentiment that African Americans should be protected from discrimination with regard to access to public housing projects. In response to the planned discrimination, the spokesman for the Permanent Committee for Better Schools in Harlem stated that "at a time when Negro and white Americans are dying on the battle fields to preserve our Nation, it seems shocking that such a project could even be proposed."[16]

However, despite the public subsidization of MetLife's development, Moses and the LaGuardia administration considered Stuyvesant Town a private project, and its management had more discretion to discriminate against nonwhites in order to maintain segregation. The Board of Estimates, a city board charged with land-use decisions, was set to vote to approve the Stuyvesant Town plan. On the night before the vote, Frederick Ecker stated his case for the whites-only policy: "Negroes and whites don't mix. If we brought them into the development it would be to the detriment of the city, too, because it would depress all the surrounding property."[17] Robert Moses fully endorsed Ecker's stance, as Moses not only believed strongly in the right of private companies to choose their own tenants, but he also had concerns that fair housing mandates could dissuade private-sector firms from participating in his other planned slum clearance projects. Writing in support of legislation designed to protect MetLife's right to discriminate, Moses warned that "if control of selection of tenants" is "to be supervised by public officials, it will be impossible to get insurance companies and banks to help us clear substandard, run-down, and cancerous areas in the heart of the city."[18]

Though Mayor LaGuardia had strong reservations about the contract after becoming aware of the racially restrictive policy,[19] he signed it as written, and the plan for Stuyvesant Town went to the Board of Estimates. The Board members approved the plan within just a few weeks, and such hasty consideration meant there was little opportunity for the public to consider or debate the design and redevelopment plans. Exacerbating the narrow window for public participation was the fact that three of the most powerful men in New York City at the time, LaGuardia, Moses, and MetLife chairman Frederick Ecker were all strong Stuyvesant Town champions. Against this triumvirate of city power and amidst the backdrop of modernist planning rhetoric that proclaimed the creation of a better postwar New York, the public stood little chance of successfully opposing Stuyvesant Town's plans, or of lobbying for a racially inclusive renting policy. In the end, Stuyvesant Town's plans were approved by a vote of five to one, with the dissenting commissioner, Lawrence M. Orton, objecting because the development lacked a provision for a public school. The city's board approved Stuyvesant Town as a whites-only development and green-lit the project for construction.

A year later, in 1944, MetLife answered the charges of racism by announcing a new housing project for African Americans—the Riverton project in Harlem. This project copied Stuyvesant Town's tower designs, but on a far smaller scale, constructing only six buildings adjacent to the Harlem River at East 135th Street. With lower rents than those charged in Stuyvesant Town, architectural critic Richard Plunz concluded that MetLife's racially segregated housing developments were "a symptom of the new generation of racism endemic to the emerging postwar culture."[20] What mattered to Moses and MetLife was that the path had become cleared for Stuyvesant Town to replace the blighted blocks of the doomed Gas House District.

## Building Stuyvesant Town

With the plans approved, development of Stuyvesant Town proceeded quickly. Under the supervision of Robert Moses' subordinate Gilmore Clark, Irwin Clavin, H. F. Richardson, George Gore, and Andrew Ekin laid out the design utilizing a sixty-acre superblock between Fourteenth and Twentieth Streets, and between First Avenue and the East River.[21] The thirty-five cross-shaped buildings included a total of 8,775 apartments that were designed to hold a population of approximately 24,000 people, with a population density of between 359 and 393 people per square acre, depending on the calculation of the site's acreage.[22] With brick exteriors and copious landscaping surrounding the buildings, Stuyvesant Town's built form was reminiscent of Le Corbusier's "towers in the park" ideal that had informed European public housing. The buildings radiated out from a central oval; around the periphery of the superblock, the buildings were organized to form open quadrangles that nevertheless all faced inward, creating the impression of separation from the neighboring city blocks. Moses' influence in the development of Stuyvesant Town extended into making design recommendations, including his suggestion of varying the building heights and adding setbacks from the street in order to soften the massive scale of the development as well as the institutional nature of its design.

Despite these recommendations, Stuyvesant Town's grand scale and the homogeneous nature of its buildings led to significant criticism of its architectural and planning merits. The kindest critiques merely described the architecture as "dull," the landscape design as "pedestrian," and the planned playgrounds as "unimaginative."[23] However, prominent urban critic Lewis Mumford lobbed some of the sharpest public barbs at the very rationale for Stuyvesant Town in his reviews of the design plan in the *New Yorker* magazine. Mumford's negative evaluation of Stuyvesant Town predated Jane Jacobs' well-known critiques of Moses' modernist urban renewal projects by thirteen years, but was similarly focused on the consequences of urban renewal for community life. He complained that Stuyvesant Town reflected a growing emphasis on congested mass housing in U.S. cities that threatened a sense of place and belonging in the middle of the city. He argued that communities were being replaced with "barracks-style housing" of such high densities as to create "fresh areas of congestion that is nothing less than urban malpractice," and that such design was reestablishing the population densities associated with New York's earlier slums.[24] For Mumford, such projects dehumanized the city and made it difficult to establish a sense of community in urban places. He argued that "like Le Corbusier, Mr. Moses confuses visual open space with functional (habitable) open space," implying that while aesthetically appealing, residents would not actually use the landscaped areas within the superblock.[25]

Such criticism was not altogether justified, since residents did make frequent use of the playgrounds and other public spaces. Still, MetLife's policies lent support to some of Mumford's critiques, as the company strictly enforced an extensive set of regulations about how Stuyvesant Town residents were permitted to use the community's public spaces.

Adding to his critique of the development, Mumford argued Stuyvesant Town's tall apartment blocks were only practical for bachelors and childless couples, since families would likely prefer houses or lower-rise apartment buildings "where young children may still be under the eyes of their mother while she is at work about the flat."[26] Mumford was also concerned with the development's highly visible security guards; he complained that Stuyvesant Town "is the architecture of the Police State, embodying all the vices of regimentation one associates with state control at its unimaginative worst."[27] Other critics were similarly concerned that, in addition to Stuyvesant Town's inhuman scale, the superblock created a city within a city, where residents were intentionally enclosed and separated from the rest of Manhattan's urban chaos by the insular and sheltering nature of the buildings.[28]

Despite these critiques of the overall development, the apartments contained unusual and desirable amenities for New York residences, especially in comparison to other public-led housing developments of the period. For instance, Stuyvesant Town provided a variety of apartment types, from one-bedroom apartments to units that, in theory, could accommodate up to nine family members. Kitchens had windows, a rarity in similar high-rise housing complexes, and though room sizes have been described as simply "adequate," the quality of construction was lauded, with relatively thick walls impeding noise transfer between apartments.[29] Indeed, even Lewis Mumford admitted that Stuyvesant Town residents seemed to have favorable opinions of their home, as evidenced by the letters from tenants who wrote to the *New Yorker* to defend their community against his initial critique. Mumford demurred, acknowledging in a somewhat amusing way that

my monograph on Stuyvesant Town has brought other letters, from tenants who wish to defend the apartments they live in against my criticism. Quite properly, they declare their quarters are the equal of anything

Manhattan can offer elsewhere at two or three times the rental, and they feel that they are in heaven. On that limited basis they are right, and nothing I have said in disparagement of the project should diminish their pleasure.[30]

This acknowledgment was tempered, however, by Mumford's glib justification that Stuyvesant Town residents were simply unaware of how many superior forms of urban housing existed in other cities in the United States and beyond.[31]

Mumford's condescension toward Stuyvesant Town's original tenants and their comprehension of what good housing should resemble may have arisen through an elitist attitude toward the intended residents of Stuyvesant Town, given that the new neighborhood was designed to provide rent-controlled, middle-income housing for veterans and their families. In part, Mumford's paternalistic iciness toward the residents may have been leveled at the significant controls that MetLife sought to impose on the people who were permitted to rent in the community. Beyond the stark issue of racial discrimination, Stuyvesant Town's leasing agents conducted highly detailed background research on prospective tenants. Potential renters at Stuyvesant Town would have to apply for housing with the understanding that MetLife's inspectors would evaluate their current living conditions to ensure that some unspecified standard of housekeeping and appropriate lifestyle was present. Original residents' recollections of the MetLife inspectors' visits in advance of being approved to move into Stuyvesant Town were a common and unifying bond between the earliest residents. Further, this tenant screening policy did nothing to assuage Mumford's early pronouncement that the development was designed to be a dystopic nightmare of strict surveillance that created a setting of "impersonal regimentation, apparently for people who have no identity numbers but the serial numbers of their Social Security cards."[32]

Of course, Stuyvesant Town was not built on virgin land. In order to construct it, the city needed to eradicate the old Gas House District and move out the 3,400 families who were residing there. Such displacement weaves the construction of Stuyvesant Town into broader urban change narratives of the mid-twentieth-century American city. Stuyvesant Town was an early and massive example of mid-century urban renewal

projects and their consequences. Both then and now, many have criticized urban renewal projects for displacing families and disrupting vital
social networks. Research on the psychological consequences of social
displacement from African American neighborhoods shows that it is
associated with short-term disruption of social ties, declines in income,
the triggering of depression symptoms, and a long-term reduction in
community political mobilization.[33] As Northeastern cities from Boston
to Pittsburgh have sought to redevelop land, working-class, poor, and
minority neighborhoods with strong legacies of social capital building
have been faced with erasure.

Nevertheless, in the case of the Gas House District, appropriate concerns over the treatment and fate of displaced residents must be balanced with caution about tendencies toward romanticizing the past. It is
not uncommon for nostalgic residents and sentimental urban boosters
to overlook the negative as they eulogize the days of yore and exagger-
ate the liveliness and well-being of those who reside in struggling urban
communities. For instance, despite the high rates of criminality and
housing obsolescence present in the Gas House District, scholar Samuel
Zipp preferred to emphasize the district's "lingering vitality."[34] Using
photographic records taken from MetLife archives and plat maps, he argued that Stuyvesant Town supplanted an area of varied urban form and
function. Zipp went so far as to write, "the neighborhood may not be
bustling, but much of it looks almost prosperous. Many of the four- and
five-story tenements that line the streets look kept up, as do other odd,
older houses mixed in. There are at least two theaters, a Murray's Five
and Dime chain store, numerous ornate churches, and two schools."[35]
Though such local flavor is important, the problems of the Gas House
District were not contrived and should not be minimized. Robert Moses,
while certainly biased in his perspective on what structures needed to
be razed, defended demolition of the Gas House District by noting that
"the dismal walkup cold-water tenements just off the good residential
section were built on a 60 to 70 percent [land area] coverage, and most
of the rooms were dark and airless."[36] In short, whereas the narrative of
wanton displacement of a vital working-class community by a new class
of bourgeois barracks-dwellers fits with the standard critique of modernist housing, Stuyvesant Town's reality fails to conform to the narrative put forth by some critics of Moses and his development.

As part of the public-private partnership to construct Stuyvesant Town and similar developments, the City of New York obtained the land required for the development by using a combination of street closings, utility easements, and eminent domain.[37] MetLife was required to provide adequate housing for residents who were displaced by the urban renewal project. It organized a Tenant Relocation Bureau to assist in the resettlement of families whose neighborhood was to be torn down, with Moses recalling in his memoir that the relocation company was headed by experienced real estate executives who were engaged "full time to finding places in better buildings for those to be moved and also providing bonuses and cash subsidies."[38]

Moses naturally claimed that nearly all of those who were dispossessed benefitted from the provisions created by MetLife, although later commentators would dispute those claims. By the summer of 1945, MetLife warned the evicted tenants of the Gas House District to vacate immediately. The Tenant Relocation Bureau provided a list of available apartments and offered transportation to view alternative housing options, but many evicted tenants could not afford the units on this list.[39] A small number of tenants moved into public housing administered by the City Housing Authority, but demand outstripped supply, and new construction for public housing was tied up in political disputes between developers and the city.[40] As Moses moved forward with demolition, tenants were forced to "self-relocate," spilling over into crowded public housing and slums nearby.[41] In general, condemning and clearing the Gas House District did not improve the substandard housing conditions of evicted tenants, many of whom ended up living in squalor in nearby blighted slums, residing in housing that was worse than in their former neighborhood.[42]

This marks the beginning of the story of rent control in New York, to which Stuyvesant Town's construction was intimately tied. Rent control covers a set of legal measures enacted at the municipal scale to increase the supply of affordable rental housing in places where market rates are considered prohibitively expensive. Rent control legislation was first implemented in the United States during World War I as a response to acute housing shortages, but some communities continue to employ it to address a broader array of perceived housing problems. For instance, New York City's primary reason for subsidizing the development of

Stuyvesant Town was to provide new opportunities for middle-income housing in the heart of the city.[43]

In the case of Stuyvesant Town, the Redevelopment Companies Law originally required that MetLife employ rent controls for twenty-five years and was later extended by ten years, serving as an important component of the successful transformation of a blighted New York City neighborhood into a safe and stable housing community for the middle class, including veterans returning from the war. When rent controls came under threat in the late twentieth century, the modern history of Stuyvesant Town came to highlight the deepening encroachment of an ideology that considers housing development to be a source of profits and homes to be commodities, rather than the basis for community.

## The Community-Building Years

By 1950, Stuyvesant Town's population had reached 31,173, reflecting the appeal of modern housing developments as well as the strong demand for affordable housing in the heart of Manhattan. These rents were affordable to many middle-class families, but were far outside the reach of most of the displaced former tenants of the Gas House District. Three years after opening for occupancy, median family incomes in the Stuyvesant Town apartments between East Fourteenth Street and East Twentieth Street were $5,301 (in 1949 dollars),[44] and the median rent was $76 (in 1950 dollars). By comparison, median family incomes in New York City were $5,105 during the same period, and Manhattan's median rent was $43. Median family incomes and rents were significantly higher north of East Twentieth Street into Peter Cooper Village at $7,778 and $100, respectively. This difference in incomes and rent can be attributed to the features of the newer Peter Cooper Village buildings, between Twentieth and Twenty-Third Streets. Because these apartments were larger and featured air conditioning units, MetLife was able to set rental prices at double the amount of the average rental contract for Manhattan, and 1.6 times the amount of average rental contracts in Stuyvesant Town. The original tenants of Stuyvesant Town buildings recalled the rift between themselves and Peter Cooper Village tenants. As one longtime resident said,

At Peter Cooper you had to make more [money] . . . They were the rich people . . . The rents were higher. The rooms were bigger. They had certain things, like one of our friends, my girlfriend's cousin, lived at Stuyvesant Town, and then later, because it had air conditioning they moved to Peter Cooper. And when I went to their apartment . . . the apartment was much larger.

Though they lived in a housing development that discriminated against African Americans through MetLife's selective rental policies, Stuyvesant Town residents often perceived their community as ethnically diverse. After all, at the time, the mix of Jews, Catholics, and Protestants distinguished their community from many of New York's white ethnic enclaves that were dominated by people from one nationality or religion. However, Stuyvesant Town had an incredibly racially homogeneous population during its first years of occupation, with whites comprising more than 99 percent of its residents and with only 7.5 percent of its residents identifying as foreign-born, mostly from countries in the former USSR, England/Wales, Ireland, Germany, Poland, Austria, and Canada.[45]

Regardless of Stuyvesant Town's racially discriminatory policy, African Americans in search of quality housing in New York wanted access to these new apartments, as well. In 1948, with the support of community members such as Shad Polier of the American Jewish Congress, three African American World War II veterans brought a lawsuit against Stuyvesant Town to the New York Court of Appeals, hoping for permission to apply to be tenants. The court dismissed their complaints on the grounds that "the legislative intent [of the RCL] is clear to leave private enterprise free to select tenants of its own choice."[46] Accordingly, the courts upheld the right of MetLife to engage in racial discrimination as late as 1949.

In 1948 approximately 1,800 residents formed the group "Town and Village Tenants Committee to End Discrimination in Stuyvesant Town." According to the granddaughter of one of its members, the committee conducted surveys that showed that two-thirds of the tenants opposed MetLife's racially exclusionary policy.[47] In fact, one tenant, Lee Lorch, a college professor who was leaving the city, protested the discrimination by inviting an African American family to move into his apartment. Lorch was a vice chairman of the tenants committee and had been abruptly dismissed from his position as a mathematics professor at the City College of New York. Many believed that his dismissal was a reaction to his pro-integration activism. MetLife was charged with racial discrimination for attempting to evict this family and thirty-six other Stuyvesant Town residents who were members of the tenants committee. Soon after, several of these tenants moved out of the development in protest. According to reports in the *New York Times*, scores of organizations and thousands of individuals became more vocal in their opposition to Stuyvesant Town's practice of racial discrimination, and these voices were becoming difficult to ignore.[48] Nineteen members of the tenants group continued their campaign to end discrimination by taking their case to court and then winning the lawsuit. Finally, in 1952, Stuyvesant Town's management granted its first lease to an African American family. However, informal exclusion of African Americans seems to have persisted well into the 1960s and beyond. According to the U.S. Census, there were fifty-two blacks living in Stuyvesant Town and Peter Cooper Village in 1960.[49] By 1970 that number had increased to 354, a mere 1.4 percent of the nearly 25,000 residents of the community.[50] One of the longtime tenants we spoke to was unequivocal in stating that despite the lawsuit, MetLife discriminated against African Americans well into the 1970s:

> I worked as a security guard in the '70s and was able to get some of the facts about how that process took place, and it was very clear. In fact, it was plastered all over the newspapers that Metropolitan had a particular—I'll be careful about the way I say it—but I think you know what I mean. Their waiting list was very carefully looked at.

Tom Walter, who is African American, and his wife Jessica Walter, who is white, are both in their mid-sixties. They moved into Stuyvesant Town in 1967 and raised their three children there. They were able to get past the informal exclusionary policies because Jessica handled all the paperwork and face-to-face meetings with management in addition to having personal contacts at MetLife. At the time, Tom was not aware of any other African Americans living in Stuyvesant Town. He also described Stuyvesant Town as "very racist," but said that he felt "very much at home" in the community because he had grown up in a "very racist area." He described being followed by security, having doors slammed in his face, and said that he knew several African American families who left the community because of the treatment they received from their neighbors.

America's postwar demographic trends quickly disproved Lewis Mumford's earlier premonition that Stuyvesant Town would become a barracks for single professionals and childless couples. Because Stuyvesant Town's original residents were exclusively veterans and their wives, its postwar "baby boom" was magnified. In the decade between 1950 and 1960, the population of Stuyvesant Town and Peter Cooper Village remained at capacity, shifting downward a bit from 31,000 to 28,000, and yet Stuyvesant Town became known as "the rabbit farm," with thousands of families raising their children in the neighborhood. Corrine Demas, who grew up in Stuyvesant Town during the development's early years, considered it as an "accidental utopia," for whites at least, that was home to a considerable number of children;[51] 7,332 children were living in Stuyvesant Town and Peter Cooper Village in 1960.[52] Many former residents verify that Stuyvesant Town was a remarkable place for raising children and for being a child. The physical layout and community amenities added to residents' sense of security.

Further contributing to Stuyvesant Town's residential stability was the controlled rent provided by the RCL, which ensured that families could stay if they chose, and they usually did. Many original Stuyvesant Town residents retained their apartments for as long as their circumstances would allow, with the consequence that some could still be found in Stuyvesant Town in the mid-2010s. This conforms to research that has shown a "market-distorting" consequence of rent-control policies, wherein caps on rental rates have deterred aging residents from downsizing into more economically "rational" housing stock as their household composition has changed through births, marriages, retirements, or the death of partners. The residential stability of the community eventually led to the process of "aging in place" that would become highly significant in the later period of Stuyvesant Town's story. However, during the community-building years of the 1950s and 1960s, the compound effect of rent controls, valued location, and urban amenities increased the sense of community in a neighborhood that some had criticized as a dull, featureless fortress along the East River.

The large number of families with children added to an increasing sense of place for the new community, and families' longer lengths of residence translated into meaningful social ties and a strong sense of belonging that critics like Mumford believed could not occur in such a high-density housing development. Original tenants such as Ellen Himes recall the unique sense of community that was fostered within Stuyvesant Town's tower blocks:

> You didn't even close or lock your doors. Everybody was so friendly, so happy to be home, to have a home, and to be pretty much on the same wavelength. It was a very happy time. I remember when [my husband] Lawrence died [that] there was a man who had the same last name we had. He said, "What can I do for you?" and I said, "Well, he's supposed to be buried in white. Can you get him a suit?" [He said], "He'll be buried in white." And the man . . . got him his burial suit. It was really sweet.

For the next several decades Stuyvesant Town's residential composition remained largely unchanged. With residents firmly rooted in their modern apartments, prospective tenants began to request slots on a waiting list, remaining in a holding pattern for several years, hoping for a vacancy. However, at the same time, this residential stability protected a vibrant moderate-income community within an expensive city and created a sense of place in the midst of a changing late-twentieth-century Manhattan. Indeed, in the broader context of New York's housing market, Stuyvesant Town functioned as a stable northern border against the nearby East Village crime and disorder of the 1970s and the gentrification that exploded there in the 1980s and that continues to this day.[53]

## Selling Out: The Transition to Market Rate

Over the years, the hard rules of rent control devolved into the softer system of rent stabilization. In the 1990s, MetLife enacted a series of Major Capital Improvements, including rewiring the electrical system and replacing windows throughout Stuyvesant Town. These were large-scale projects that were costly enough to allow MetLife to pass on some of the expense to tenants in the form of rent increases. Such capital improvements continue, with mixed reviews among the current tenants.[54] In general, tenants appreciate the benefits of some of the improvements, but many also complain that some of the upgrades are excessive, unnecessary, and perhaps most importantly, designed to attract young people rather than improve the lives of current residents. In fact, many long-standing residents suspect that lavish upgrades are, in truth, a management tactic to push out rent-stabilized tenants and convert their apartments to market rate.

In 1997, New York passed a law stating that once an apartment's rent exceeds $2,000, it must become deregulated.[55] At that point, a landlord may ask any price that the market will bear. Around 2000, some of the rent-stabilized apartments in Stuyvesant Town hit this threshold, and MetLife converted them to market rate. In 2001, MetLife made an attempt to expedite such conversions by initiating a $50 million project to improve the site's grounds, including upgrading the playgrounds, lighting, and landscaping. MetLife officials knew that the more the property improved, the faster rents would increase, and the more attractive the community would become to prospective tenants willing to pay market-rate rents.

Changes in the Stuyvesant Town waiting list reflect these improvements, rent increases, and conversions to market rate. In the past, rental applicants had to wait several years for a rent-stabilized apartment. For instance, in 1991, the wait for an apartment on the Stuyvesant Town side of the complex was five years, and for the more spacious Peter Cooper Village, the wait was more than ten years.[56] With the conversion to market rate, fewer rent-stabilized apartments were available, and the waiting list for rent-stabilized apartments was terminated, marking a sea change for the community.

Significantly, in 2002, the year that MetLife engaged in major renovations and introduced a tenants' concierge service to better compete in New York's luxury apartment market, management also removed from the property a plaque honoring the MetLife chairman and placed it in the archives.[57] The removal of the plaque, inscribed with the quotation "that families of moderate means might live in health, comfort and dignity in park-like communities and that a pattern might be set of private enterprise productively devoted to public service," symbolized the end of an era for Stuyvesant Town and its residents.[58]

A comparison of the demographics of residents of Stuyvesant Town and Peter Cooper Village in 1950 and then in 2000 shows that much had changed in Stuyvesant Town even before the transition to market rate. In terms of family composition, the young married couples with children from the 1950s are Stuyvesant Town's elderly residents of today. Unmarried singles with roommates have largely replaced those who left, as have young families, some of whom are the adult children of the original residents. It is not uncommon to meet adults who grew up in Stuyvesant Town and now raise their own children there. In terms of ethnicity, Stuyvesant Town has shifted from almost completely white to mostly white. In 1950 it was overwhelmingly white, with only 114 African Americans residing there; now it is 76 percent white, with Asians being the next largest ethnic group.[59] In terms of social class, as indicated by residents' occupations, it has become far more professional, as well.

## The 2006 Sale of Stuyvesant Town

After owning Stuyvesant Town for nearly sixty years, MetLife announced in the summer of 2006 that it was placing the community on the auction block. This was not the first time that MetLife had considered selling the property; this first occurred in the mid-1970s as the original tax exemption for Stuyvesant Town was set to expire. MetLife demurred after a successful tenant-led bid to extend the exemption while bringing the properties under New York's Rent Stabilization Act. By 2006 things had changed. For one, MetLife was decades removed from the point at which its leaders felt obligated to provide veterans and their families with low-cost Manhattan housing; it became a publicly traded company in 2000; and it had already divested itself of its other major residential properties. At the same time, New York's social geography changed to include far-flung bedroom communities in neighboring states where middle-income families could live out their dreams of home ownership. In addition, the real estate market was at a boiling point, with public investors representing sovereign funds and domestic pension funds; also, private investors were aggressively seeking real estate deals, aided by the ready availability of loans to support bids. Therefore, the conditions were perfect for the creation of a frenzied bidding war for a prime piece of residential real estate on Manhattan's East Side.

Residents were troubled when news began to emerge about a potential sale. Daniel R. Garodnick, a New York City Councilman who was raised in Peter Cooper Village and now lives there with his wife and children, was incensed about the sale: "It's not every day that 20 percent of your district goes up for sale—this is going to be a mess. People are going to be very scared about the future."[60] Concerned that the sale would lead to widespread evictions, Garodnick contacted a wide array of actors who could assist with plans to protect the properties, including colleagues at his former law firm, leaders of the tenants association, local political leaders, labor representatives, and real estate developers. Garodnick and his allies decided to attempt a tenant-led bid to buy the site, and began to determine how to finance the anticipated $4 billion sale price.

The sale of Stuyvesant Town attracted a large number of interested real estate developers, each with its own evaluation of how many billions of dollars the properties were worth. These calculations were based on the limitations on rent increases imposed by rent stabilization, modified according to how aggressively each bidder thought they could supplant rent-stabilized tenants with market-rate renters. Darcy Stacom, a second-generation New York real estate broker, handled this transaction. Her team put together sales information explaining the ways that this unique property could be leveraged to bring returns for the successful buyer. For example, the sales book suggested that doormen, health club amenities, an elite private school, deluxe stores, and development rights to construct traditional high-rise buildings amidst Stuyvesant Town's park spaces could all work to generate returns on the investment price—not to mention the aggressive tactics to remove rent-stabilized tenants to make way for market-rate renters. All of this meant the erasure of the property's former role as a bastion of middle-income housing, re-imagining the space as something that would appeal to a different, more affluent population.

Initially, both Ms. Stacom, whom the *Wall Street Journal* has called "the Queen of the Skyscrapers," and MetLife considered the tenant-led group to be an "unqualified bidder" that could not be expected to compete with dedicated investor groups, and thus declared it ineligible to be considered for a real estate deal. However, elected officials pressured the company to take the bid seriously, and MetLife provided the group with the bid book outlining the specifics of the properties and sale process. Stuyvesant Town tenants were excited by the prospect of a tenant-led purchase and rallied to the cause; the sale also incited fair housing activists who considered this a community that symbolized the endangered nature of affordable housing in Manhattan.

Despite the significant changes that this sale would mean for a large section of Manhattan's housing, former mayor Bloomberg's administration kept the process at arm's length, having earlier promised MetLife that the city government would not interfere. Indeed, the Bloomberg administration had good relations with New York's elite real estate sector, and had business relationships with Tishman-Speyer's patriarch, Jerry Speyer, through development partnership agreements.[61] Discounting the original social intent of the LaGuardia administration's tax breaks, land acquisition, and zoning changes to create Stuyvesant Town, Bloomberg went on the record to assert MetLife's right to sell the property:

> MetLife owns it and they have a right to sell it—a lot of people want to live there. That's part of the problem. When people want to live somewhere prices go up. When they don't, prices go down. The character of this community will change, but it will change slowly, over time. And it would change whether it is sold or not.[62]

Ultimately, development firm Tishman-Speyer, whose website declares it to be "one of the leading owners, developers, operators, and managers of first-class real estate in the world," outbid the tenant group and other interested bidders. It partnered on the sale with BlackRock Realty, which assembled the investment funding necessary to complete the transaction. To secure the purchase, Tishman and BlackRock amassed an international portfolio of investors including the California Public Employees' Retirement System, the California State Teachers' Retirement System, the Church of England, the Government of Singapore Investment Corporation, and other interests from countries including Denmark, Canada, Japan, and South Korea. Tishman's and BlackRock's enthusiasm for the project, their property development profile, and the claims of investment returns of 13 percent proved alluring to these investors. Indeed, there seemed little reason to doubt the ultimate success of the Stuyvesant Town project. BlackRock's managing director Dale Gruen explained it in these terms:

> New York City's housing market has yet to experience a significant slow-down. Prices are high and continue to rise, which is depressing affordability. In fact, housing affordability, which takes into account home prices, incomes, and mortgage rates, recently dropped to a record low. Above average job growth, favorable demographics and a record-low for-own housing affordability are driving strong demand for rental units. Against the backdrop of limited supply of new rental units, vacancy rates are ex-tremely low and rent growth is strong. These strong trends are expected to persist, and we currently rank New York as one of the nation's best apartment markets for investors.[63]

Tishman took over the two complexes, paying $5.4 billion for the property and making this transaction the largest sale of a single property in U.S. history.[64] The price averaged out to over $450,000 per unit, but the rent rolls covered only 58 percent of the monthly mortgage payments on the property, leaving Stuyvesant Town's middle-class, rent-stabilized tenants justifiably concerned. The selling price left little mystery as to what the new owners planned to do with the property. The only way for Tishman-Speyer to feasibly make a profit on the deal would be to fully convert the once middle-income housing development into a luxury apartment complex. During the period of time that it owned the prop-erty, Tishman-Speyer was highly motivated to continue what MetLife had initiated: ejecting rent-stabilized tenants and converting their apart-ments to market-rate units as quickly as possible.

Two important events interfered with the steady march of Stuyves-ant Town's market-rate period, and these events ushered in a new era of uncertainty. First, the 2008–2009 housing crisis caused the property's market value to drop significantly. A second landmark event was the 2009 Roberts decision in which the New York Court of Appeals ruled that Stuyvesant Town's owners had improperly deregulated apartments while also receiving a J-51 tax abatement. This "double dipping" contin-ued until tenants sued and won. The 2009 Roberts decision required Tishman-Speyer to live up to a commitment to forgo the "luxury decontrol" deregulation provisions allowed under the 1993 Rent Regulation Decontrol Act in exchange for tax breaks the company continued to receive.[65] By the end of 2009, it was clear that Tishman-Speyer had overestimated the number of rent-stabilized units they would be able to convert to market-rate rents. This meant the company was unable to continue to make the monthly payments on the property and needed to turn the development over to a special servicer in order to avoid foreclosure.

The trouble in Stuyvesant Town soon sparked the interest of tenants in other communities, as well. Independent Plaza North, a building complex in Tribeca housing 1,300 tenants, was the unqualified recipient of tax breaks from 2004 to 2006.[66] The tenants were unaware that their landlord, Laurence Gluck, and his company, Stellar Management, had left the stabilization program in 2004 after acquiring the property in 2003, but had continued to accept the tax breaks "unknowingly," according to Gluck. A tenant who inquired whether the tax breaks required rent stabilization brought attention to the matter, so the city asked Gluck to repay the amount, and the company "retroactively declared he never received them."

Hence, Stuyvesant Town's story is not merely one of a large-scale urban housing development. The LaGuardia administration originally conceived of it to accommodate 24,000 middle-income tenants in postwar New York, so Stuyvesant Town represents an early example of a publicly subsidized private development. It also showcases the conflicts that arise when citizens seek rent-controlled housing and developers pursue higher profit. In essence, Stuyvesant Town's history is bound with that of mid- to late-twentieth-century capitalist development in New York City and elsewhere. However, many scholars and policymakers now argue that the commodification of housing has contributed to, if not caused, housing cost burden, involuntary displacement, foreclosure, eviction, homelessness, a wide array of negative outcomes for adults and children.[67] This all suggests that critical urban theorists are correct in asserting that housing is not merely a piece of wealth, but that it has a lifespan that extends far beyond most consumable goods, and as such, it has long-lasting effects on people's lives.[68]

Stuyvesant Town could not have been created without the partnership between the City of New York and MetLife. In return for generous twenty-five-year tax abatements, powers of eminent domain, and the architectural services of Robert Moses' planners, MetLife created a large-scale housing development targeted to whites with moderate incomes. Stuyvesant Town could only cater to families with moderate incomes because of the strong rent controls. New York's rent control legislation changed over the subsequent decades, but in the 1990s, Stuyvesant Town's rental units were still covered by some form of rent stabilization, hence generating less revenue for the landlords than would otherwise have been possible in Manhattan's robust housing market. Nevertheless, to its residents, Stuyvesant Town provided a sense of place and community, aspects of urban life that are commonly overlooked in heated debates over the economic merits of rent-control legislation.

Economic imperatives over the built environment also trump social imperatives in the context of the neoliberal development that came to characterize cities in the late twentieth century and which continues today. Many have argued that neoliberal administrations denigrate collective consumption and institutions, instead favoring the reification of free-market principles that seek only the highest possible rates of return for every parcel of land in the built environment.[69] Under such conditions, developers and city officials who seek to dispose of rent-stabilized properties in favor of market-rate rentals conveniently forget the publicly subsidized origins of developments such as Stuyvesant Town. However, these goals are not uncontested, and the community has responded to the potential sale of its buildings with a level of mobilization unmatched by those who were dispossessed by the 1940s construction of Stuyvesant Town.[70]

In chapter 2, we focus on the voices of longtime residents. These stories explain the difficult circumstances that brought residents to Stuyvesant Town and highlight the obstacles that longtime residents overcame in their journey to secure rent-controlled housing in a community that was in high demand. This chapter also brings us into the present, as longtime residents describe their perceptions of recent changes in Stuyvesant Town's management, policies, and tenant composition, and especially how these factors have affected their quality of life, their feelings of security, and their peace of mind about the future.

2

# Stayers Then and Now

## *Getting and Keeping a Slice of Stuy Town*

It is easy to find positive sentiments about growing up in Stuyvesant Town. One former resident wrote that the neighborhood has had the unique power to draw New Yorkers back in again after they have squandered years living elsewhere, searching and failing to find the same sense of community: "We lived intimately with our neighbors . . . We knew our neighbors by their floors as people in small towns associate neighbors with their houses."[1] Today, many of these same Stuyvesant Town residents, now in their later years, are far more jaded and pessimistic.

This chapter evokes the sense of place held by long-term residents of Stuyvesant Town. The firsthand accounts of these residents' early lives provide a contrast to the Stuyvesant Town of today, and their contemporary experiences shed light on the ways in which the transition to market-rate housing has affected them. From its inception, Stuyvesant Town's selling point was that it was intended to be a good place to raise a family in the heart of Manhattan. In general, long-time residents used positive terms to describe the Stuyvesant Town of their childhoods and younger adulthoods. The community felt like an urban oasis where neighbors felt safe and left their doors unlocked. Mutual trust and a willingness and desire to participate in community life—a sociological concept known as collective efficacy—were the norm. However, these residents are now more ambivalent in their evaluations of Stuyvesant Town. Many residents still believe that Stuyvesant Town offers an ideal environment for aging in place, but they also express dissatisfaction with the changes to the community, and they share a profound fear that at any time they could lose their homes.

## The Social Dynamics of Stuyvesant Town Back Then

Irish and Italian Catholics and East European Jews were the first to move to Stuyvesant Town, eager to start families after World War II and ready to begin their independent lives. Jewish celebrities and public intellectuals, including comedian Paul Reiser, opera singer Beverly Sills, Pulitzer Prize–winning author Frank McCourt, and journalist David Brooks have all recounted memories of their lives there. In 2000 Corinne Demas, a college professor and author, wrote an entertaining memoir about her childhood entitled *Eleven Stories High, Growing Up in Stuyvesant Town, 1948–1968*. New York University's oral history, "Archives of Irish America," also features interviews with prominent members of New York's Irish community who raised their families in Stuyvesant Town.

Yet beneath sentimental stories of the old days, residents describe a harsher truth. They detail the difficult circumstances that led them to seek out new housing decades ago. They tell of the long and unpredictable waitlists, the scrutiny they endured from management as they took on the process of applying for Stuyvesant Town's rent-controlled housing, the need for special social connections to gain priority, and the denial of basic rights to privacy that most people take for granted today. Even so, they insist that it was all worth it to get an apartment that would be roomy and affordable enough for raising a middle-class family in the city.

### The Ethnic Cultural Context

After World War II, Irish American migration patterns in New York were such that many middle-class married couples began moving into Stuyvesant Town.[2] By the 1960s, Stuyvesant Town had become known for being heavily Irish American, as well as Jewish. As one resident we interviewed stated, some people considered Stuyvesant Town to be "the projects for white people."

Still, New York's Jews and Irish remained culturally distinct in many ways. For instance, many Irish and Italians in New York enrolled their children in Catholic schools in an attempt to shield them from secular society, whereas Jews were less committed to Jewish education and far more focused on their Jewish cultural identity.[3] The National Jewish

Welfare Board conducted a survey of Stuyvesant Town's Jewish residents in 1950, painting a distinct picture of a secular subculture among Jews.[4] Most in the study were young married families with children, many were well-educated professionals who were involved in Jewish organizations, most were either fluent in Yiddish or understood it, but only 10 percent actually belonged to a synagogue.[5]

In addition to professional and educational class divisions and differences in levels of religiosity, the liberal Jewish outlook and the cultural value Jews placed on vocal dissent became sources of contention as Irish Americans and Jews became more politically separated.[6] Coming out of a war against fascism, many Jewish tenants were active in social justice causes pertinent to Jews and other minority groups. For instance, the American Jewish Congress, a liberal Jewish defense agency, filed lawsuits against New York's medical schools that used quota ceilings to limit the number of Jewish students.[7] Along with three African American veterans, and other organizations such as the American Civil Liberties Union and the National Association for the Advancement of Colored People, the American Jewish Congress co-sponsored a lawsuit against MetLife for discriminating against blacks in the all-white Stuyvesant Town.[8] Thus, Jews became the face of instigation and integrationist activism in Stuyvesant Town until African Americans were finally allowed to reside there in 1950 after the retirement of MetLife chairman Ecker, who had initiated the discriminatory tenancy policies discussed in chapter 2.

Older residents whom we interviewed were aware of Stuyvesant Town's reputation as a white community unwelcoming to people of color; as one stated, "Long before our time, when it first started out, it has a very bad history of racism, of course. Black people were not allowed." Tom and Jessica, the interracial couple mentioned in the previous chapter, expressed a positive view of Stuyvesant Town in general, but expressed ambivalence about what it had been like many decades ago. Tom elaborated on the prejudice and discrimination that his family had faced on a daily basis:

> I have mixed feelings about it. On one hand, I felt, coming from New Jersey, very much at home here because [Stuyvesant Town, like New Jersey,] wasn't anything like the city. As soon as you leave Stuyvesant Town, you know that you're in the city. And so, it was nice in that sense. On the other

hand, since there were no other blacks that I knew of at the time—I think there was one other black, but I think she was an employee—in any case, I was not treated too nicely by a lot of people. More than once, even after I had been here five years, I would be followed to my door by other tenants and by security. A lot of times, even your neighbors who knew you would slam the door in your face. That's the God's awful truth. And a few years later, when they started to accept a few blacks in the community, a number of blacks that we coincidentally became friends with stayed here a year or two, and they couldn't stand it because of the treatment they got. You know, people looking at them like they were animals in a cage. It was a very racist community.

And so, those households with residents of color lived under their neighbors' "white gaze,"[9] feeling scrutinized and diminished, which created additional barriers to community assimilation and inclusion.

Clearly, the fact that Stuyvesant Town's origin story is tarnished by racial discrimination detracts from any saccharine portraits of the community. Stuyvesant Town's longtime residents' personal testimonies bring to the fore the lingering effects that anti-black discrimination has had on residents' quality of life, not just in the short term, but long after the community had become officially integrated.

### Tough Times for the Middle Class: Pushed to Live in Stuy Town

Those who study migration have shown that some factors "push" people into the decision to move, and some factors "pull" them to certain locations. For Stuyvesant Town's longtime residents, family life cycle was often the main push factor as married couples needed more room to raise a family, and aging people needed elevator access and maintenance services. However, obstacles or so-called frictional factors impeded their choice of where to live.[10] Many who moved to Stuyvesant Town were faced with the difficult situation of needing an apartment located close to their Manhattan jobs, while contending with limited financial resources and the city's sparse stock of family-sized apartments. The choice became even more difficult for those bold enough to insist on locating their families in a relatively safe neighborhood or a community with acceptable schools.

Evelyn Takemoto, a longtime resident in her late fifties, is a co-owner of a small advertising company. For years she has been separated from her husband, who is also her business partner, but she continues to work with him at their nearby studio office. As she put it, "I'm your all-American WASP. He's your all-Japanese rural rice farmer." The couple raised two daughters in Stuyvesant Town, both of whom are now graduates of prestigious colleges with professional jobs, one in finance and one in design.

Evelyn recalled her family's decision to move to Stuyvesant Town when she was a pregnant mother of a two-year-old. She said that she and her husband were desperate for an affordable two-bedroom apartment. Though their apartment was located in the less desirable section of Stuyvesant Town, and the children were zoned to attend a bad school in a poor, high-crime neighborhood where the drug epidemic was in full effect, the living situation was ideal for balancing their family needs, cultural and parenting values, and careers. The family eventually secured need-based scholarships for the children to attend the private United Nations International School:

> I didn't care [about the downsides of Stuyvesant Town] at that point. I was just in heaven. We always loved the neighborhood. We liked being artistic. We wanted it gritty. We came to New York to do advertising . . . We knew we were committed to New York City. With my husband's career as a photographer and mine as a sales agent, we were a "mom and pop" business. We didn't want to do the commute. We couldn't do a commute, and he's Japanese, so the idea of nannies, babysitters, and preschools—none of that had a chance. We were full-time parents, so we had to be close, and he had a studio on 20th Street, so we were back and forth between his studio and our apartment.

Ken Smith, a fifty-eight-year-old attorney for the city, moved to Stuyvesant Town with his wife and daughter in 1980. After nine months on the waitlist, he was overjoyed to move to Stuyvesant Town, which he considers a respite from the city, but one that is convenient to his nearby government job:

> We did some apartment hunting at a certain time, and you see all sorts of apartments depending on your price range. A lot of New York apartments

in our price range were small, and less than ideal, and Stuy Town has a lot going for it. The apartments are all pretty much standard sized. Different numbers of bedrooms, but the rooms are decently sized. There's a lot of light and air and cross-ventilation. You're never looking at an airshaft or into a neighbor's window. You have a little feeling of space. It's maintained well. It's a little bit of a break from the street grid, so inside there's a little relative peace and quiet, and yet you have the convenience of being essentially in midtown Manhattan. So I think anyone who needs or wants to be in Manhattan would probably look at it as not a bad place to live.

Walter Geller, a fifty-four-year-old social worker, moved to Stuyvesant Town when he was around two years old. After starting a family in Brooklyn, he and his pregnant wife returned there to be closer to his wife's job. Walter now commutes to his job in Westchester County and shares the apartment with his retired wife and their twenty-nine-year-old son, as he eagerly anticipates his own retirement. Walter is typical of longtime residents in that he felt no need to romanticize the circumstances that led him to Stuyvesant Town, nor did he downplay the fact that he had once actually dreaded the prospect of living there. In fact, Walter emphasized that he was quite reluctant to return to the impersonal, artificial atmosphere of the apartment complex that was his childhood home, especially after living in a more "natural" neighborhood. The only reason Walter acquiesced was sheer practicality:

> I did not like it one bit, because . . . Well, there are a lot of reasons. We enjoyed living in Brooklyn. It was different [from Stuyvesant Town]. It was like another little apartment building. It was sort of a brownstone, and the whole feel of the neighborhood was a lot different. Coming back here to the same place with the big buildings and the red bricks, and walking into practically the same apartment you grew up in? It was not a thrill.

Beatrice Hanley, a seventy-three-year-old longtime resident from Ireland, described herself as very outgoing and as "a very contented senior citizen." A single woman, Beatrice reported that she had never "met the right person," but is active in the community through her work as a teacher and volunteer, and she has many friendships with neighbors. Beatrice takes great pride in her loyalty to the neighborhood stores and restaurants and her efforts to learn the names of the employees there. She continues to work part-time in the afternoons and evenings for the Department of Education, traveling all over the city as a home instruction teacher to teenagers who are unable to attend school because of severe emotional and psychological problems. Like many residents, Beatrice arrived to Stuyvesant Town at a desperate time in her life:

> I wasn't feeling well, and it was at that time I was diagnosed with cancer. And I got a call one day from MetLife. I was on the waitlist for a while, and you had to be on the list at that time, so I said, "Yes. I would love an apartment." 'Cause I had to stay [in the U.S.] to undergo treatments—chemo and radiation. And so they said there was one available on First Avenue. And I didn't know the difference between First Avenue and Second Avenue. I came and put the deposit on it, and I moved in, and I wasn't that well. I had no furniture at the time, just enough to survive, a bed and chairs. I didn't know what I was going to do, whether I was going to remain here for a year or two, or whether I was going to [die] . . . I was sick.

Seventy-eight-year-old Morris Cann and his wife, seventy-five-year-old Cathy Wilson, arrived at Stuyvesant Town in 2001 after four long years on the waiting list. Morris insisted that at the time of the move, he was against Stuyvesant Town as a destination, but Cathy "brow-beat" him into it. Cathy explained that the couple had been living in a nearby Lower East Side walk-up close to her publishing job, but the physical toll of aging forced them to adjust their living situation. Though they clearly take pride in being physically active and exercising regularly, life in Manhattan presents challenges to even the young and hearty. Unfortunately, Morris is hard of hearing, and Cathy has respiratory difficulty and mobility limitations:

> The year we moved in here I broke my ankle, and I was mighty glad to have an elevator. We had lived [in our other apartment] for a long time, and I just wanted to move to a place with an elevator. I couldn't walk up there. I was too old, and we applied here because I have friends who were in Stuyvesant Town . . . We like the neighborhood because it's handy. There's a convenient laundry, a convenient wine shop, convenient post office, convenient pharmacy.

Morris and Cathy have become concerned about living on a fixed income in a poor economy, a worry that is not eased by the changes in Stuyvesant Town. Arguably, older people are mindful of the budgets in general, but Morris used the word "survival" as he explained that their apartment provides them with more than desirable housing amenities. It represents his perceived need for a contingency plan:

> It's so full of light, and it's so massive, and it's something that, in case we get into financial trouble, we could sublet the middle room . . . So we don't worry about the downturn, the economic situation. At least we have recourse. And naturally, it would shrink the standard of living because people would prefer their privacy, but the main thing is survival . . . I used to go to lunch and dinner at places, to restaurants. But now, because of the economic situation, I'm speaking of stocks and bonds, assets and shares, she does more cooking.

Cathy said that she and her husband have been "sufficiently scared by the [late-2000s economic] downturn not to go out so much," and now they tend to eat "more beans and rice." The couple is very concerned about their financial security, and because of the uncertainty surrounding Stuyvesant Town, about their housing stability, as well. Cathy explained: "I actually love it here. I just hope that we can stay, too."

Though purely sentimental accounts of life in Stuyvesant Town appear elsewhere in journalistic accounts, memoirs, and personal essays, a deeper analysis of longtime residents' stories provides a more balanced and nuanced view of the factors that drew people to the community and explain what it was like to live there at an earlier time. Many residents arrived to Stuyvesant Town at a difficult time in their lives, looking for a larger but affordable apartment in which to raise children. Some arrived while struggling to get by on a single income, but also desiring a more feasible commute to Manhattan jobs. Stuyvesant Town has also come to represent an ideal home for older people on fixed incomes. In other words, for many longtime residents, Stuyvesant Town is not a romantic neighborhood, but neither does it symbolize the rebellious, unconventional identity to which so many New Yorkers aspire. Still, until recently, it is undeniable that Stuyvesant Town conjures up a particular image of

New York: a New York where people of modest means can find afford-able and appropriate housing in a community designed for families.

*The Indignities of Affordable Housing: Pulling Strings, Withstanding Scrutiny, and Pressure to Sign a Lease*

Today, in the post-default era, the staff members who work in Stuyves-ant Town's leasing office regularly field calls asking whether there is a waiting list for rent-stabilized apartments. What were the old days like for those who wanted to move to Stuy Town? In explaining her journey to Stuyvesant Town, one longtime resident reported that she had spent approximately six years languishing on the waiting list. When asked why the list was so long, she said: "In those days, nobody moved, and the [grown] children remained here, the children of the original tenants who are gone now."

Many longtime tenants mentioned that one needed to have social connections to get a Stuyvesant Town apartment in a timely fashion, particularly associations with MetLife. Several seemed resentful that today's market-rate tenants are able to move directly into the roomier Peter Cooper Village apartments that longtime tenants coveted in their younger days. In the old days, families could only gain access to Peter Cooper Village apartments after a long period of living in Stuyvesant Town's smaller apartments. Even then, in order to be upgraded, resi-dents had to reapply and wait; a bit of social capital could go a long way in getting an apartment that could better accommodate a family.

Walter Geller highlighted the social advantages that helped his par-ents secure a Stuyvesant Town apartment when he was a boy. He also ad-mitted that he had leveraged his family connections to get a Stuyvesant Town apartment later in life, which resulted in MetLife's management office swiftly accepting his application:

> It was very easy for me because my parents lived here, and my father had worked for Metropolitan Life Insurance for many years. All I needed to do was write a letter, and at that time we got an apartment right away. There was a long waiting list then, but because of the history [my parents and MetLife] have, I guess we got special consideration.

Ken Smith also explained his efforts to pull strings to get an apartment:

> It took a while. We wrote several letters to let them know how inter-
> ested we were. My wife's cousin [a tenant] wrote a letter on our behalf
> to the general manager at the time, who was somebody she knew from
> having been there a long time, and I think he was a longtime general
> manager. Whether that made any difference, I don't know. But as I said,
> it took about nine months, and then we got the word that we had an
> apartment.

Tom and Jessica both reported that they used personal connections to hasten the move up the waiting list. Tom, a retired security guard, had worked for Stuyvesant Town at one time and knew people who lived there. Plus, Tom still kept in touch with someone who worked there and he pulled some strings, as Jessica explained:

> I either worked with or had friends who lived here, and they had raved
> about it and said it was great and said, "Why don't you apply?" Although
> other people had said the waiting list is long. But you can try. And as
> it turned out, Tom worked in a place where one of the clients was the
> resident manager here, and he had known him for a while. I guess, in
> the course of conversation, Tom mentioned that we had put our name
> on the waiting list, and within a few months after that, we were being
> interviewed.

In describing their application process, Tom stressed that his family's story represents an especially unique case because they are an interra-cial couple. He described the way he and Jessica tried to avoid the racial discrimination that they anticipated by using their social networks and by strategically assigning Jessica to handle all face-to-face meetings with management:

> My case was a particular case, partly because I had a working relationship
> with the manager. That was one part of it, and the other part is that Jessica
> is white, and so she was able to come down and do all the preliminary
> paperwork for that. So, I basically kind of sneaked in the door.

Ilene Canegula, a sixty-eight-year-old resident, has lived in Stuyvesant Town for twenty years. She and her adult daughter had originally decided to move there together, but Ilene now lives in the apartment alone. Overall, she enjoys the opportunity to live in the city as a single person rather than in the family-oriented suburbs where she resided before her divorce. Ilene also likes that Stuyvesant Town's apartments are large, that the community is relatively quiet, it has no through-traffic, and that it is convenient to so many other neighborhoods.

Ilene also had an inside advantage in securing an apartment. Her father had been a maintenance worker at Stuyvesant Town from the time it first opened until he retired. She did not grow up there because her father had wanted their family to live in what he called "the country," the suburban environment of Queens, rather than in the city. Ilene and her husband raised their two children in Westchester County, then later moved to the city, and eventually divorced after twenty-three years of marriage. She had applied to Stuyvesant Town, but had no luck getting an apartment. Then, after encountering "the big shots" from the development at her father's funeral, a gesture of respect that she thinks would be unlikely to occur at today's Stuyvesant Town, she was promised an apartment there. She described the process:

> Finally, they came through with an apartment, and you're not allowed to look at them. I had never been inside a Stuyvesant apartment, so my daughter and I went with a clipboard, and we interviewed the people in the building where I would have lived. And it was facing Fourteenth Street. And I asked one guy, "Does the noise bother you?" He said, "Nah. I sleep through anything." I asked another person. They said, "It's very noisy." But the apartment that we would've gotten, I saw the birds landing on the ledge. And I thought, "That's all I need to do, is be cleaning and watching out of the corner of my eye at the birds landing on this particular windowsill." I don't know why they picked that one. I declined the apartment, and my mother went hysterical saying, "Now these are hard to get into." I said, "Ma, I'm not living with pigeons on my ledge. I cannot do that." So then I was offered this apartment, and I knew it was in the back of the complex.

The social connections and special favors that allowed applicants to get on the waiting list and be moved up the queue did not insulate applicants from the next stage of the process: the interview. Longtime residents recalled the arduous hurdles that followed the initial application, wherein Stuyvesant Town's management team interviewed and presented leases to those tenants who had reached the top of the waiting list. Such interviews were conducted in prospective tenants' homes. MetLife management attempted to communicate to applicants that the interview was merely a formality, but in truth, it was a standard procedure for interviewers to inspect the applicant's home, peek into closed cabinets, and ask intrusive questions. Arguably, such personal investigations are more closely associated with public housing projects than with private rentals.

Perhaps not surprisingly, typical interview questions included queries to review and verify facts, to check for inconsistencies, and to test whether applicants had been truthful in filling out the forms. However, MetLife's interviewers often delved into private matters, as well, routinely making inquiries about each household member's hobbies, patterns of comings and goings, guests and friends, and typical bedtimes. Some have speculated that these questions were linked to anti-black discrimination policies, such that MetLife was on the lookout for tenants who might bring African American guests or tenants to the community. Lines of questioning investigated applicants' daily behaviors and general lifestyles, as Tom and Jessica explained:

> TOM: They were very selective in those days. The procedure was someone on the staff would sign your lease and just have a conversation with you, and basically just see . . .
>
> JESSICA: How you lived.
>
> T: To verify that you lived where you said you lived, and how you lived. Every tenant was interviewed in those days. Every tenant was interviewed in their home, wherever they lived at that time. That was their procedure. [The interview] was very, very homey. You know, just casual. It didn't sound formal or feel formal. They just came and would chit chat, basically.
>
> J: It ended up that the gentleman who interviewed us lived below us. Not in this apartment. We were in a two-bedroom first. It was funny.
>
> T: Yeah. He was our next-door neighbor.

Perhaps most surprising, management rewarded those applicants who passed the lifestyle test by presenting them with a lease that they would have to sign on the spot. The catch? The lease was for an apartment that applicants were forbidden to view beforehand, just as Ilene described above. Thus, future tenants withstood the scrutiny of the application questions, in-home observations and interview, and strict lease terms, all for the privilege to live in an apartment they were not allowed to inspect—a violation of tenants' rights that would shock even the most jaded urban apartment hunter today.

Furthermore, many tenants reported that rental agents heavily pressured them into making rash decisions and signing leases, a practice that continues to this day:

> First, they'd tell us we were accepted, because you have to fill out all these forms telling how much money you have and what you earn and everything. Then they said we were accepted. Then I'd call and say, "Is there an apartment and everything?" "Well, not quite. We're working on a letter." It's evasive, and I thought, "What's going on?" And then I heard about the market stuff, and I thought, "We're cooked. That's it." Then I got a call very suddenly, "There's a block of apartments that are rent-stabilized that we have decided to open. Do you want one?" And I said, "Yes." And I took it on the spot. [My husband] was away. I couldn't even ask [him]. I had to do it right away. You're not allowed to look at them here.

Ken shared a similar story:

> We had to fill out an application. I remember that we were visited in our apartment at the time on Fifty-Ninth Street and Tenth Avenue from a representative [of MetLife]. At the time, it was run by Metropolitan Life. They owned it, and their employees were the rental staff and maintenance staff, so basically you did things their way . . . One thing you could not do then was see your own apartment. You had to take it more or less sight unseen, but having visited my wife's cousin, we knew basically what the layout of the apartment would be, so it was fine.

Though Stuyvesant Town's rent-stabilized tenants did not have the privilege of seeing the apartments beforehand or adequate time to think things over, longtime residents felt certain that living there would ensure a lifetime of housing stability as they moved through their lives and into their retirement years. This sense of security would leave them unprepared for the real estate drama that would unfold in their golden years.

## Now: Aging in Place in Stuyvesant Town

Today, the United States is witnessing two important demographic phenomena: the "graying" or rapid aging of a large segment of the population, and older people living longer lives than in the past. Though New York City is known for having a young, hip, vital population, it is also aging disproportionately compared to the rest of the nation.[11] Given this profile, city planners, health professionals, and families have been forced to ask themselves what the ideal residential environment is for older populations.[12] In cities like New York, where apartment living is typical, many residents are content to age in place. The universal design principles that apartments feature (typically a single-floor layout and an elevator, with differing degrees of secured building access that may feature doormen) provide a living situation that relieves older people of the burdens often found in suburban communities, such as social isolation, the need for a car, or the challenge of climbing steps in a house. Because so many of Stuyvesant Town's older residents are longtime tenants who have aged in place, the neighborhood has become what housing policymakers call a "NORC," or naturally occurring retirement community. New York City contains many NORCs, such as Chelsea's Penn South, the Bronx's Co-op City, Queens' Forest Hills Co-op, and Phipps Plaza West.[13]

Stuyvesant Town offers much to its senior residents on a fixed income, some of whom receive need-based assistance. They appreciate that it is located adjacent to what some call "Bedpan Alley"—two major hospitals and a Veterans Administration hospital. Seniors enjoy the perks of Stuyvesant Town and generally feel satisfied with the responsiveness of the maintenance staff when requesting repairs, painting, or exterminator services. However, what brings some seniors the greatest source of relief is their exemption from rent increases. Ilene explained:

> I'm much older now, and I'm under the SCRIE (Senior Citizen Rent Increase Exemption) Program. If you qualify for it, your rent gets frozen,

and you are not subject to paying MCI (major capital improvement) increases. So right now, if I were to live anywhere else I would be a fool, because my rent is at a certain level, and every two years I bring my income tax papers, and they look them over, and whatever the "ishkabibble" they do, I qualify, and that's it. It definitely is a perk, but most people don't apply for it, and the reason they don't apply for it is because they don't want anyone to know about them [getting assistance]. I'm not that proud.

To be eligible for this program, tenants must be at least sixty-two years old, reside in a rent-stabilized or a rent-controlled apartment, have an annual household income of $50,000 or less (after deductions including all income taxes and Social Security taxes in 2015), and pay more than one-third of the household's aggregate disposable income for rent.

The success of NORCs is dependent on the cooperation of the apartment complex's management in helping its aging tenants.[14] Indeed, in the past, the Stuyvesant Town Peter Cooper Village Tenants Association has worked with NORC consultants, such as the NORC Supportive Services Center, Inc., to address the special management issues related to its aging population. For example, when New York City officials were preparing for Hurricane Sandy in 2012, Stuyvesant Town's management issued a special alert spearheaded by the Tenants Association and Councilman Garodnick, asking tenants to check on elderly neighbors' preparedness for the storm. The Tenants Association also helped residents who suffered losses during and after the hurricane when tenants waited months for management to restore basic services while paying full rent. Specifically, the Tenants Association facilitated and negotiated resolution of a master complaint, resulting in a one-time rent reduction for more than 1,500 tenants affected by the storm.[15]

However, Stuyvesant Town's older tenants believe that management has not adjusted the services to meet the needs of the core, longtime tenants who have aged in place. For instance, when management renovated building lobbies in recent years, it did not install ramps for wheelchairs, leaving older people sitting at the bottom of the steps, helpless when the wheelchair lift was not functioning. Management decisions to adapt the design, service initiatives, and policies have been increasingly geared toward the newer residents' preferences and conveniences (e.g., Little League, adult sports teams, an indoor sports facility called "The Courts," and dog-friendly social activities) over the needs of older and longtime residents (e.g., maintaining the ban on cycling on pedestrian walkways and enforcing noise regulations).

These kinds of discrepancies between supply and demand of affordable age-appropriate housing, community features, public infrastructure, and supportive services are the negative and unintended consequences of a cohort aging in place. Still, compared to seniors who age in place in suburban and rural places, Stuyvesant Town residents arguably face far less risk of physical and cultural isolation, major problems that older people face when they stop driving.[16] An inexpensive, dependable, and accessible ride by bus, train, or taxi is just outside of their building should they seek goods, services, or the company of friends and family.

### Out with the Old and in with the New?

In the eyes of some longtime residents of Stuyvesant Town in Manhattan, the ruin of their apartment complex has come in stages. First, the development's managers opened a green market . . . which drew large crowds of nonresidents, and they scheduled noisy music concerts . . . Then they allowed vendor carts onto the property: neon-colored trucks that sell tacos, Greek food and desserts on the tree-shaded paths. And in August, they sent notice that all residents who kept property in the free storage spaces in the basements of the buildings would have 30 days to remove their belongings, a decision that provoked so much ire it was soon reversed. Now, a seasonal ice-skating rink that opened at the end of November has again put management and many residents on a collision course. A number of residents view the rink as another amenity that the property manager, Rose Associates, is using to try to lure new tenants who are willing to pay higher rents and who have no sense of the role the complex has played in providing low-cost housing to middle-class residents. (*New York Times* blog post, 2011)

Like most longtime residents, Ilene was eager to describe the changes in Stuyvesant Town's population composition, citing the three most visible groups: elderly stayers, New York University students, and "families choosing to raise their kids in the city":

I had a friend visit me from the suburbs one day. We passed by Bleecker Street playground. She goes, "I didn't know they had children in the city." That was really pretty stupid, but people in the suburbs at that time had really no idea what the city was like, and just to hear her say that was like, "Are you for real?" But there are an awful lot of young children here. And other than that, you've got the elderly that are still here. The younger people that are moving in. As a result of what Tishman-Speyer has done, we now have NYU students. So, to me there's only three categories.

Walter also noticed an influx of families with children: "There were a lot more older people. Not as many little kids. There are a lot more in this building now than there were."

Cathy and Morris also commented on the unlikely assortment of people now living in Stuyvesant Town, attributing the mix of people to the housing shortage in New York and the fact that apartment hunters cannot be as selective about neighborhoods as they were in the past:

> MORRIS: Many different kinds of people. A lot depends on money, money, money. And all sorts of business people, creative people, old people. It's very diversified, and so it depends on the individual's status of money and convenience and opportunity.
>
> CATHY: I think it's also a whole different scene. When we were looking for apartments years and years ago, you kind of said to yourself, "Oh, what neighborhood would I like to live in? I might like to live here, or I might like to live there. What do I pay? Oh, I could pay that or I could pay that." You know? It's just totally different. The housing stock has gotten smaller and smaller and smaller.

The influx of younger market-rate residents has caused many older residents to feel that their needs are no longer management's priority, and some even feel harassed by Stuyvesant Town's management. Of course, New York City residents have no shortage of horror stories about their conflicts with landlords and real estate management companies. The *Village Voice*, a weekly city newspaper, publishes a "Ten Worst Landlords" list every year that details landlords' various affiliations with powerful city officials, notes any city violations, and features anecdotes from tenants who have uselessly pleaded with landlords for help with their concerns.

New York is especially notorious for landlords who use harassment tactics to turn over apartments and raise rents. The *New York Times* has featured numerous stories about landlords' "overzealous tactics as they move to evict tenants from their rent-stabilized apartments and convert the units into market-rate housing."[17] In 2010, after settling such a case, New York State Attorney General Andrew M. Cuomo made the following pronouncement: "Landlords who harass tenants harm all New York City residents by displacing longtime tenants from stable neighborhoods and exacerbating the affordable-housing shortage. In these tough economic times, the preservation of affordable housing is of the utmost importance."[18]

Evelyn went so far as to assert that the newcomers are part of a grand scheme to eliminate older residents:

> They're working so hard to get rid of us. They just check if you own property anywhere. I've had friends who've been called up for non-lease renewals because they own property elsewhere, but this is still their primary residence. They've just been put through the mill to get legal defense to defend the fact that this is home. They check. Management checks their car registration, their checking account, their voter registration, and they go far and wide . . . It's been absolutely just heartbreaking, some of the stories I've heard of people who don't get their leases renewed and the cost that they have to incur to defend their home.

Beatrice acknowledged Stuyvesant Town's quick population turnover as well, but she dismissed the idea that management has been taking an active role in shifting the age structure of the tenants. Instead, she pointed out that the presence of young people is partly the natural result of the aging population dying off: "There's constantly people here passing." However, she did acknowledge that the newcomers create an atmosphere that bears little resemblance to the family-oriented sense of place that she experienced in Stuyvesant Town when she was a teenaged girl visiting her relatives there:

> There'd be people walking around, people with baby carriages. The children of the original tenants, and then I don't know if they got apartments or not. Or [if] they moved in with their parents. I'm not sure, but what-

ever. You could see all different age groups. Not as many young as you see today.

## Unwanted and Unused Upgrades and the Loss of Valued Amenities

Older tenants often reported that they do not have a use for the new amenities that Stuyvesant Town now advertises. Many complained about cutbacks to services that have impacted them, such as management firing the unionized painters and hiring non-unionized staff. Cathy and Morris took a typically cynical view of the upgrades that Stuyvesant Town management has implemented in an effort to attract younger, market-rate tenants. With modest means and nowhere else to go, the couple harbors deep fears and anxiety about the extravagant spending of their landlord and what that means for Stuyvesant Town's solvency:

> CATHY: Putting in all those gardens and everything, and putting in some services. They had to do something to attract the market-rate people 'cause there isn't any doorman.
>
> MORRIS: But now we're worried that the management might be in financial trouble and have to go bankrupt, and then where would all the tenants go? How will we get any services?
>
> C: What are we gonna do when they go over the cliff?
>
> M: If the management abandons us, and we don't own any apartment, and we're dependent on them, what happens after the management goes away?
>
> C: Also, the gossip. The workmen say that they've cut back a lot already. The maintenance man told me he has to work a whole extra building, squeeze it into his shift. And last time I had the plumber, this older man, and he was tired, and he says they've cut, I don't know what percentage, but a big percentage. And the same so that the plumbers have to work twice as hard, but he said, "I'm not complaining. I'm not complaining. I like my job."

One could argue that older tenants' feelings of insecurity are highly subjective and not fully grounded in reality. For instance, like Morris and Cathy, Evelyn described the ways in which gossip has fueled her concerns about her future housing situation. For many longtime residents who are financially constrained and content with the Stuyvesant Town that they had known, property upgrades can be perceived as superfluous. These tenants merely seek to maintain the basic amenities that they have heard are threatened, amenities that they have always valued and to which they have grown accustomed.

For instance, Evelyn seemed less interested in sharing cherished memories of the good old days than venting about her current and recent problems with management. Among these, she was forced to get an air conditioning unit and pay for it as part of an upgrade, and most recently she has been distraught over management's decision (reversed since the interview) to discontinue the practice of allowing tenants to have storage space in her building:

> The other concern I have that's up and coming is that we've always had trouble with our storage space, footlockers. And that's where I keep all of my Christmas ornaments and the girls' clothes and school things, and all the memorabilia of life. A person can't just keep [it all] in a little closet. . . . We got this fear, we got wind that they were going to discontinue that. I did rent two U-haul units here. So I'm paying another $160 on top of my rent to keep all-season clothes and other things there. But I do have about six big footlockers in wherever the storage units are for my building, and I'm very frightened that they're going to put U-haul units in those spaces to just bring in a little bit more rent—put every inch of space to work. And I don't know what I'm going to do then. Then I'm going to have to get a U-haul out of the city. It's where people would keep their baby carriages, their trunk, and their cribs and things, but everything had to be—except for cribs, baby carriages, strollers, and high chairs—everything else had to be in a footlocker or a suitcase. Nothing could be just loose and random. And way back then, we tenants had access to storage, so if I only wanted to bring one thing in and out, I didn't want the guys to haul up a big footlocker. It takes a couple days' arrangement. You used to be able to [get it yourself]. And they would bring the trunk up. It'd take a couple days of arrangement of calling and scheduling. You had to be home. You would sign. You'd get a card ticket with a number that matches what they look for and then the same thing in reverse. If you only had a little bit to change in and out of a trunk, they

would grant you access to storage, so you would join the serviceman and go downstairs.

Beatrice, in contrast, reported that she approves of the upgrades:

I think when the new people took over, Tishman-Speyer, they wanted to change the aura of the place, so they—in good faith, I would say—they planted a lot of trees. And they did a lot of paving, which is beautiful. [They] put new lighting in, lighting fixtures, and they did quite a bit which I'm very pleased with. 'Cause I love trees and flowers and everything . . . I love all the new paving they did. It's very nice, and they have done a lot of beautiful work around the Oval. I mean, it's spectacular. And they put a lot of money in, more than they had, never thinking the recession was coming, but they did a beautiful job, and they're still trying to maintain it. They're putting new steps in now in the back of our places here, and they are trying to make it as nice as they can, but they are losing money . . . You'd think I work for Tishman-Speyer. I don't have anything to do with it. Except for I pay my rent. But like, they put a lot of money in, and nobody really expected this.

Still, Beatrice's comments are contrary to the general pattern; she represents what research methodologists call a "negative case." Generally, longtime residents were adamant that management intended to use the upgrades as an instrument to increase rents, attract market-rate tenants desperate for Manhattan apartments, and squeeze out the older residents. Almost certainly, management would counter that maintaining an aging property in an expensive real estate market requires higher prices, and large numbers of stabilized tenants make it hard for landlords to keep up with needed maintenance.

## This Isn't "Sex and the City"

When asked about what it was like to be aging among the young newcomers, longtime residents seemed especially perplexed that young, unattached people would want to live in Stuyvesant Town. Many recalled their own negative opinions of Stuyvesant Town as an appropriate or desirable destination for relatively young people. However, some longtime residents seemed to have difficulty appreciating that New York City has changed considerably in the last twenty years, and the East Side and Union Square in particular have experienced significant urban renewal, making the area that surrounds Stuyvesant Town far more attractive to unattached young people than was the case in recent decades or when longtime residents first arrived.

Ken remarked that even back in the day, when he and his wife moved to Stuyvesant Town as a young couple, the neighborhood seemed so old-fashioned:

> We used to joke about it, because for us it still had—as it does now—it had that green sort of oasis at the Oval, but it was all very roped off, chained off. Literally, you weren't supposed to walk on the grass any-where. We were young enough that we used to sort of laugh at ourselves and where we were living, and it was sort of staid, sort of regimented. They had their own ways of doing things, but we did feel welcome, and we met nice people, and we liked the neighborhood.

Cathy and Morris also expressed confusion about young single peo-ple choosing Stuyvesant Town as a home in the city. Though the couple acknowledged the upside of the apartments, such as city views from large windows, ample daylight pouring into the rooms, spaciousness, and easy access to maintenance services, they said that Stuyvesant Town never fit their self-image: "It was a boring, middle-class, conventional place where stodgy people lived and didn't have any character, but my values changed 'cause with getting older, I did not want to be extremely elderly and live in a walk-up."

At the time of their move to Stuyvesant Town, and Cathy and Morris had a strong emotional attachment to the East Village, a diverse, lively neighborhood. Though Stuyvesant Town is located nearby, it failed to conform to the couple's bohemian identity. However, eventually they adapted and modified their opinion of Stuyvesant Town, a surrender to their changing circumstances.

Several longtime residents asserted that management's advertising Stuyvesant Town as an exciting, young, luxury destination was just hype. Walter insisted that this strategy is just a way for the landlord to justify high rents, and stated that in fact, Stuyvesant Town has not undergone as much of a transformation as potential tenants may think:

> In some ways it hasn't changed at all. The people who bought the place five years ago [Tishman-Speyer] have made a huge effort to make people believe these were luxury apartments, and it just didn't work because they're not. And the people who live here and have lived here a long time live here because of the same reasons—because it's affordable, safe, and relatively pleasant.

Cathy agreed that it is preposterous for the landlord to brand Stuyvesant Town as glamorous or sophisticated:

> It's very middle class. We used to laugh at it years ago when everybody was a bohemian. It was the last word in boring bourgeois. Who would want to live there? Your grandmother would want to live there. Oh, it was stodgy and conventional, cookie-cutter apartments . . . Our architecture is drab. Very. It's terrible, but so what? [Laughs] So what? Nice apartment. Who cares? I mean, maybe there are people who have discretionary money, and they may decide what kind of neighborhood they'd like and not like. I don't think it has any cachet, you know, people who live on the Upper East Side probably don't [want to live here].

Ken also commented that people seeking luxury should probably look elsewhere: "People who would want a different level of luxury, a better level of luxury, would not choose it."

As Walter explained, Stuyvesant Town as a neighborhood is not well integrated with retail and restaurants, it is relatively far from some of the more heavily utilized subway lines, and it lacks the status or exclusivity of nearby neighborhoods with varied styles of architecture, wealthy residents, and full-service buildings. He seemed mystified by market-rate tenants because he rejects the idea that Stuyvesant Town has been sufficiently upgraded to merit such high rents:

> It's the same floors. The toilets are still lousy. They still give you a paint job every three years. It really has not changed. Certainly for the rent-stabilized tenants, the affordability factor has always been there, and that's

what makes it very attractive to people. Paying twice as much rent as I am paying now would not appeal to me. So the people who were paying all that, and much, much more, I'm sure their experience of this is very, very different. People who are interested in living here, meaning they don't live here already, you got to be fairly wealthy because if you're moving in, you've got to pay market rates. And this apartment is probably close to $5,000 a month, and so they're either fairly wealthy or there are five people that are willing to pay for this kind of place.

Luxury or not, Stuyvesant Town's propinquity matters. Close to NYU, hospitals, and trendy neighborhoods, a higher-income market is interested in residing there. Like so many longtime residents, Ken agreed that the middle class has been priced out of Stuyvesant Town:

> The pricing structure, of course, has all changed since when we moved in. We still have stabilized rent . . . I think probably now the people who would not be attracted to it, would basically be for reasons of price. Some people would be priced out of it who previously would not be . . . I think probably the big consideration now is that it's expensive.

Longtime tenants view the amenities, some of which are open to people outside of the complex for a fee, as a commercialization of the community and a further divide between the haves and have-nots. Some have observed that the fee-based amenities divide the younger families, as well. Referring to Oval Kids, Ilene, a longtime resident, said:

> One of [the mothers I babysit for] asked me, "Would you like me to get a membership, so you can play there with the children?" I said, "Are you kidding? Are you really kidding?" If it's cold, I can take them somewhere else. I don't need to sit around and talk to other nannies. And I heard at Christmastime they had a Santa, but only for the people who paid. How do you like that? Is Santa not for everyone?

Ilene's observation highlights how the changes in Stuyvesant Town, particularly the addition of fee-based amenities that are not accessible to all tenants, have made class differences more visible in the community. The floor-to-ceiling glass windows that encase each of the four amenity spaces are highly conspicuous on the Oval. Children walking with their parents past Oval Kids can see brightly colored toys and other children having fun, but they are not allowed to participate if their parents have not paid the membership fee. Since opening in 2007, occasional activities are open to "non-members," and the Oval Lounge has been converted to Oval Café, which is now open to the public. Management has also removed the harsh signs warning non-member residents that they are forbidden from sitting at the tables or even on the chairs. It is unclear whether these changes are in response to tenants' complaints or whether they are just management's attempts to improve the economic viability of some of the offerings. Regardless, the relaxing of the restrictions and removal of signage has ameliorated some feelings of exclusion that residents have experienced within their own community.

## Surveillance, Intimidation, and Aggressive Eviction Tactics

People who live in rent-stabilized apartments are reluctant to let them slip away from their possession and are often interested in passing the property on to other family members. The topics of "succession rights," renewal leases, and eviction protection are especially heated among older tenants, as some have grown children who live with them and care for them over extended periods of time. These younger family members often want the rights to the apartment after an older relative dies.

This topic arose when Evelyn explained that her two adult daughters share in her disappointment about the changes to Stuyvesant Town and the surrounding neighborhoods:

> They both just absolutely love New York, loved growing up here, loved the era they grew up in here, in this neighborhood of being a little rough and tumble and working class, but they don't like what they see now . . . They're sorry to see what's going on in this particular community in the worst way. 'Cause they could never afford to move back, and that's what hurts. They really always dreamed that they could come back to New York. They could take this apartment, and we still have to sort that out, as to succession, 'cause they both want to. They don't want anyone else to live here if something were to happen that we couldn't be here anymore . . .

One child can take it, but you have to prove that they've been living here for two years. They have to be living here for two years.

When asked about how management would know who exactly has been living in the apartment and for what period of time, many residents seemed certain that management monitors apartments and encourages residents, staff, and delivery people to "spy" on tenants in search of lease violations. Laura Dunn, a forty-three-year-old African American single mother, again fueled by rumors and discussions with people working in the building, said that she was beginning to feel paranoid about management's surveillance practices. She provided evidence for the legitimacy of her concerns:

A couple years ago, a Fed Ex guy came to my door, and it was a package for me. It must have been before the kids were born because there wasn't anybody around. And I was signing it, and we were talking, and he was like, "You know, your folks here are really coming down hard on us." I said, "What folks?" He said, alluding to management or whatever, he said, "They're wanting us to check in with them to see if there are people illegally subletting apartments." And I said, "Really?" And he said, "Yeah. Really."

Even Beatrice, who seemed eager to come to the defense of Stuyvesant Town management, stated that she has witnessed acts of intimidation and has heard rumors about management harassing older, rent-stabilized tenants. She said this kind of chatter has stoked her own fears:

I've [read] articles about Stuyvesant Town, where MetLife investigated seniors, older people, saying it was their second home. You probably have met some of them already. That caused me a lot of anxiety and grief, because some of them are only [gone from the building] for brief times. There are still a lot of seniors that I know in this building . . . The problem that I could see or I have seen recently in the last two years is that they were checking on people's identity and finding out that some of the older people in the rent-stabilized apartments . . . They were trying to get people out, so I think that was one bad thing that they did. They did an investigation into taxes, whatever form of privacy they invaded. I know people personally that have left through intimidation.

## Thanks for the Memories: The Stuy Town Way of Life Comes to a Close

Many long-term residents complained that with the changes in population and policies, Stuyvesant Town has lost its sense of place, its community cohesiveness, and its friendliness. Cathy felt this way and explained that hers was a subdued version of the general dissatisfaction among longtime residents: "We haven't been here long enough to grumble like the *real* old-timers. The real old-timers have said that the management and neighbors were friendly, and it hasn't been friendly for a long time." Even Walter, who was originally reluctant to move back to his childhood home, said that his memories of growing up in Stuyvesant Town were mostly positive. He seemed especially satisfied with the fact that he was able to attend a high-quality school and his family felt safe from crime, a combination of community features that New York City families cannot take for granted.

Many residents shared memories of Stuyvesant Town's events, organizations, children's playgroups, and babysitting pools. They were especially pleased with the fact that in the old days the residents, themselves, organized such activities. For instance, Tom and Jessica, both musicians and singers, had organized a music program to showcase residents' talents, a contrast to the management-sponsored concerts held on the grounds of today's Stuyvesant Town:

> TOM: On the good side—and actually not related to being a security guard, because Jessica and I are musicians—we initiated, along with another lady who was our neighbor who's passed on now, music programs in the summer.
> JESSICA: In the beginning it was just us out on the playground. [A neighbor] knew that we were musicians, and she knew that in Stuyvesant Town there were a lot of other talented people.
> T: Yeah, not only Beverly Sills.
> J: But she suggested it would be nice to have a talent show to showcase the people in the community. Now, they don't do it anymore. They

have the thing in the Oval though, the jazz. But in the beginning it
was showcasing the people here, and each year they would do it. And
it was quite a big deal, and the whole playground would be filled.

T: Anyway, it's actually exciting to be a part of that history, the fact that
we had a little influence in bringing music to the community.

Many longtime residents stressed the importance of living someplace
where tenants "stay put." They were proud that they have continued to
maintain the friendships that they had formed when they were still raising their families in Stuyvesant Town. One man explained how these relationships with neighbors span generations and allow residents to have
shared histories and memories:

We have a nice relationship with a couple I mentioned, the retired police officer and teacher. We'd go out together occasionally. With the kids
growing up at the same time, we'd be at a lot of the same places: basketball games, softball games, soccer games. So we're very comfortable with
them and our other neighbors, also boys. Friendly people. During the
last transit strike when everybody was figuring out how to get to work, I
happened to be coming out of the building, and the husband was driving
his wife down to work—she works near where I do—so I hopped in the
car with them. So those are probably the people that we're friendliest with
on the floor, but we've also made friends with other people in the building that you see over the years—a few older people, very nice people. You
live somewhere long enough, so you're around. Somebody has a baby
or unfortunately, somebody dies. So one of our upstairs neighbors on a
different floor, a very nice woman who was a widow herself, lost her husband at a young age, probably four or five kids. She died about a year ago,
and we see her children in the building. One of her sons is probably in his
twenties, plays basketball at the Y where I play on Sunday mornings, and
he's one of the guys who can play who tolerate me.

Still, others have taken it a step further, maintaining old friendships
while forming new ones with the younger families. Beatrice, again more
extroverted and atypical, was proud to say that she knows everyone on
her floor and feels grateful that she can rely on neighbors to help her
carry groceries, to assist her when she is ill, or just to socialize. Her floor

has experienced less tenant turnover, so she has been able to establish friendships with neighbors who are younger, but who intend to stay. She described her special relationships with some of these neighbors, such as the man who lives in the apartment above hers:

He's directly up top . . . He's single, and he's a wonderful neighbor. When I was sick he brought up my mail, did the shopping, and if I go away for a few days, he takes care of everything for me. He'll come in and water the plants and take care of the apartment. And he's a wonderful neighbor, and my family likes him a lot. And he has his own life now. I just left him a note to say, "Does he want breakfast in the morning?" And he said, "No." He was out for the weekend. But we do have breakfast together about once a month, and we go across the street. It's like payback time to him for all he does for me.

Beatrice then described the newer families whom she has come to know:

Further down, there's a young family, David and his wife, and their lovely little boy, and he's either three now or four . . . And I can't tell how many times, now it wouldn't be every week, it might be every couple, they'll knock on the door and say, "Did you eat? We have steak." Now, they've been here a good while, but not as long as the rest. And there's a man here for many, many years, an older man, and his wife died, and he's a nice person. He will help me carry things if I need to carry heavy things. And then there's another apartment that has people who go to work very early. They work for television. They invited me down [to the television station] in the morning if I wanted to go down and see everything. And then, there's two across the hall, and they have a daughter, and she's just leaving for Chicago tonight, the girl. Lovely girl, and they are marvelous friends, and we go out for dinner occasionally across the street, and we have a bite to eat or something, at the Indian restaurant. They're very nice . . . Unbelievable, the people on the floor here. Just the two apartments beside me have changed . . . Two young couples that moved in here in the last year, and the other apartment now is empty. And the others are all the same. So this young couple of Indian ancestry would feel comfortable at a party with everybody on the floor, I invited everybody on the floor for a party to welcome them. And they couldn't get over us . . . We have become great friends. They even invite me to parties up there for their age group, and we have become great friends.

Several middle-aged residents have even formed networks to look out for their older neighbors. For instance, Nora Lewis, an eighty-two-year-old widow who lives alone, reported that neighbors bring her food and take her to church. Ilene also proudly reported on her own efforts to organize the neighbors to help an ailing resident. Still, the residents generally agree that the modern era marks an end to the celebrated Stuyvesant Town way of life. In the next chapter, we provide a closer look at longtime residents' experiences by focusing on the single case of a woman named Ruthie. The arc of her narrative reveals how longtime residents have made sense of their past and current lives in Stuyvesant Town as they have aged in place.

3

# Aging in Place in the City

*Ruthie's Story*

Ruthie Goldblum's bright, clean two-bedroom Stuyvesant Town apartment is located on a high floor facing the Oval. On a Sunday afternoon the sun shines through lace curtains, scattering a pattern of light onto the vintage furniture and the fading family photos that decorate the wall. "These weren't here when I moved in," she joked, pointing to the photos. Her coffee table and end tables are trimmed with gold paint and are draped with aged, delicate handmade doilies that match the curtains.

At eighty-three years old, Ruthie is what many longtime Stuyvesant Town residents call an "original." She has lived in the community since it first opened in 1948 and has no plans to leave her cherished apartment, let alone her beloved Manhattan. Here, she described her personal experiences of raising three children in a two-bedroom apartment and then years later, dealing with the difficulties of aging in place alone as a widow in Stuyvesant Town.

Ruthie was excited to share her vivid memories of Stuyvesant Town, where she made lifelong friends and watched her three children play freely and safely outside. As she proudly provided a tour of her apartment, she presented the view from the master bedroom window and pointed to the Oval and its fountain to the north, which has long served as a centerpiece for community social life: "I met a whole group of people here that I still know. Some of them are still living here. We call ourselves the 'original' tenants." Ruthie's story highlights longtime residents' sentimental attachments to their homes and neighborhood and the particular sense of place that Stuyvesant Town evokes for them. It provides the groundwork for understanding their perceptions of the changes that have taken place since they first arrived.

## Moving In

New York City's postwar housing crisis left very little housing available, and as discussed, part of MetLife's process for vetting prospective Stuyvesant Town tenants included representatives inspecting applicants' current homes. Shortly after Ruthie and her husband, Hersch, applied for their first apartment there, management associates visited her mother's home, where the couple was residing:

> You applied for Stuy Town, and a few of my friends did. All of a sudden, wherever you lived, the doorbell would ring, and [someone would say], "I'm from Stuyvesant Town, and I came to investigate and inspect where you live and how it's kept." This was my mother's apartment. You know, you could have a dirty mother or something. Anyway, they investigated and looked in cabinets and such and wanted to know where you sleep, and just everything! And then you waited for a reply.

Ruthie and Hersch passed the inspection, and just a few months later they moved into their first Stuyvesant Town apartment, a one-bedroom unit. Years later, after their first child was born, they applied to move into a two-bedroom, and once again, MetLife's management insisted on inspecting their apartment. Though it was an intrusion, Ruthie considered herself fortunate to secure what she called a "family-sized" apartment in Stuyvesant Town. Many of her friends were not as lucky:

> A lot of friends did not get in, you know? I don't know what the reason was. They never tell you. They just never call you back for an apartment . . . You had to give them how much money you made. You had to give your whole life's story to them.

She went on to speculate that these friends who MetLife rejected might not have met the income requirements for residency in Stuyvesant Town. Though these were rent-controlled apartments, MetLife sought to fill them with middle-income tenants, and many returning veterans earned insufficient wages to qualify. Ruthie explained that she and Hersch had to prove they were worthy, and it was a struggle:

We moved in at $55 [a month]. That was expensive because the guys just got out of the Army. But they had to have a job. You had to show them your income tax return, or something saying what you're making and everything. Just to pay the rent. That's all they care about. $55 sounds like nothing, but it was *not* nothing. It was expensive then. It's all according to the time. When I was a kid, you bought three bananas for a nickel. Three rolls—Kaiser rolls—for a nickel, and now, it cost me ninety-nine cents for two bananas.

Ruthie was correct in noting that $55 a month was not a modest sum in 1948. Suburban communities were starting to boom at around this time, and for about the same price, she and Hersch could have achieved the American Dream by buying their own suburban home. In Levittown, New York, located just twenty-five miles from Manhattan, families were snapping up four-room suburban tract homes for less than $60 a month, and with little to no money down.[1] Often, real estate developers offered these houses as rentals with the option of purchasing after one year. Thanks to Federal Housing Authority and Veterans Administration programs, renting could cost more than the total price of a mortgage, principal, interest, and taxes, so buying a house soon became the norm across the country.[2]

However, Ruthie and her husband, like others of her generation who moved into Stuyvesant Town and stayed, wanted to make their life in the city. Following the first residents who moved into Stuyvesant Town in August 1947, Ruthie and Hersch arrived in 1948. By 1949, tenants occupied every unit, and veterans and their families lived in 98 percent of them.

## Raising Children in Stuyvesant Town

Ruthie and Hersch referred to Stuyvesant Town as a "godsend." For them, finding an affordable apartment was the only thing standing in the way of expanding their family:

I wanted to have a baby, and my husband said, "No, not until we have an apartment. We're not going to raise a baby in an unfurnished room." And that's what happened. Everybody moved in, and the next year we all had babies. And then you had the Catholics and the non-Jews who weren't religious, and the Jews who were. Two years later, you had more babies! When I moved into Stuy Town I lived on Avenue C in a one-bedroom. You had to have a child to get a two-bedroom apartment, and I didn't have any. And then when Isaac was born, we were overcrowding the apartment because I only had one bedroom. My girlfriend had lived next door, and she found out from the people living here that they were moving. Well, every day I called them up. I wanted to live here because of the school district. P.S. 40 was the school in this district, and my girl-friend lived next door. I wanted to live next door. Every morning I would call the people, and they'd be working, and they'd say, "Mrs. Goldblum, we have not found out who is going to get the apartment." And then they called me, and told me.

Ruthie's concerns about finding an appropriate apartment and a quality school mirror young families' concerns in today's Stuyvesant Town. With two-bedroom apartments financially out of reach, families often will rent one-bedroom apartments that management has converted into two bedrooms by installing a temporary wall. This floor plan consists of a small, windowless living area and two reasonably sized bedrooms.

A few years later, Ruthie gave birth to their second child, a daughter, and submitted an application for a three-bedroom apartment. This time, the couple faced a long wait to find an apartment that would better ac-commodate a family of four. In fact, it took ten years before Stuyvesant Town management contacted them with the news that a three-bedroom had become available. By then Ruthie had given birth to a third child, Maggie, but their eldest child had already grown up, gotten married, and moved. In addition, Ruthie and her family were reluctant to say goodbye to their home; they had established a strong attachment to their location on the Oval and their neighbors:

They really didn't make enough three-bedrooms, because I waited ten years when I put in an application for a three-bedroom apartment. I waited ten years, and they called me two weeks after my first daughter got married. So, I said, "Hey, it's right across the street from the post of-fice, and I didn't like it there. It was on the top floor, and on the top floor you have the pipes of the heat across. And [Maggie] started crying, "All of my friends live in the Oval. I don't want to live there!" And I said, "You know what? I love my apartment, and if I can raise three children in a two-bedroom, I can raise two children in a two-bedroom." So, I stayed here, and I'm not sorry.

Ruthie described the various ways she coped with raising three children in a two-bedroom apartment. The children shared the master bedroom, and she and Hersch were relegated to the smaller second bedroom. She explained how this living arrangement forced the couple to become creative with their parenting skills. After all, with three children sharing a room, the couple could not very well punish them by sending them to their own isolated bedrooms: "I couldn't say, 'Go to your room. You're being bad!' I would say, 'Now, you sit down there, and don't you dare move 'til I tell you.' And then, of course, they'd tell me that they call it the 'punishment chair.' I couldn't say, 'Go in your room!' There was no room!"

The contentious practice of constructing makeshift walls to improve privacy in Stuyvesant Town apartments is not a new phenomenon. Ruthie's father eventually erected a wall in the kids' master bedroom to provide privacy to the two girls and her son, Isaac. However, this solution was short-lived: "My father built a wall because Maggie's friend had a wall. My father was in his 70s when he built it, and years ago when you had to paint, they would come six weeks before and plaster. Now, they plaster and paint, and it doesn't stay." Ruthie was uncertain whether the recent shoddy paint job in her apartment could be attributed to management cutting corners on painting supplies or the fact that they have hired less experienced painters. However, she went on to explain what happened to the makeshift wall that her father had built to give Maggie some privacy:

When they came up to plaster, they saw the wall and sent me a letter and called me up and said it was a fire hazard . . . They said that if there was a fire here, they would have to walk through [her son's room] to get out. Then, they had to take the wall out, but we got a bamboo divider . . . The girls used to just open it up, and Isaac had his own room, and they had theirs. And then when Isaac got married, Maggie said, "Ma, I want my own room!" And she did.

Many original tenants eventually moved away from Stuyvesant Town, often to the suburbs, or as they retired, to a warmer climate. However, Ruthie wanted to remain because she likes living in the home where she raised her family, she is attached to life in Manhattan, and most of all, it made sense to stay since Hersch worked nearby. She said that she has no regrets:

> I love this city. I never wanted to move out. All my friends moved out to the Island [Long Island] after a while. They lived here a number of years, and they moved out to the Island. My husband worked on Fourteenth Street and Fifth Avenue, and he walked to work and walked home. I said, "What am I, crazy? I'm going to make him commute [when] we [can] live right here?" Well, I don't see the point in moving out. But everybody that moved out, some of them went to Florida and died, and I'm still happy here. So, why? I was very happy.

Ruthie provided an unsurprising list of reasons that some of her neighbors exited Stuyvesant Town when she was younger. Some wanted houses with more space and private yards. Understandably, some told her that they were simply fed up with the hassles of apartment life, such as noisy neighbors and unaccommodating landlords. Others just decided that they would prefer to live in a warmer climate. For many people, a longer commute to work seems like a reasonable trade-off for a home that better meets a family's needs. However, Ruthie was unwilling to compromise on a long commute from the suburbs that would result in a loss of family time and would place so much distance between herself and her beloved city. She also described her perception that some of her friends had become competitive about the fact that they were becoming homeowners and she was still living in a rental, or that they had more space than she did: "Some of my friends [think] if *you* wanted to buy a house, [then] I wanted to buy a house. If *you* wanted a bigger house, then I wanted a [bigger house]. That's how it is in Florida— 'You can't have more rooms than me.' I mean, I don't know. What's the competition?"

With the postwar population boom and so many children around, as mentioned in the chapter 1 comparison of Stuyvesant Town to a "rabbit farm," Ruthie insists that Stuyvesant Town was an ideal place to raise a family. She emphasized that the community made it easy for children to form bonds with each other, become close with neighbors, and play spontaneously. In contrast, she is highly critical of the suburbs, which she considers to be insular places that require planned activities and scheduled play dates. She thinks the city's population density leads to familiarity and more natural opportunities for social interaction, so adults and children can form friendships with neighbors:

> First of all, we had a lot of friends. There are so many friends, so many friends. It's wonderful. I think it's great for children. Because, look, if you buy a house on the Island, or wherever you buy a house, you don't know who is living next door. And you might not have any children on the whole block. Maybe only children from school. Here, there's always children.

As a parent, Ruthie also valued Stuyvesant Town's feeling of safety as an essential aspect of its identity as a New York City community for families. For example, at the local grocery store, D'Agostino, on Twentieth Street, Stuyvesant Town's mothers would leave their babies outside in carriages while they shopped. (Though today, in the space where the market once stood is Oval Fitness, Stuyvesant Town's gym that costs approximately $80 a month for membership.) Ruthie felt so certain of her children's safety in her community that she allowed them to go to the playgrounds unaccompanied by an adult: "Francie, the oldest, would say, 'I want to go downstairs.' I'd say, 'Okay, go downstairs, and when you want to come up, call me.' She'd call me from this window."

One of Ruthie's fondest memories of raising her children in Stuyvesant Town is of the daily preschool program that the development's recreation department administered:

> They had a [preschool] group. Gee whiz! They would get together and play around. They would play games. And then, when you were ready to go to school—this was preschool—when you were ready to go to school, they had a graduation. I took a picture of my daughter in a cap and a gown. I mean, it was wonderful, and that was something I did every day.

Stuyvesant Town once offered this supervised children's activity free of charge to all residents, but today in its place is "Oval Kids," which

Figure 3.1 A page from a MetLife brochure for Stuyvesant Town from February 1952 entitled "Stuyvesant Town—This is YOUR Home," showing an activity that the recreation department organized for families. The subtitle for this section of the brochure is "Children are Happy in Stuyvesant Town." Reproduced with permission of MetLife Archives.

requires a special membership of $60 in addition to the price of classes.

Many who grew up in Stuyvesant Town continued to live there as adults and went on to raise their own children in the community. Ruthie's two oldest children used Stuyvesant Town as a starter home when they first got married and had children before they eventually purchased homes in the suburbs:

> When Francie and Isaac each got married, as soon as they got engaged, they put in for an application because they were considered a tenant. Francie said, "Look, we're getting married June 7th. I want the apartment at the end of May." They got it because they were tenants, and they were next in line for whatever [apartment became available]. Isaac did the same thing, and [he and his wife] got it. They lived here five years and saved up money, because the rent was not as high as now, and they bought houses.

Ruthie is clearly proud of the life that she and her husband provided for their children in Stuyvesant Town. Living there afforded the children many opportunities that were not readily available in other neighborhoods in the city or elsewhere. They had open spaces, playgrounds, and organized community activities in the comfort of a neighborhood with a higher degree of safety than most because of the private security officers. As residents of Stuyvesant Town, her children also had rights to affordable apartments when they were ready to start their own families, which allowed them to save money to buy their own homes later. However, Ruthie's conception of Stuyvesant Town as an ideal place for families has been tempered by recent changes. She now believes that management's focus on young singles has transformed the feeling it once had as a "bubble" that protected children from the adult world of New York City: "I have to tell you, if you had to raise children in this city, this was the best place. The best place in the world . . . There's so many things different now."

## In and Out of Work Life

Ruthie often waits at the Stuyvesant Town stop for the M23 crosstown bus that goes between the east and west sides of the city. Though in her eighties, she still works two days a week at Baruch College. When she started working nearly seventy years ago, she was already ahead of her time and a savvy negotiator:

> I graduated at eighteen [years old] on a Friday and went to work on a Monday. I went to work for accountants and lawyers, and I did statistical typing. So, they offered me $18 a week, and I said, "No, I can't. I need $20." And they said, "Why do you need $20?" And I said, "Because I have to give my parents $10." So, whatever was left was mine, and I needed that two extra bucks, and they gave it to me.

Ruthie continued to work even after marrying Hersch, but she eventually quit her job in order to spend time with her husband while he was stationed in Florida. Shortly after, Hersch found out that he was up for furlough, so Ruthie contacted her boss immediately to ask for her job back:

> I went there, and they said, "We'll take you back only on one condition: as soon as you become pregnant, we have to know." Because years ago you

couldn't have a belly at work. As soon as you became pregnant, "Out!" So stupid. Because I did nothing for all those months [while pregnant and not working].

In the years that Ruthie was not employed outside of the home, she was an industrious homemaker. Because Hersch walked past the children's school on his way to work, he was responsible for morning drop-off. This freed up Ruthie to complete the laundry, cooking, and cleaning before she picked up the children from school in the afternoon. She proudly described the lack of leisure in her daily routine as a housewife:

When the kids were a lot younger, I never had anybody coming in early in the morning for coffee. I never had friends. I didn't want to have friends coming in early in the morning and sitting down. You know, you have a cup of coffee, and it lasts for three hours. Every morning after 8:00, you would see me dusting the windowsill. I mean, I had a routine, and I had a washing machine. You were allowed to have a washing machine then. And [I had] a dryer that fit over the bathtub from one end to the other, so you can hang your clothes to dry. So, I used to do laundry every morning. If I had a pot roast or something that took long to cook, like a stew, I would put it in [the oven] in the morning.

Ruthie's description of her busy, solitary, no-nonsense routine contrasted with her earlier description of sociability and having a lot of friends in the community. When asked about the contradiction, she indicated that many of the Stuyvesant Town mothers used to fritter away their mornings gossiping with one another, which she neither approved of nor participated in.

Though Ruthie enjoyed her stay-at-home mom days in Stuyvesant Town, it was not long before a chance encounter with a neighbor led to her return to work:

When my daughter, Maggie, was eight years old, one of my friends [Judy] who I met in Stuy Town, she had a daughter who was Maggie's age, and they were friends. And Judy would say to me, "Why the heck don't you try and find a job?" I said, "You find me a job, and I'll go to work." And she did. She was working, and she said, "Ruthie, how would you like to work for two weeks?" I said, "Doing what?" She said, "Typing envelopes." I said, "Judy, oh my God. I haven't typed in fifteen years." Well, she took me into the interview, and I went in, and I told him the truth that I hadn't typed in fifteen years. So, I sat down, and you know when you ride a bike and you fall? I sat down, and I started to type. This was a two-week job, and my first in seven years. I worked part-time for a while, and I left after the kids went to school. Then, in the summer I worked longer because they went to camp.

Ruthie, like many mothers, preferred working part-time, but this made her ineligible for benefits, such as paid time off. So, within a few years she resumed working full-time:

So, my boss called me in one day and said, "I want you to sit down and figure out how many hours a week you work." It came out to like, thirty-three and a half hours a week. She said, "For thirty-five hours you can get all the benefits." I had no benefits, and if you didn't work you didn't get paid. So, that's when my boss said, "You're a schmuck! For another couple of hours, two and a half hours, you can get your benefits." So, I worked full-time.

By the mid-1960s, Ruthie was part of the growing cadre of working mothers, and her Stuyvesant Town address, near Manhattan's bustling Midtown, gave her convenient access to a broad range of employment opportunities within a short distance of their home and the children's schools.

In fact, Ruthie's urban lifestyle and return to full-time employment in the mid-1960s contrasts sharply with the depiction of suburban housewives popularized by Betty Friedan's 1963 book *The Feminine Mystique*. However, working full-time as a mother of three, Ruthie and her family made difficult trade-offs. She explained that her children were helpful around the house, but she would still come home to a second shift of household chores after a full day of clerical work at the college. Ruthie described how the family coped with their new lifestyle and how she struggled to let go of control while upholding her strict housekeeping standards:

We had a family meeting. They always had to make their beds, and they'd say, "Did I do a good job?" and I'd say, "You did a wonderful job!" But, of course, then I'd straighten it up. And then, if I had a chicken to roast, Francie [the oldest child] would put it in the oven. Just put it in the oven, not touch it, you know? Maggie would set the table because she was the youngest. I mean, everybody chipped in, and it was fine.

Working also expanded Ruthie's friendship networks, in that she became friends with women who were younger and had not yet settled down. These women, whom she had called the "kids" at work, are now grown with their own children, and they remain close friends. Ruthie attended her colleagues' weddings, their children's Bar and Bat Mitzvahs and christenings, and eventually *their* children's weddings. She told a story about one of her work friends who wanted to live in Stuyvesant Town when the waitlist was still active:

She said to me one day, years ago, "Ruthie, I'd love to live in Stuyvesant Town." I said, "Do me a favor. Go get yourself an application, fill it out, and forget about it for a while. It's going to take a while, maybe even a few years." But, what does it hurt to fill out an application? Before you know it, years went by, and she's been living in Stuyvesant Town for thirty years now, and loves it.

With her children grown and out of the house, Ruthie continued to work at the same local college for nearly twenty years. She retired briefly at age seventy, but her boss convinced her to come back a few years later. Ruthie accepted, but only on her terms:

They said, "We'd like to ask you to come back." I said, "Only for part-time and under my conditions. If I want to take two or three weeks off in the winter, or I want to go away in the summer." They said, "Whatever you want to do." So, I retired thirteen years ago, but went back to work ten years ago. I only retired three years. Really, I still consider myself retired.

## The Senior Years in Stuyvesant Town

Ruthie has continued to be able to afford her Stuyvesant Town apartment, but many seniors on fixed incomes are unable to keep up with rent increases. While retired, she had qualified for the Senor Citizen Rent Increase Exemption (SCRIE) program, but her return to work raised her income just above the threshold, disqualifying her use of it:

> When I retired I applied for SCRIE, and I got it! That was before I started to work. I didn't know that every two years you have to fill out the application or else they think you're cheating them. Then one year I made $21,000—$1,000 more [over the maximum income to qualify at the time], and they wouldn't give it to me.

Ruthie explained that her rent is currently $1,057 a month. If she had continued to qualify for SCRIE, her rent would have been reduced by hundreds of dollars a month. She described the reasons that she continues to work, despite the financial disincentive:

> I'd rather work, anyway. It gives me two days a week where I get up and get dressed, and I'm amongst people. I love it. I mean, we have Indians and Hispanics, Asians, and African Americans, and just the United Nations! I love every one of them. They're great to me. And you're amongst people. It keeps your mind going. But they're all just wonderful, and a lot of them are all new people, so it's like a revolving door. But whoever comes in, I get along with them. So, it's good for me to get out of the house.

### When an Improvement Is Not an Improvement

Ruthie has lived through many changes during her life in Stuyvesant Town, both for the better and for the worse. Overall, she has strong positive sentiments toward her community. Pointing again out the window, and down to the Oval, she explained that the property has always been beautifully maintained, way before Stuyvesant Town's market-rate period: "And I'll tell you they [MetLife] really kept it beautifully. This is not new." Below, Ruthie describes her perception of the upgrades and policy changes in Stuyvesant Town and explains the reasons that she is so critical of the changes. Many of the improvements have received poor reviews from older tenants.

Ruthie first described air conditioning as a problem. She said that management gave Stuyvesant Town residents the option of installing window air conditioning units for a monthly fee plus the cost of the air conditioning unit. Many of the current tenants could not afford these costs. Ruthie still does not have air conditioning in her apartment:

> I couldn't afford it for a long, long time. I would've had to, when they first came in, I would have had to pay $127 [up front for the air conditioner] plus $19.90 for each air-conditioner a month. Plus you had to remove the window. I don't know if they charged you [for that] or what. And you had to buy the air-conditioner, I think, from a certain place. But that's a lot of money.

Ruthie also recalled that she felt pressured to opt in at the initial offering because management had warned her that the price would go up later. She then explained that management eventually installed air conditioning in all apartments and required new tenants to pay the fees: "That's one of the things. When a tenant moves out, they put in the air-conditioners, and then you have to pay for it. They tell you it's free; it's not free." Even so, Ruthie seemed content with her window fan and the ceiling fans that she had purchased and which the handyman from the local hardware store installed for her. She later dismissed the implication that the cost of air conditioning was her main concern: "It's not that. It's that I don't like air conditioning . . . so I have fans."

Around 2005 MetLife installed energy-saving heating sensors in Stuyvesant Town with the stated purpose of more efficiently regulating apartments' steam heat. Afterward, many tenants reported that their apartments were either too hot or too cold. Even today, residents with overheated apartments routinely open windows or even run air conditioners in the winter; on the very same evenings, some of their neighbors run space heaters to keep warm. Ruthie reported that her apartment is often too cold in the winter, so she routinely calls maintenance to adjust it. She recalled an encounter with a repairman who came to check on her heat on one cold winter day:

I always call them, and I say, "It's freezing." He would take this thing and look at it and say it's sixty-eight degrees. I said, "You know what? You can tell me it says 112 degrees. I'm cold." I said, "If your mother was living in this apartment, she would tell you it's cold, and you wouldn't like it with your mother laying there. If your mother complained, you wouldn't like it! So, don't tell me it's sixty-eight degrees."

Still, Ruthie admitted that she feels colder as she's gotten older, "There are times, it's not too bad now, but there are times I'm cold. When you get older, you get colder."

Temperature concerns continue to plague Stuyvesant Town residents. During a cold snap in January 2014, the tenants association's Facebook page was flooded with discussions about how to manage the cold in apartments with insufficient heat, and the association offered strategies for coaxing management to respond. Many tenants complained about cold apartments for days and weeks without reprieve. At the other end of the spectrum, some residents posted images of internal temperature gauges reading over 80 degrees. Complaints to Councilman Garodnick's office prompted him to write a letter to CWCapital, asking that they "take all necessary steps to make sure apartments are getting the proper level of heat."[3]

* * *

Ruthie also has concerns about her apartment's modern video intercom system. Near the front door inside of her apartment, a small monitor displays an image of the entryway whenever someone buzzes from the lobby. At first glance, this would seem to be an improvement over the old system, which activated the buzzer through the household telephone line. Ruthie explained why she views the video intercom as a hindrance, especially for older residents with mobility problems:

A lot of things that they're changing I didn't like. I preferred the telephone. Now it's the intercom. I'm in the bedroom, and when that intercom comes on, I don't always hear it. Then, I have to walk from the bedroom to here. And sometimes people think [I'm not home]. Before, we just had our regular phone. It just rings. I loved that. I have the phone right there! I didn't have to get up! Now, I have to get up to find out who it is. I know who it is. If I expect it, like with you, I don't have to run in. I didn't like that.

Residents have reacted negatively to what they see as excessive improvements that fail to cater to older people, and at times, diminish their quality of life. The landscaping efforts have been a much debated topic on the Oval, along the pathways, as well as in Stuyvesant Town's cyber community, drawing largely negative, and sometimes extreme, feedback from residents. Ruthie also opposes the new landscaping, finding it to be extravagant and ceaseless: "Now, they're doing all these trees. It's so expensive. So much money. And it's not even attractive. Some of the trees aren't even attractive. And the flowers. Do you think he [the gardener] can take away a couple of trees? It's pretty, but it's overdone. It's just too much."

Ruthie also weighed in on other highly visible changes in the community, including the influx of students, the relaxed rules about walking on the grass, and the recent introduction of dogs into the community. For fifty-five years Ruthie lived in Stuyvesant Town with its acres of grass strictly off-limits. She feels a sense of injustice because she and her children were not able to walk, play, or picnic on the grass, and now that she is older and her kids are grown, the grass is a free-for-all:

I don't mind them walking on the ground, but the grass? Never could you walk on the grass! The first time I saw this, I remember I said, "For fifty-five years I wasn't allowed!" I remember when they allowed this a few years ago, I said, "I was never able to walk on the grass!" If the kids were ever to walk on the grass they [security officers] took your name and wrote you a letter [of reprimand]. They were really very strict. I'm angry that they didn't allow me to do the things that they're [new residents are] doing now, but we have different owners.

Ruthie also shared her ambivalence about the new policy to allow dogs in Stuyvesant Town. She has a fondness for dogs, but she resents the inconsiderate owners:

A lot of the things I don't like, you know? I don't really like the dogs. I have such compassion when I see these things on T.V. where they beat the animals and things like that. So, I really don't object, except people are not always going to pick up [after their dogs]. I always look out of the window and see them. They are walking in the grass, and doing their things in the grass, and I say, "You better pick it up." You know? That's what I object to. And it's not that there's noisy dogs here. It's not that it affects me, by them barking. I never hear anything like that. I don't know what they do. They must drug them.

Like many Stuyvesant Town residents of all ages, Ruthie had objections about the laundry rooms, which even younger residents described as having a "competitive" environment. When Stuyvesant Town was built, there were five central laundry facilities with attendants who did the wash. Today, each building has its own unattended laundry room. In general, residents complain about one person taking too many machines, clothes disappearing, and broken machines. All of this is compounded by the increasing population density in the buildings, which has placed more pressure on the limited laundry resources:

You go down, and you have a lot of the nannies. They picked seven machines, and I say that's not fair. Of course, they're not going to be down here at seven in the morning. But when I come down there's never a machine. And then sometimes, you look in the dryer like, "Is there anything here?" All they put in there is a pair of panties and two socks! They just spread everything out. So how are you going to complain? You have to have somebody there watching it. So, you learn the time to go down and things like that.

To corroborate her complaint, in our fieldwork, one author observed a heated argument between a Latina housekeeper who worked for one of the newer residents with children and an older resident in the laundry room. The older resident had struggled to cart one load of laundry down to the basement and was upset that a woman who did not even live in the building was using all the machines at once. The housekeeper was completing the entire family's laundry for the whole week. In addition, the housekeeper was watching a Spanish-language talk show on the television, which the tenant thought was unfair, since she believed tenants, rather than housekeepers, should be allowed to choose what to watch while doing laundry.

Although Ruthie's complaints about improved intercoms, walking on the grass, and dogs may sound petty or like sour grapes, her concerns echo those of many long-term residents who believe that Stuyvesant Town has changed in ways that have consistently disadvantaged them. Moreover, considering the long history of tenants being forced to follow arbitrary policies, it is not surprising that they resent changes to policies they had come to accept and even appreciate.

With the end of the waitlist and the transition to market-rate apartments, the rules governing who is an acceptable tenant were simplified, or perhaps abolished: anyone who could afford it could secure an apartment in Stuyvesant Town. In one sense, this may be seen as a leveling the playing field by increasing opportunities for people who are not "in the know," do not have connections with management, or are not the children of current residents. It is clearly better that management no longer inspects prospective tenants' apartments in order to discriminate. Whether one keeps a tidy home is no longer relevant; instead, tax returns, credit ratings, and co-signers rule the day.

However, one downside of this change has been an increase in transient and student residents. The students have drawn particularly negative attention from many residents. Ruthie has also noticed the influx of students into Stuyvesant Town in recent years, which she contrasted to the scrutiny she faced before moving in: "They take a lot of students. I don't really object to it. I understand I'm lucky. They have parties. They've had the police up, or the guards up, and things like that." It's notable that Ruthie, a longtime tenant, feels she is "lucky" to have an apartment that she can afford in a community she loves when the prices around her are increasing rapidly. She mentioned that she does not blame *all* of the students for engaging in disrespectful behavior: "Some of them are lovely, but some of them are disrespectful. It's the *person* and their friends, but I have not been involved with any of that, thank God."

Though she has not personally had serious problems with any students, Ruthie went on to share a story about her new neighbors upstairs:

We have neighbors. It's the new people that moved in, and I don't know what the heck they do. I rang the doorbell one day and said, "Excuse me. I'm your neighbor downstairs. What in the world do you do? You're a skinny guy. How could you make so much noise when you walk?" My son said when you walk barefoot it makes more noise. So I said, "You don't have any carpeting." See, you have to have carpeting. So I said, "I want you to know I didn't report you to Stuy Town. I wouldn't do that." But, I let him know. One night there was a woman there. How did I know? She walked, and you could hear the heels!

Instead of informing on them, Ruthie chose to handle the loud neighbors personally, by going up and speaking to them. Management's policy is that tenants are not to confront their neighbors with noise complaints, but instead they must directly report them to security, even for small matters. Though the policy is intended to protect tenants and reduce direct conflict between neighbors, many residents prefer to handle minor issues among themselves without involving management, when possible. Others believe that complaining to management is pointless anyway, so they are better off trying to handle neighbor conflicts themselves.

## Aging in Place

Despite her complaints, Ruthie still loves living in Stuyvesant Town and made it clear that she has no plans to leave the community. She feels grateful that she still has a few neighbors who look after each other:

It's funny. We were three women only on this floor. I was the baby of the three. One of them, with all her money, they sent her to a home, and she died shortly after that—when she could've lived here and died here. And then we have another friend upstairs, so I kid them. I'm the baby, and they say, "Watch over the elderly." When they get down [depressed], you go make sure they're okay. The elderly watching the elderly. But I was sitting and having breakfast, and she's very hard of hearing, Jeanette. She used to use a walker. She can't walk one step without it. And her door squeaks, so I opened up the door, and I said, "Jeanette!" She's not hard of hearing. She's deaf! So I said, "Jeanette! Jeanette!" [She's] trying to pick up the paper with her cane. She pushes the papers into the house. I don't know how long it lays there before she picks it up. So she says, "How did you hear me?" I said, "Your door squeaks!" She said, "I wanted to get some WD40." I said, "No, don't! I'll never know if you're there!"

Ruthie's relationship with Jeanette reflects the value of aging in place for the seniors in Stuyvesant Town, who often look out for each other. A squeaky door might be perceived as an annoyance to a new resident, but for Ruthie it signals that all is well with her friend. She provided other examples of ways that she and Jeannette help each other, such as with shopping and collecting coupons for groceries. Ruthie then went on to describe how Manhattan is the ideal city for aging in place: "There isn't anything [you can't get]. You can't starve! They deliver for $6! I mean, Chinese, $5.95. They deliver it. It's the most wonderful . . . You can't starve. You can't have dirty clothes. You have everything."

Some might find the notion of Manhattan as ideal for older residents to be counterintuitive, and they may wonder why so many older people continue to live in Stuyvesant Town rather than move to the suburbs or assisted living, which are often perceived as safer and more convenient for older people. Indeed, in chapter 2, we discussed the emergence of naturally occurring retirement communities and the ways in which housing must be adapted for this population. Whatever the difficulties are, Ruthie reiterated that the quality of life is better for seniors who live in the city. She feels safe and finds the public transportation especially helpful for older people with limited mobility and for those who are unable to drive safely. For instance, Ruthie wanted her newly widowed sister, Miriam, to move to Manhattan after she sold her Long Island house. Ruthie thought Manhattan would be perfect for Miriam, because she would be near her and their other sister. However, Miriam's adult children convinced her to remain in the suburbs:

> Miriam, my sister, lives in Heritage Village in Westchester. I begged her, when she moved out of her house in Seaford, in the Island, to move to Manhattan where she'd have both her sisters. So her daughters said, "You're a candidate for a mugging because you're a little old lady using a cane." So, they just frightened her. I said to my sister, "I don't know why parents are afraid of their children." . . . When my husband died, not one of my kids said, "Ma, are you going to stay in the apartment?" They knew I would stay. Where would I go? Now, my sister really didn't want to stay there, but her daughters scared her. So, she has a beautiful home, and she's miserable.

Ruthie explained that her sister is lonely in the suburbs. She cannot drive, and public transportation is limited, so she is dependent on others. In contrast, Ruthie described how she rarely feels alone in Stuyvesant Town:

> I said to her, "In the worst weather you see someone walking." I can look out my window at 3:00 in the morning, there's somebody walking. There are always people. You don't see a soul out in the Island. You never see people. They walk out of a house and into a car. Nobody walks. So, I'll say, "Abbie and I are going to the movies." Miriam says, "Aw shoot, I wish I could go." Yeah, I feel so bad for her because she has a lot of trouble with her knees so she uses a cane. But, what the heck? So, I don't feel that I'm really alone. We had a group of friends . . . Of course, some of them died. So, I don't know. I keep myself busy somehow. Somehow, I do. It may not be exciting [to you], but at my age, it's exciting.

As much as Ruthie appreciates her life in the city, she realizes that she lost out in some ways by staying in Stuyvesant Town and renting for more than sixty years, when others bought homes, creating more stability for themselves and building an asset to pass on to their children. Still, she is without remorse:

> You want to know my rent? $1,057. But, look how many years I'm living here. Listen, for sixty years I pay the rent, and when I die what am I going to get? The rent money? Isaac [her son] is smarter [because he bought a house]. But I didn't want that. I was happy right here. And, of course, my husband worked right here; that's what it really was. So, with it all I'm very happy here. It's convenient. Wherever I have to go, to my kids or whatever like that, it's easy. It's a bus, or a train, or they pick me up. It's all according to what's happening, but for me it's wonderful. I love this city. I never want to move out.

Ruthie's story is emblematic of the experiences of a significant population in Stuyvesant Town, longtime tenants who are aging in place. She has lived in Stuyvesant Town since it first opened; she raised her children in the community, and hopes to stay put until the end of her life. Ruthie's residential experiences and strong sense of attachment to Stuyvesant Town embody the ambitions of its founders, "that families of moderate means might live in health, comfort and dignity in park-like communities." However, her story raises the question of whether such a life is possible or desirable in today's Stuyvesant Town or whether the life that Ruthie seeks to preserve is a relic of the past. The next chapter explores how urban housing policy in New York City has changed over the years and the implications of such changes for Stuyvesant Town's current and future generations of residents.

# 4

## Neoliberalism, Deregulation, and the Challenges to Middle-Class Housing

Any study of Stuyvesant Town must take into account the fact that Manhattan has always been one of the most expensive U.S. locations in which to live. However, with the skyrocketing demand for limited space over the past two decades, Manhattan housing costs have reached a threshold that is pushing middle-class families out of the borough. Critics of policies that are aimed at expanding access to affordable housing in New York, and in Manhattan in particular, sometimes invoke the commonsense notion that not "everyone" can live in Manhattan, and that commuting from outer boroughs is a feasible alternative to increasing the number of affordable units within Manhattan. Clearly, only a limited number of people can comfortably and sustainably inhabit Manhattan's 22.7 square miles. However, there is also a strong desire to ensure economic diversity throughout the city, as illustrated by the resonance of the "tale of two cities" narrative popularized during Bill de Blasio's successful 2013 mayoral campaign.

Further, Manhattan's rising prices have spilled over to the outer boroughs, limiting the options for families who have been priced out. For instance, the gap in median rent between Brooklyn and Manhattan is closing. In 2008 Brooklyn's median rent was $1,000 less than Manhattan's; by May 2015, the gap was $419.[1] In fact, Brooklyn is considered the country's least affordable housing market compared to historical averages, followed by San Francisco and Manhattan.[2] A Brooklyn resident earning the median income would have to spend 98 percent of his or her income on payments to own a median-priced home. And as for Queens, in May 2015, the median rent was up to $2,597, gaining rapidly on the median rent in Brooklyn of $2,933, and in Manhattan of $3,380.[3]

Public housing, rent control, and rent regulation have been staples of New York City housing. However, recent changes to urban housing policy favor business-related real estate actors, such as landlords and developers, and have had a negative impact on the availability of middle-class housing in New York City and Stuyvesant Town. This chapter brings into relief the recent history of threats to middle-class residency in New York City. These threats are manifold, but stem from the way that neoliberal housing policy has unfolded in the city, including the shifting role of the government in subsidizing and regulating New York City housing.

## The Ascendance of Neoliberal Housing Policy and Rise of Deregulation

In the context of New York City housing, *neoliberalism* refers to policies and practices that favor free-market solutions over regulatory interventions. This commonly means that property owners can charge rental prices at whatever the market will bear and are not limited by government-imposed regulations, such as rent stabilization. Other manifestations of neoliberal policies in New York include public subsidization of private investments through tax abatements, tax incentives, and low-interest loans.[4] Neoliberalism is the prevailing paradigm in many societies worldwide, and although it cannot be considered monolithic or uncontested, it is expressed prominently in cities because they are the primary engines of economic growth and power.[5]

Neoliberal policy is evident in some form in most, if not all, North American cities. It is heralded by city government officials who have been increasing their reliance on entrepreneurial modes of governance.[6] It is boosted by the expectation of intra- and inter-urban competition[7] and the anticipation that communities and the private sector will take over the functions and services that the local state declares to be uneconomic or outside of the public good.[8] During the past thirty years city administrations have experimented with neoliberal policy, creating significant and obvious changes to urban-built environments, all in an attempt to enhance urban economic growth, or to mimic policies occurring elsewhere.[9] This is a subject for ongoing research, as academics and activists alike strive to describe the global spread of neoliberal policies while remaining sensitive to local variations in how they manifest.[10]

The deregulation of rental properties specifically, and land-use policies in general, is part of a broader political effort at the city, state, and national levels to create neoliberal economic environments with little consideration for social aspects of policy.[11] The 1950s marked the beginning of a paradigm in which market-based housing strategies gained legitimacy, with nongovernmental approaches to lower-priced housing becoming the preferred alternative to government-based efforts.[12] Prominent economists argued that the solution to housing shortages was simply to construct more housing and increase rental units' profitability in order to encourage people to become landlords.[13]

The contemporary acceptance of free-market solutions is such that many city officials, business elites, and even some community groups insist that these policies are a neutral form of localized economic development.[14] It is common practice for government officials, in collaboration with real estate actors, to participate in neoliberal experiments such as tax abatements, development corporations, place-marketing, public-private partnerships, and other forms of urban space and land-use consumption.[15] Federal and local officials work with private developers to enhance the *exchange value* (i.e., the worth in the marketplace as a commodity) of properties for the owners, often sacrificing the *use value* (i.e., the value to people who use or consume it) for existing residents. Such government involvement in redevelopment that seeks to further privatize the housing market only works to legitimate the displacement of middle-income residents who are priced out of the city.[16] However, to fully appreciate the impact of neoliberal policy, it is necessary to understand New York's two important historical solutions to middle-class housing shortages: subsidizing housing and enacting rent regulation.

## Government Strategies to Cope with Manhattan's Housing Shortage

New York City is well known for its housing assistance programs, making the gradual shift toward free-market housing policies more pronounced. A pioneer in the realm of housing policy, it is the home of the United States' first tenement laws, the first comprehensive zoning ordinances, and the country's first public housing project.[17] Indeed, from 1987 through the 1990s, the city's spending on housing was three times as much as that of the next thirty-two largest cities combined.[18] Even so, the city lost 39 percent of its apartments for low-income residents from 2002 to 2011.[19] Further, 61 percent of low-income renter house-holds spent at least 50 percent of their income on rent, an increase from 46 percent in 1999.[20]

The housing supply for poor New Yorkers is dwindling and their circumstances are especially dire, but low-income residents are not the only ones who need help securing affordable housing. The city's tight housing market also affects nonpoor segments of the population, such as those who are rent-burdened and pay a large percentage of their income on housing costs. Aside from the extremely rich, virtually every New Yorker has struggled to find adequate, affordable housing, and the middle class is no exception. Efforts to deal with this social problem have resulted in what some have called a tug of war between landlords and the government.[21] Two major ways in which the federal, state, and city governments have intervened on behalf of middle-class citizens are to subsidize housing construction and to regulate existing housing.

## Subsidizing Middle-Class Housing

The term "subsidized housing" conjures drab, uniform, government-built and managed (and often, mismanaged) housing projects riddled with crime, poverty, and other social problems. However, government officials in cities, counties, and states regularly use subsidies and tax incentives to encourage private developers to build housing for both low-income and middle-income households, and developers make a great profit from such deals.[22] This type of business-oriented economic development often involves loosening regulation to lower private companies' operating costs, including the price of land and taxes. For instance, owners of New York City condos and co-ops can receive tax abatements, which reduce their property taxes for a period of time. Another example is redevelopment programs, such as New York City's Hudson Yards project, for which the city has granted hundreds of millions of dollars of real estate tax exemptions to build apartments, skyscrapers, a retail mall, offices, parks, and cultural spaces on underutilized land.[23] As part of the planned project, city bonds have paid for a subway extension. Former Mayor Michael Bloomberg called this "one of the largest private developments in U.S. history," though in fact it is partially publicly funded and is costing the city nearly $1 billion.

Stuyvesant Town's older residents have asserted that their landlord has intentionally enacted policies to replace older residents with younger residents and young college students. Indeed, historically, city planners have also used housing policies to engineer specific population composition profiles in communities. For instance, Robert Moses used Title I of the Federal Housing Act of 1948 to create housing developments insulated from the poor, which prevented middle-class households from leaving the city and attracted residents who aspired to live and work in Manhattan.[24] Title I permitted the government to subsidize and incentivize the private development of so-called blighted areas through tax breaks. With government assistance, developers could replace low-income communities with housing for better-off residents. Nicholas Dagen Bloom's 2008 book, *Public Housing That Worked: New York in the Twentieth Century*, documents the New York City Housing Authority's efforts to ensure the success of government-subsidized housing by protecting against undesirables, creating projects with "model tenants" (including the adoption of a points system for rating applicants), and advocating for the social control provided by "tightly managed communities."

In 1955, Robert Moses helped to create the Mitchell-Lama program. The state-created program provides "affordable rental and cooperative housing to moderate- and middle-income families" and resulted in the construction of 269 developments with more than 105,000 apartments.[25] The program kept rents low by offering perks to real estate developers who were interested in constructing affordable rentals or co-ops: they could acquire land for free or at a low cost, they would receive exemptions from property taxes, and they would have access to mortgages subsidized to be lower than market rate.[26] Today, New York City has 54,000 Mitchell-Lama units and waiting lists are long. Applicants must apply for each development separately, but can submit an application for multiple apartments at once if the waiting lists are not closed. Given New York's high rents, politicians have attempted to intervene to preserve middle-class subsidy programs by increasing the barriers that prevent Mitchell-Lama landlords from buying out of rent restrictions and evicting tenants. For instance, in 2007, former governor Eliot Spitzer attempted to slow the loss of Mitchell-Lama units by declaring an end to the practice of granting landlords "unique or particular" permission to raise rents in buildings that are leaving the program. In other words, the owners of almost 18,000 apartments that were built before 1974 cannot claim that leaving the program is a "unique and peculiar" situation that allows them to implement large rent increases, and tenants can continue to live as rent-stabilized residents.[27]

In more recent decades, New York City adopted a series of so-called Ten-Year Plans. In 1985, the Koch administration faced a three-pronged housing crisis: (1) a rise in housing costs and prices; (2) an increase in homelessness; and (3) President Ronald Reagan's cutbacks to federal housing assistance. In response, Koch implemented the Ten-Year Plan for Housing, an expansion in housing programs that was unprecedented in scale.[28] Koch announced that the plan would be a "five-year $4.4 billion program to build or rehabilitate around 100,000 housing units for middle-class, low-income, and working poor families and individuals."[29] By 1988 he amended the plan to a ten-year period, a $5.1 billion budget, and 252,000 housing units receiving assistance.[30] The plan included the renovation of 82,000 units in occupied tax-foreclosed buildings (i.e., "in rem"), the construction of 42,000 units in vacant buildings, the construction of 37,000 new units, and the upgrading of 87,000 units in privately owned buildings.[31] David Dinkins became mayor in the middle of Koch's ambitious plan, and was burdened with costs and management issues associated with rehabilitating buildings, sustaining them, and filling vacancies.[32]

Mayor Rudolph Giuliani's subsequent housing initiatives (announced in 2001) centered on rehabilitating and preserving housing, with a $1.2 billion "public/private partnership."[33] This translated into three major goals. First, he planned to put aside 1,100 vacant units owned by the City of New York and place them into the private sector.[34] Second, given that it is expensive for the city to own dilapidated buildings, Giuliani planned to transfer them to new landlords.[35] Third, he planned to expand the Alliance for Neighborhood Commerce, Homeownership, and Revitalization (ANCHOR) program, which now reports that it is "a neighborhood revitalization initiative that has created over 300,000 square feet of new commercial/retail space and over 1,000 units of middle-income housing on vacant City-owned land" using a "combination of Federal, State, City, and private funds to finance new retail space along targeted commercial corridors."[36] Giuliani's plan was to use the ANCHOR program to subsidize mixed-use residential/commercial retail developments, totaling 3,067 units and 875,000 square feet of commercial space.[37] The funding for all of these goals was "contingent on reforms of the Buildings Department and the City Building Code; rezoning land for residential development; and passing legislation aimed at removing organized crime from the construction industry."[38] Of course, the September 11th terrorist attacks occurred months after the mayor's proposal, but Michael Bloomberg continued to pursue these reforms.[39] This makes sense given that programs put forth by the city's Department of Housing and Preservation Development tend to be seamlessly implemented across mayors' administrations.[40]

Former mayor Bloomberg adopted his own Ten-Year Housing Plan. One part of the program involved a plan to build 1,676 new middle-income housing units in fourteen housing developments, the majority of which would be restricted to households with incomes of $56,700 to $124,075 for a family of four.[41] The city provided nonprofits and private developers with housing subsidies for these and later planned twenty-six more. Bloomberg's plan also focused on maintaining the city's existing middle-income apartments, including the affordable housing developments built from the mid-1950s to the mid-1970s (e.g., Mitchell-Lama complexes), many of which the city had converted to market rate.[42]

However, Mayor Bloomberg's plan was complex and uneven. For instance, he included the construction of single-family homes and high-rise apartment buildings, but as few as 20 percent of units would be reserved for affordable housing, allowing developers to make a large profit. Landlords would be required to limit rentals to those who met the income limits, but these arrangements would vary in term length, with some requiring income limits for decades and others remaining affordable for as little as five years. This means that some landlords would face prolonged limitations to resale value, while others would be able to sell at market rates relatively soon.[43]

Thus, rather than just supplying housing vouchers, Bloomberg's plan was to add housing production programs through renovating or building new units, including middle-class units, as part of a ten-year plan. One major positive finding on the impact of such efforts is that they contribute to larger neighborhood revitalization and have positive spillover effects, such as increased property values in distressed neighborhoods where such housing is often sited.[44] Still, such ten-year plans are not *primarily* focused on middle-class housing, and to the extent that they address the middle class, homeownership is often a central goal (e.g., the New Homes Program for families making under $75,000 and the Nehemiah Program selling houses to those making as little as $27,000 a year), though some new middle-income rentals have been developed using city-owned land and city financing (e.g., the New Housing Opportunities Program gives below-market mortgages to developers who construct moderate-income rental housing).[45]

In 2004, Mayor Bloomberg reported a plan to create "an ambitious middle-class housing program for the 21st Century."[46] Under the plan, 32 percent of units were slated for moderate- and middle-income New York families. The other 68 percent would be considered affordable to citizens earning less than 80 percent of the area median income, which in 2004 was $50,000 for a family of four.[47] One of the tools he highlighted, his "middle class housing initiative", stated the intent to use capital funding to create 22,000 units on large sites in all boroughs for citizens earning between $50,000 and $100,000. This would be financed through creating a new housing development entity that would issue bonds, expedite public land development, and retain ownership to keep the housing affordable, as well as expand existing affordable housing programs to serve more middle-class people, and implement a cross-subsidy program that would include a market-rate component to subsidize other tenants.

Bill de Blasio's 2013 campaign for mayor prominently featured a "tale of two cities" platform in which he promised to prioritize income inequality, declining quality of life, and a shrinking middle class as major blights on New York City. Affordable housing was a key component of his campaign, as he called for "a dramatic expansion of affordable housing" and noted that, "we have a crisis of affordability on our hands." Mayor de Blasio's affordable housing plan called for building or preserving 200,000 units of affordable housing over the next ten years. He formalized this ambition in a policy book published during the 2013 mayoral race entitled "One New York, Rising Together":[48]

> It's a crisis in many ways built on New York City's success. We are a safer, more welcoming city than we were decades ago. People from all over the world come to study, to work or to start a business here. And that success

story has put pressure on our housing stock. Coupled with ever-rising economic inequality, it has created a painful reality where more and more New Yorkers are spending more and more to cover their housing costs, and entire neighborhoods have lost their affordability. Affordable housing is part of the bedrock of what makes New York City work. It's what underpins the economically diverse neighborhoods New Yorkers want to live in. It's critical to providing financial stability for working families, helping them get ahead and build a better life. And that is why today, we are laying out a comprehensive plan to build and preserve 200,000 affordable units over the coming decade, to support New Yorkers with a range of incomes, from the very lowest to those in the middle class. This is a plan to get ahead of the curve, to protect neighborhoods, and build our city's next generation of affordable housing. It's about knitting communities together. Our affordable housing policies must reach every New Yorker in need, which is why this plan thinks big about the changes we need to make—in government and in the private sector—to make this a city where everyone rises together, and everyone has a safe and decent home. If you're in a community where affordability is disappearing, we want to protect it. If your family lives in a rent-regulated apartment, this plan is focused on helping you keep it. If you're a senior trying to remain in the neighborhood you helped to build, we are fighting to help you stay.

In the 2013 election, three out of four voters in New York City cast their ballots for Bill de Blasio, bringing him into office with a clear mandate to address the "affordability crisis." Mayor de Blasio's election indicates voters' strong support for policies aimed at expanding affordable housing and maintaining what he called the "economically diverse neighborhoods New Yorkers want to live in." The extent to which de Blasio will be able to realize these ambitions remains to be seen. In February 2015, the mayor referred to Stuyvesant Town when he announced a plan to build 11,250 units of affordable housing on 200 acres at Sunnyside Yards.[49] The announced sale to the Blackstone Group in October 2015 was viewed by the mayor as an advance in his affordable housing plan. However, if rent-stabilized housing units are neither replaced nor the number of units is increased, middle-class families face few affordable options in Manhattan. In the wake of the losses during the Bloomberg administration,[50] and with the decline of stabilized housing and increasing rents in formerly affordable communities found in Brooklyn, Queens, and the Bronx, housing is likely to remain a challenge for the foreseeable future.[51]

## Rent Regulation

Prior to the ascendance of neoliberal dogma, New York City had very different housing policy priorities. Rent regulation emerged as part of a federal initiative to address acute housing shortages after World War II. Though inconsistently applied, federal, state, and city levels of government have intervened with solutions to preserve and encourage middle-class housing, though at times these efforts have actually undermined middle-class residence in the city.

New York City's efforts to improve the health of citizens and maintain positive housing conditions date back at least to the New Law Tenement House Act of 1901.[52] They are also evidenced in the city's compliance with the United States Housing Act of 1937, which created the Federal Public Housing Program in order to improve poor citizens' dangerous and unsanitary housing conditions.[53] In 1942, in response to wartime inflation, President Franklin D. Roosevelt signed the Emergency Price Control Act (EPCA) into law.[54] In anticipation of housing shortages, this included apartment rent controls for most counties in the state of New York.[55] By 1943, the Federal Office of Price Administration froze New York City rents at March 1, 1943 levels.[56] Thus began New York's current rent-control program, the longest running program in the United States. The federal government administered the program until it expired in 1951. At this time, the state took over; between 1962 and 1984, both the city and state administered the program, and then state resumed control and still does.[57]

But soon, little by little, city and state governments began to decontrol apartments. For instance, in 1953 the city decontrolled vacant apartments in one- and two-family homes, it allowed for luxury decontrol (i.e., decontrolling apartments that reach a certain rent threshold or those occupied by tenants whose income increased to exceed a certain limit) of specific kinds of high-rent apartments in 1964 and 1968, and it adopted vacancy decontrol (i.e., decontrolling apartments between tenants, usually after upgrades) for all units in 1971.[58] This triggered action from tenants who were afraid of unaffordable rents and losing their apartments, and it eventually resulted in rent stabilization. By 1974, the New York State Legislature passed the Emergency Tenant Protection Act (ETPA), an amendment to the New York City Rent Stabilization Law that introduced rent stabilization to properties that previously had been market rate; this restored rent regulation to many decontrolled apartments.[59] In a city of renters, citizens viewed this form of rent regulation as a necessity for meeting the vital need of affordable housing, but rent stabilization was less tenant-friendly than rent control. Rent stabilization usually comes with income restrictions stipulating that tenants can be evicted if their income exceeds a certain threshold and that the legal rent amount cannot exceed a certain amount or the unit will be deregulated. The vast majority of New York City's regulated apartments are rent-stabilized, not rent-controlled. As of 2014, about one million units in the city were subject to rent stabilization and 27,000 were subject to *rent control*,[60] which applies only to tenants who have continually occupied an apartment since 1971, when the city adopted rent decontrol for all units. Economic conditions and pressures to deregulate rents and generate capital threaten the security of rent-stabilization policies.

New York City's policies in the mid-twentieth century were in keeping with larger societal ideals grounded in justice and pragmatism, in which housing was viewed as a right,[61] but the fiscal crisis of the 1970s changed this. The combined loss of the tax base because of deindustrialization and middle-class suburbanization, the high costs of services, and the debts used to offset the budgetary shortfalls all drained New York City's coffers, leaving the city nearly bankrupt.[62] Both the mayor and governor expressed concern to President Ford in 1975 that civil unrest might result.[63] It was in this climate that neoliberal rhetoric found a welcoming environment, as the city and state retreated from providing housing and began to deregulate units in order to stimulate economic growth. As geographer David Harvey put it:

> The management of the New York fiscal crisis pioneered the way for neoliberal practices both domestically under [President] Reagan and internationally through the IMF [International Monetary Fund] in the 1980s . . . It emphasized that the role of government was to create a good

business climate rather than look to the needs and well-being of the population at large.[64]

The 1980s and early 1990s brought forth several noteworthy changes. The 1983 Omnibus Housing Act consolidated rent control and stabilization issues under the Division of Housing and Community Renewal, abolishing the Conciliation and Appeals Board and the New York City Division of Rent Control.[65] The Act eliminated a pro-tenant policy, the option to renew a lease with a three-year lease.[66] The 1990s marked the beginning of an especially significant weakening of protections for rent-regulated tenants. The Rent Regulation Reform Act of 1993 not only deregulated vacant apartments, it also deregulated those occupied and regulated apartments that would become vacant and that rented for at least $2,000 per month between July 7 and October 1, 1993.[67] It also stated that owners could apply to deregulate their rent-regulated apartments when the lease expired if the rent was $2,000 or more a month as of October 1, 1993, and if the tenants earned a combined household income of more than $250,000 in each of two preceding years. Further, the state stipulated that landlords could decontrol certain rent-controlled tenants one year after landlords applied for decontrol.[68]

Soon, landlords' efforts at organizing for deregulation and higher profits gained steam. In 1997, the Rent Regulation Reform Act of 1993 was amended. The state legislature reduced the household income "means test" needed to qualify for stabilized housing from $250,000 to $175,000, a stricter standard for luxury decontrol that put more tenants at risk for losing their apartments.[69] In other words, landlords could now disqualify tenants with an annual household income of more than $175,000 for two consecutive years if they had a monthly rent exceeding $2,000. This would free landlords to evict tenants, increase rents, and seek out market-rate tenants.[70] Stabilized tenants would need to prove to landlords that their apartment was their primary residence for at least 183 days of the calendar year.[71] Finally, when a stabilized unit would become vacant, the landlord would be free to convert it to market rate.[72] These changes are a major departure from the past and are the foundation of New York City's current neoliberal housing climate in which politicians and real estate actors advocate for the expiration of rent regulations, the elimination of rent stabilization extensions, and easier ways to implement luxury and vacancy decontrols.[73] However, apartments in buildings receiving J-51 tax benefits, such as Stuyvesant Town, are not eligible for high-rent vacancy deregulation as long as the benefits continue. This would later become the subject of the tenants' class action lawsuit.

In 1997, as state renewal of rent regulations approached, public opinion was in favor of it, with at least 70 percent of New York City residents agreeing that, "rent regulations were necessary to provide affordable housing and to prevent rents from soaring."[74] At the same time, editorial columns in newspapers from the *New York Times* to the *Wall Street Journal* strongly advocated for the elimination of rent regulations.[75] What triggered further deregulation? New York governor George Pataki, a believer in the free market, campaigned with Majority Leader of the New York State Senate, Joseph Bruno, to end rent control.[76] They employed information from conservative think tanks to spread the pro-market populist argument that rent stabilization is unfair, reduces housing construction, hurts small business owners, and benefits wealthy tenants.[77] In response, tenant organizations and their supporters held protest rallies, resulting in a 1997 extension of rent regulation, albeit with fewer regulated units.[78] Rent regulations were extended again after similar lobbying efforts and protests on each side in 2003, 2011, and most recently in the Rent Act of 2015.

Still, the efforts to deregulate apartments have been quite successful in decreasing the stock of affordable housing. The New York City Housing and Vacancy Survey and other data from 2011 show that: (1) New York City had 1,030,000 rent-stabilized housing units, comprising 47 percent of the rental stock in 2014; (2) most additions to the rent-stabilized stock resulted from two tax incentive programs, one for low-income housing projects and one for newly constructed buildings; (3) the largest category of units removed from the stabilized housing stock were "high rent/vacancy" deregulations (comprising 71 percent of deregulations) and 63.9 percent of these were in Manhattan alone; and (4) New York City's rent-stabilized housing stock lost at least 105,242 units between 1994 and 2011,[79] though 2013 and 2014 brought a net gain in stabilized units for the first time in a decade.[80] The Rent Act of 2015 extends rent law protections through June 15, 2019.

## And Now? The Impact of the Mortgage Market Bubble

Neoliberal policies and practices flourished in New York City in the early- to mid-2000s. At this time, U.S. mortgage markets were highly active and bullish, because of the deregulation of the financial services industry and development of structured products, including mortgage-backed securities and asset-backed securities. The U.S. mortgage market changed after the Savings and Loans crisis of the early 1980s. Legislation that was intended to restructure the industry spurred an increasing reliance on mortgage securitization, where capital markets rather than depositories or traditional regulated commercial banks funded mortgages.[81] In, addition, lenders developed what some have called "innovative," "affordability," or "exotic" mortgage products to increase property buyers' purchasing power.[82] Investors considered such products to be highly useful in distributing risk when assembling large real estate transactions and when trying to increase the number of mortgage originations. This is reflected in the following quote by finance scholar Frank J. Fabozzi:

> Asset securitization provides various benefits for borrowers. Corporate issuers may find it more cost-effective to raise funds via asset securitization than to offer a typical corporate bond. Asset securitization can be used as a tool to manage risk-based capital requirements by regulated financial institutions, such as banks, thrifts, and insurance companies, throughout the world . . . a financial institution can securitize assets that expose the institution to higher interest rate risk and retain certain customized parts of the asset securitization transaction to attain an improved asset/liability position.[83]

At the time, economic orthodoxy held that liberalizing financial markets is socially desirable, because the mechanics of mortgage-backed securities enables lenders to provide housing loans to purchasers who traditionally would not have qualified, hence increasing homeownership rates, upward social mobility, and neighborhood growth.

Of course, in retrospect, lenders' capacities to offer subprime loans would prove to be disastrous, and as Manuel Aalbers noted, the expansion of mortgage markets could be read not so much as a means to increase homeownership as it was "to further the neoliberal agenda of private property, firms and growing profits."[84] In either case, the availability of capital raised the prospect of large returns to investors. Realizing this potential, however, required opportunities to trade, whether through "flipping" properties at higher prices or, in the case of rentals, flipping tenants at higher rents. These pressures to trade led property owners, lenders, and investors to engage in increasingly risky moves, causing elevated mortgage default rates and home foreclosures and signaling an impending crisis. When the mortgage market bubble finally burst and became the financial crisis of 2007–2008, the rapid sclerosis of capital markets began to create major problems for investment firms, which had overleveraged themselves at the height of the bubble.

These forces affected the Stuyvesant Town property that Tishman-Speyer and BlackRock Realty purchased from MetLife. Here, the increased availability and attractiveness of speculative financing options for purchasing real estate coincided with MetLife's desire to exit the business and allowed for Stuyvesant Town's highly leveraged buyout. Of course, the debt load involved in the Stuyvesant Town deal also created tremendous pressure to trade which, in a rental community where many tenants paid below-market rents, equated to pressure to replace existing tenants with more profitable ones. Ultimately, the focus on profit-seeking encouraged by neoliberal policies relegated the health of communities to a secondary concern. Although this trend harmed the middle class throughout the United States, the precarious position of the middle class in New York City with regard to housing magnified its effects because, simply put, middle-class New Yorkers have so few affordable, high-quality neighborhood options.

*Contemporary Housing Trends in the "Luxury City": Vacancies Down and Rents Up*

Given that Manhattan is the most expensive place in the United States in which to reside,[85] it is not surprising that most residents are renters. The 2014 home ownership rate in Manhattan was 24.8 percent, compared to 32.5 percent for New York City as a whole, and 64 percent nationwide.[86] Even when people do own their homes, more than 90 percent of the time, they live in a condo or co-op unit rather than the single-family houses commonly found in boroughs like Staten Island or Queens.[87] As a result of the high demand, low supply, and excessive costs, only about 19 percent of New York City's population lives in Manhattan, but the borough contains 25 percent of the city's housing units, and it remains a highly desirable location because it offers easy access to urban amenities and close proximity to jobs.

None of this information would come as a surprise to anyone who has looked for an apartment in New York City. New Yorkers are well aware of three facts about housing in their city: (1) the demand for housing greatly exceeds supply, as indicated by the 3.45 percent vacancy rate, which is significantly below the 5 percent threshold that state law requires for rent regulation to continue;[88] (2) many residents spend a very high percentage of their income on housing as evidenced by the fact that the median gross rent-to-income ratio, or the proportion of their income renters spend on rent, was 33.8 percent, the highest in the history of the Housing Vacancy Survey[89] (30 percent of households pay 50 percent or more of their income for rent); and (3) 12.2 percent of rental housing is overcrowded,[90] having more than one person per room, on average. Thus, when an affordable apartment becomes vacant, it does not stay vacant for long unless the owner keeps it off the market or offers it at a rent higher than the market will bear. For instance, a Manhattan apartment spent an average of forty-five days on the market in 2014, which is four days fewer than the previous year.[91] Notably, rent-stabilized apartments are especially overcrowded, with 20.9 percent designated as overcrowded or severely overcrowded (more than 1.5 people per room).[92]

From the 1930s through the 1970s New York City rents increased incrementally, but the cost of renting surged during the 1980s, 1990s, and 2000s.[93] City, state, and federal government policies were favorable to business and real estate actors. In addition, mayors' appointments and decision making aligned with free-market policies, such as commercial rezoning plans that allow smaller buildings to be replaced with office and residential towers and financing agreements for public transit and public space upgrades.[94] As a result, Manhattan has become a city for high earners,[95] with places like Brooklyn inching higher in cost as residents and landlords move faster and faster to purchase and rent properties there. Specifically, the median rental price for a Manhattan

Figure 4.1 Manhattan Population Density Map.
*Source*: U.S. Census Bureau

apartment reached an all-time high in 2013 at $3,860.[96] The median rent in November 2013 for a one-bedroom Manhattan apartment was $3,065, and a two-bedroom rented for $4,795.[97]

In the first decade of this century, Manhattan's vacancy rate fell dramatically from an already low average of 2.94 percent in 2002 to 1.94 percent in July 2013, compared to a national rental vacancy average of almost 10 percent.[98] The low vacancy rates and the decreases in the number of subsidized housing units have only increased the city's concentration of wealth. Further, wages have not been keeping up with rents, and real income has fallen, both of which place a higher rent burden on many New York City residents.[99] These factors combined have pushed middle-income individuals and families out of the borough altogether.

Many elected officials and political hopefuls give speeches about their own modest middle-class roots and pledge their allegiance to middle-class families who are struggling to get by in New York City, but many, like former mayor Bloomberg, also loudly celebrate New York as a "luxury city" catering to the upper class and global elites who dine at the hottest new restaurants, shop in expensive fashion boutiques, and plan vacations to exotic locations.[100] After pop star and Nashville-based country singer Taylor Swift purchased a $15 million penthouse in Tribeca, the New York City tourism office named her its 2015 Global Welcome Ambassador, much to the chagrin of some locals who lament that rich outsiders have taken over the city's housing, culture, and image.[101]

However, putting aside efforts to brand the city as a home for the 1 percent, New York City's many competitive economic advantages over other cities require a diverse workforce to support industries and populations. It is not enough to create middle-class jobs; Manhattan's workers need someplace to live that is reasonable in terms of cost of living, quality public schools, transit and commute times, affordable housing, fair taxes, and broad economic opportunities.

According to a 2013 report entitled "The Middle-Class Squeeze" prepared by the New York City Council,[102] New York's middle class, which is defined as those with a household income between 100 and 300 percent of the city's median income, is indeed shrinking, causing a decline in economic diversity among the populace. Excessive inequality, such as that found in New York City's boroughs, interferes with cooperation, trust, and social cohesion as workers receive the message that they are needed to work for and serve Manhattan's rich, but they are not fit to live among them.[103]

In general, wealthier residents in the United States tend to live geographically separated from everyone else, but one of New York City's historical features is that this has been less true here. New York City is a place where the wealthy have traditionally been more likely to rub elbows with average citizens, and the current period marks a major change that has implications for the city's culture of striving, and even for the nation as a whole. After all, New York has been revered as a visible example of a place where people of modest means truly live close to elites. Even in the age of social media, one of the reasons that ambitious people move to New York is that they aspire to "make it there" in their career, or at least be closer to the more influential people in their industry. Hence, the image of New York City's urban core as the vibrant place where artists, writers, and other creative people live the mythical American Dream may become a thing of the past. Making matters worse, this group is increasingly priced out of the outer boroughs, which then pushes them to the suburbs and other cities, all so that Manhattan can be reserved for merchant bankers and those in the professional class.

Not only do cities need the middle class to balance the interests of the rich and poor,[104] but planners, scholars, and activists argue that people have a "right to the city." French sociologist Henri Lefebvre used this phrase in the late 1960s to call for citizens to participate in decisions about urban space and to fully inhabit the city center, rather than abandoning it to capital.[105] According to this viewpoint, surely perceived as radical to some, access to the city is a human right that exists as much for people in the five boroughs of New York City as it does in the shantytowns of Brazil.[106] Some commentators have claimed that neoliberal policy and the resulting price structure of housing denies poor and middle-class people a chance to live near urban centers. David Harvey, who favors an emphasis on class conflict and anti-capitalist revolution rather than Lefebvre's less radical tendency to highlight situational territorial conflicts and reform,[107] dramatically stated his fears about the loss of citizens' right to the city in this way: "I wager that within fifteen years, if present trends continue, all those hillsides in Rio now occupied by favelas will be covered by high-rise condominiums with fabulous views over the idyllic bay, while the erstwhile favela dwellers will have been filtered off into some remote periphery."[108]

## "If They *Can't* Make It There": The Middle Class in Manhattan

New Yorkers often say that they cannot imagine life anywhere else but in New York, which is to them, the greatest city in the world. Still, at some point in their lives, many New Yorkers compare their circumstances to those of people who live in other parts of the country. They cannot help but wonder if it is worth it to pay so much money to live in such a tiny apartment and pay such a high cost of living. Research shows that New York's costly utility bills, groceries, insurance, childcare, and taxes, combined with poor schools, a decrease in middle-income jobs, and stagnant wages have made residence in the city especially difficult for the middle class.[109] For example, a Manhattan resident must earn $123,322 to enjoy a similar standard of living to a person earning $50,000 in Houston. The report also showed that housing cost is the "single biggest factor" pushing the middle class out of the city. The 2006 "NYC Movers Study," funded by former mayor Bloomberg, found that people cited housing cost as their number one reason for leaving New York; in contrast, back in 1993, a study concluded that the top three reasons for fleeing the city were not related to housing cost, but rather quality of life issues such as crime, safety, and neighborhoods.[110]

In much of the country, when one thinks of middle-class neighborhoods, what comes to mind are communities that are primarily residential, with low crime, good housing stock, high rates of homeownership, quality schools with high standardized test scores, households with high median incomes and educational attainment levels, a population with a low representation of people in poverty or extreme wealth, desirable amenities nearby (e.g., green space and community events), and residents who identify with the community, trust each other, and engage in meaningful interaction with their neighbors.[111]

However, in New York, middle-class neighborhoods are more difficult to define because few neatly fit the standard U.S. profile. Middle-class neighborhoods in New York are scarce, and some might argue that none exist in Manhattan.[112] Part of the reason for the short supply of middle-class neighborhoods is that middle-class residents have become diffused and can be found scattered across the city.[113] Research has shown that increased income segregation in the United States has led to the segregation of affluence, which, combined with segregation of the poor, leaves fewer middle-class neighborhoods in metropolitan areas;[114] as such, Manhattan presents an extreme case of declining housing options for the middle class. Consequently, many choose to exit the city altogether.

In the eyes of many New Yorkers, the very idea of a middle-class Manhattan neighborhood has become an oxymoron. Bloggers on housing websites recommend the outer boroughs for middle-class residents, especially families with children. Also mentioned in derogatory terms are bourgeois neighborhoods like Murray Hill, until recently relatively affordable, but with a reputation for being "dowdy" and appealing to former fraternity boy types. Tellingly, in recent years, even these kinds of lower status, generic neighborhoods have become expensive.

Stuyvesant Town, the antithesis of a trendy neighborhood, has become more out of reach to middle-income people. For instance, using 2013 American Community Survey 5-year estimates, the median household income in Manhattan was $69,659 and approximately 17.4 percent of households had an income higher than $200,000. In Stuyvesant Town, the median household income was $95,771 and the percentage of households with an income in excess of $200,000 almost tripled over a decade, going from 6 percent in 2000 to about 16 percent. Indeed, Stuyvesant Town has changed along with the rest of Manhattan, though it is still considered middle class for now.

One Stuyvesant Town resident explained that a rent-stabilized apartment was the only realistic option for her when she was a graduate student juggling classes and work in Manhattan. Karen Douglas, a thirty-seven-year-old professional who now works in human resources, reported that she is grateful that her housing costs have remained mostly stable and that her relatively long tenure in the community has helped her to form relationships with her neighbors and maintain local friendships. She views the latter as a privilege in New York, where the population churns and people commute to work and school from far-flung boroughs:

> There's just so few options . . . I was so grateful for having got this apartment. I knew I would like to do grad school, and I decided on NYU, which was so expensive. I mean, I got some scholarship money, but it allows me to be able to walk to my classes and stay in Manhattan and have an easy commute to my internship . . . I feel like I didn't have to move somewhere far out and find new local friends and new places, like I could just start school and still live in the city, which was wonderful . . . I've never had a really good salary until now, so for me it's never been about trying out different cool neighborhoods and fancy places 'cause it's never been something I've been able to. I've never made it a priority. That's not to say that when I go to friends' places who live in cute walk-ups with old moldings and high ceilings and corrugated ceilings or whatever [that I wouldn't like to live there]. Sure, I would love to try different neighbor-

hoods here, but it's just so expensive . . . Unless I were to win the lottery or have this windfall of money, I'll probably always live in Stuy Town if I stay in Manhattan. I mean, unless I got some amazing deal elsewhere.

Ultimately, Karen did relocate. She went to the middle-class, more affordable, and diverse community of Sunnyside, Queens. Though it is just three train stops from the city, it offers far less than Stuyvesant Town in terms of access to shopping, restaurants, culture, green space, and other city amenities.

Thus, Stuyvesant Town represents a rare combination of elements that make it recognizably middle-class to observers, but it still fails to conform in every respect to what many people think of as a middle-class neighborhood. It is safe, and as advertised, the "secure enclave" is park-like and surrounded by green space, trees, walking paths, and playgrounds. It has amenities desirable to middle-class people, such as a gym, game courts, and children's play spaces. However, Stuyvesant Town's location is less than ideal for many people as it is relatively far from the subway, and it sits on the far east side of the city. If the housing blogs are to be believed, market-rate residents still consider the rent costs to be high for what they get. Forty-four-year-old Amy Duran, a stabilized resident, believes that market-rate tenants pay way too much:

> When I see the Peter Cooper Village/Stuyvesant Town advertisements for luxury apartments, I laugh. 'Cause I'm like, "There's no luxury here." There are things like the gym, I guess, that cost a fortune . . . I don't think it's luxury. I feel like I pay what it's worth, and the [market-rate] people pay much more than it's worth. Do I sound harsh?

Also, Stuyvesant Town's design, which many have likened to a sterile, institutional public housing project, lacks the charm of older Manhattan neighborhoods and the sparkle of newer luxury developments. As the effort to enhance profit has escalated, Stuyvesant Town's apartments and buildings' common areas have taken on a dated, dingy, musty feel and odor. Further, the units are not exactly up to middle-class lifestyle standards; tenants must do laundry in communal basement laundry rooms where machines are often in disrepair, many units feature tiny kitchens, sound travels between the apartments, heating pipes bang, faucets sometimes release brown water, and tenants cannot control their apartment's temperature. In addition, staff and management treat the residents with less respect than those who live in the city's doorman buildings. Even so, in such a tight housing market, relatively large Manhattan apartments are in high demand, regardless of their lackluster features and absence of social cachet.

Despite these drawbacks, and in light of declining options, Stuyvesant Town still represents a haven for the middle-class Manhattan workforce and their families, a group crucial to the city's economy, social structure, and functioning. Many residents fear that their ability to stay is tenuous, and they are unsure of their other options in the city as they wait to see how the sale of the property to a new investment consortium will affect their tenure. What is clear is that for the individual tenant the forces at work in the New York housing market are beyond one's control, determined rather by elected officials, judges, landlords, and investors. As these forces push against the city, Stuyvesant Town is both an exemplar of the evolution of the New York City housing market and a stark reminder of what is being lost in the climate of neoliberal housing policy. Given the high price per square foot of Manhattan real estate, most housing units are rentals, and the majority of residents will remain renters for their entire lives if they choose to stay in the city. The most they had hoped for, as costs were rising and developers were making deals, was to hold onto their affordable apartments while continuing to enjoy the sense of community in a place where their neighbors had planned to stay put and remain invested in local quality of life. However, even these seemingly humble aspirations have proven too much to expect.

Against the backdrop of the global financial crisis, real estate developers' decisions combined with deregulation of rentals brought forth sudden and extreme changes in this rent-stabilized neighborhood on Manhattan's East Side. In the next chapter, we explain the ways in which landlords and tenants reacted to these economic realities. Our interviews with Stuyvesant Town residents provide an in-depth understanding of the real-life implications of housing regulation, both for housing security and for a sense of community.

# Landlords' and Tenants' Strategies for Coping with the New York City Rental Housing Market

Landlords and tenants have each developed distinct strategies to navigate New York City's housing market. This chapter outlines some of these tactics within the context of Stuyvesant Town's transition to market-rate housing, and it reports residents' perspectives on them. We describe landlords' efforts to increase profit in the wake of the 2008–2009 financial crisis, specifically highlighting the ways in which Stuyvesant Town's management attempted to extract higher rents from tenants. Our interviews show how residents attempted to use their own personal and collective agency (i.e., the capacity to make choices and act on their own) to counteract these efforts. The rich detail in residents' accounts provides a window into fears about housing insecurity and survival strategies in the face of rent hikes, and also shows how landlords use their power to alter community quality of life.

## Landlords' Strategies for Coping with Market Conditions and Maximizing Exchange Value

### Tapping into the Luxury Rental Market

In 2008, New York City was reeling from a financial crisis that marked the end of a major real estate bubble. Middle-class New Yorkers were generally worried about the economic downturn, and they were also specifically concerned about the city's extremely low housing vacancy rates (2.88 percent citywide in 2008) and that rents that were already high and were on the rise.[1] It was in this context that some landlords reacted to the financial crisis by intensifying efforts to pursue and cater to high-end renters. To the extent that developers were still building housing, they revised plans, converted old buildings, and built new ones to better accommodate the wealthy.[2] To compete with newer high-rise rentals, landlords also upgraded older buildings, including some that were only ten years old, with the hope that their apartment complexes would gain reputations as upscale residential destinations.[3]

A luxury New York City apartment traditionally includes, at the minimum, a full-service (i.e., staffed by a doorman and concierge), high-rise living situation. Usually, this also means a location in a high-status neighborhood (e.g., Chelsea's High Line, Soho, and TriBeca) or a prestigious address (Central Park West), unique architecture featuring glassy towers, oversized windows, dark hardwood floors, stainless steel appliances, personal washers and dryers, a concierge in the lobby to attend to one's personal needs, a fitness club, and in many cases, the option to purchase a unit and become an owner, as in a condo building. In the case of ultra-luxury or super-luxury "trophy" rentals, tenants with hedge-fund-executive incomes also pay for the bragging rights to addresses in buildings designed by "star" architects like Frank Gehry, with penthouses, spacious rooms, high ceilings, majestic views, and rooftop terraces.[4] Today, these kinds of luxury buildings are even ubiquitous outside of Manhattan, as in many Brooklyn neighborhoods, for example.[5]

However, even landlords who own older walkups and elevator buildings in stodgy neighborhoods now label their properties as "luxury" in an attempt to tap into the rental market of professionals with upscale tastes, hoping they will pay a premium for certain amenities. Tishman-Speyer fits into this category of landlords because of the company's efforts to convert Stuyvesant Town's affordable units to market-rate. This strategy works, in part, because demand outstrips supply and because Stuyvesant Town has a relatively desirable location. Tenants know that snap decisions are necessary in a city where high-pressure leasing tactics are the norm, rentals go fast, and the opportunity to compare apartments is fleeting.

## Condo Conversions

Back in 1964, New York State began allowing landlords to convert rental buildings into condominiums. Condo conversions, in which tenants own rather than rent units, are another way that property owners attempt to increase profitability. As business people, landlords are often concerned that their buildings are not sufficiently profitable to justify the trouble and cost of managing and maintaining them. Given that the returns on the sales of individual units are far greater than the returns on a one-time sale of an entire apartment complex, they consider conversions to be a practical way to enhance profit.[6] This is especially true of older buildings, which lose profitability as maintenance costs rise and government controls limit rent increases.[7] Landlords are also aware that urban residents desire condo conversions because they tend to be less expensive to buy than apartments in newly constructed buildings.[8] In addition, many landlords and real estate agents offer incentives to potential "outsider" buyers (i.e., buyers who are not current tenants) if they agree to sign a contract; landlords do this because the state attorney general's office requires them to get a minimum percentage of signed owner contracts in order to effectively declare a conversion. Thus, rather than selling a rental building for minimal or negative profit, and instead of tolerating the limits to profitability imposed by rent control, many landlords prefer to convert their rental buildings to condos.

Historically, tenants have often opposed conversion and have fought mightily to protect their right to rent. They do this even as they simultaneously negotiate for deep discounts, just in case they decide to purchase the unit as an "insider" (i.e., a buyer who is a current tenant, and is often offered a lower price per square foot). Since the 1980s, the law has granted tenants a large degree of bargaining power when landlords seek to convert market-rate and regulated units to condos.[9] Most approved condo conversions are non-eviction plans wherein renters have the right to remain in their apartments. However, if a tenant cannot afford to buy—even with the insider's purchasing discount—or if they prefer not to, the landlord can either sell the unit as a condo or deregulate it when the tenant finally moves out.

When a developer either partially or wholly converts a rental building into condos, the city's total rental housing stock is reduced. Furthermore, if the building is rent regulated, it subtracts from the city's rent-regulated housing stock. Some might argue that the net loss of rental units and the accompanying decline in stabilized housing stock are small losses, but in the long term the losses become more substantial.[10] As a result, some overcrowded cities with high housing costs and a shortage of affordable rental housing, such as Los Angeles and San Diego, have municipal codes that actually suspend condo conversions when the rental vacancy rate falls below the 5 percent threshold.

In general, the state of New York provides a great deal of protection to renters,[11] and New York City has experienced substantial tenant push-back on issues surrounding condo conversions.[12] However, landlords are often highly motivated by potential profits, and they find creative ways to pave the way for conversion deals that allow developers to reha-bilitate rentals into luxury condos.[13] For instance, landlords have been known to take extreme and dubious measures to push renting tenants to vacate before and during condo conversion deals. Some landlords harass tenants into leaving or offer extremely small sale price discounts to rent-ers who choose to remain after a conversion.[14]

Conversions create stress and housing uncertainty for tenants, many of whom are not in a financial position to buy property, especially now that many of the insider discounts of the past have shrunk, leaving the cost of a mortgage and maintenance far in excess of current stabilized rent. Tenants also worry about being forced to move, their right to re-main in their unit with regulated rent, and the legal fees that they are likely to incur as they seek counsel to protect their rights. Another source of agitation is the emergence of a two-class system in which owners have access to amenities that renters do not (e.g., fitness centers, concierge services, and children's playrooms). Some Manhattan devel-opers even constructed apartment towers with "poor doors," a separate entrance for tenants who reside in the portion of the building designated for affordable housing, but which were outlawed in June 2015 (though developers have found ways to circumvent the ban).[15]

Housing and community advocates note that conversion has benefits, as well. It creates a stable middle-class homeowner community, provides the opportunity for middle-class residents to build equity, and improves property upkeep, which helps prevent deterioration.[16] However, even though condo conversions can provide relatively affordable owner-occupied housing to urban residents, they often come at the cost of maintaining the limited supply of rent-stabilized rental housing because landlords increase the rents on the declining supply of units.[17] Also, rental communities with significant senior citizen populations that were once vibrant, bohemian, and diverse can transform into playgrounds for the rich. Developers who want a large return on their investments often redesign converted buildings in ways that cater to wealthy clients who are willing and able to spend millions of dollars.

## How Did Stuyvesant Town's Landlords Cope with Market Conditions? Strategies for Maximizing Profit

Over time, the various Stuyvesant Town owners and their representatives have used three major strategies to raise rents: (1) upgrading apartments and embarking on luxury marketing campaigns; (2) monitoring tenants for lease violations in order to evict them; and (3) filling apartments with transient tenants who will elevate turnover rates. Each of these is described in detail below.

### Capital Improvements to Raise Rents

As summarized in the first chapter of this book, Tishman-Speyer engaged in a speculative real estate transaction to convert affordable housing to high-rent, market-rate units. The developers did this by making relatively inexpensive and superficial cosmetic interior renovations to some market-rate units, even as the property retained its overall outdated features and lack of prestige. Management explicitly marketed the property as high end, complete with a sign in the leasing office proclaiming that luxury rentals were available.[18] The pitch that Stuyvesant Town is a complex of opulent elevator buildings may have been intended for the market of recent college graduates and professionals, but later it was extended to college students. Students tend to "pile up" in units and split expensive rents, but also remain highly mobile and transient, allowing management to implement frequent rent hikes between tenants with short leases and high turnover.

The Rent Regulation Reform Act of 1993 meant that New York landlords could convert rent-regulated apartments to market-rate occupancy if the rents were more than $2,000. MetLife, and later Tishman-Speyer, took advantage of this law and another amended New York state rent law that permits a "vacancy allowance," all in order to encourage apartment turnover. Under the new rules, when units would become vacant, the owners could increase rent by 20 percent.[19] In addition, they could charge one-fortieth of the cost of any renovations made on the apartment between tenants, such as the installation of air conditioners that Ruthie Goldblum described in chapter 3. Management also imposed an Individual Apartment Improvement (IAI) fee to increase rent. For instance, one tenant we interviewed told us that she received a new $800 refrigerator ten years ago, and ever since then, she has continued to receive an IAI fee of $10 per month. To date, she has paid $1,200 for the refrigerator and is still paying. It is these kinds of rent increases and fees that have allowed Stuyvesant Town rents to escalate so much that the maximum legal rent in stabilized apartments is often *higher* than the market rate.[20]

Leading up to the sale of Stuyvesant Town, MetLife announced that it would no longer offer rent-stabilized apartments and proceeded to use the luxury-decontrol provision to convert a large number of units to market rate.[21] As early as the 1990s, MetLife had been making plans to increase rents, including a $100 million major capital improvement campaign.[22] The project included upgrades to brickwork, lighting, landscaping, and updates to lobbies, elevators, and nearby walking paths, as well as rewired electrical systems, and new boilers, plumbing, roofs, and windows. On the surface, these might appear to be welcome changes, but many tenants, especially the middle-aged and older ones, were anything but grateful. Though residents appreciated some renovations and enhancements, they argued that others were too costly, unnecessary, and that the landlord was exaggerating the amount that was invested for such improvements, all in order to raise rents and oust the rent-regulated tenants. In one tenants association meeting, a lawyer insisted that it was perfectly legal for landlords to "gold-plate" the toilets, meaning that landlords are entitled to make overpriced improvements and pass on the costs to tenants through permanent rent increases. Of course, landlords have an incentive to pay top dollar for renovations to stabilized apartments because the rent increases will more than cover the costs.[23] In order to complete these upgrades and raise rents, landlords must apply to the Division of Housing and Community Renewal to gain approval, and at least in theory, the landlord must show evidence of the actual cost of all improvements.

After buying and overpaying for Stuyvesant Town, Tishman-Speyer attempted to recoup potential losses to the investment and continued MetLife's efforts to raise rents and force tenants out by embarking on its own set of capital improvement projects. Arguably, some of these changes were reasonable and anticipated for a property that is nearly seventy years old. For example, in 2009 Tishman-Speyer notified tenants that the company was replacing tanks and valves in the buildings. Previous to this, management distributed notices about needed basic improvements in the form of repaving, the addition of intercoms, and upgrades to roofs. Standard maintenance is essential to keep roofs and pipes functional, can prevent a building from collapsing, and can help to avoid, or at least postpone, more expensive repairs and rehabilitation. To some, capital improvements seem to signify a generous landlord who intervenes so that tenants have better lifestyles, but New York City's rent-stabilized tenants tend to believe that landlords mainly want to increase rents and profits.

Tenants seeking to preserve their current rent rates face many obstacles to gaining the ears of landlords and city officials. In terms of procedure, a landlord must apply for a major capital improvement rent increase, and then the New York Homes and Community Renewal (HCR) (formerly known as the New York Division of Housing and Community Renewal) rules on the application. At this point, the tenant receives a Notice of Application by Owner for MCI Increase.

The HCR is often considered to be "pro-developer," but tenants have thirty-five days to challenge a rent increase by participating in a process called a Petition for Administrative Review (PAR). Stuyvesant Town's tenants association devotes a significant amount of time and energy to helping tenants deal with the administrative process of appealing to the HCR when they receive an order granting the landlord an MCI rent increase. Even with assistance from the tenants association, a tenant must be very sophisticated in order to challenge the landlord. For instance, in the case of the landlord applying for a building-wide MCI, tenants should first gain counsel representation from the tenants association in order to protect their individual rights, but they should also allow the tenants association and its collective resources to handle the action. Tenants must also identify at least one neighbor who is willing to download and sign an authorization form that designates an attorney to represent the entire building's tenants. Those without Internet access must call the tenants association message center or contact the building leader or floor volunteer.

Tenants also have to contend with multiple review stages, including filing for a "Request for Information," a "Petition for Administrative Review," and participation in a tenant answer stage. For instance, from 2004 to 2009, the tenants association helped residents to petition against elevator and roof improvements and assisted tenants who sought a review of the repaving, water tank and valve improvements, and the application for new exterior doors. During this period, the landlord also applied for MCI improvements to the security system, the keycard system, and the video command center, all of which tenants sought to oppose. In 2009 Tishman-Speyer installed video intercoms after applying for an MCI and getting HCR approval; this was another item for which the tenants association sought a Request for Information, and it was followed by an increase to Stuyvesant Town tenants' base rents. Just four years later, in October 2013, CWCapital informed tenants that they were going to impose a retroactive $4.17 rent increase per room per month for the intercoms that Tishman-Speyer installed back in 2009. Aside from costs, many tenants have been critical of the video intercom system itself, with claims that the system is unreliable, and with some complaining that they were unable to use the intercoms to contact security after Hurricane Sandy. One eleventh-floor resident claimed that his broken intercom has forced him to resort to admitting guests to the building by tossing his access keycard out of the window with a weighted sock so it will land on the ground near the people who buzz into the building.[24] Tenants' skepticism about the motivations for major capital improvements has been especially high in the wake of mid-lease rent increases, stricter enforcement of late fees, and previous findings that such improvements were unjustly imposed.[25]

### Spy Town: Aggressive Monitoring of Stabilized Apartments

Though MetLife began aggressively seeking ways to raise revenue before selling Stuyvesant Town, many tenants believe that Tishman-Speyer's purchase of the property resulted in a massive debt that produced a great deal of pressure to make the deal profitable. This triggered an even more aggressive campaign to evict rent-stabilized residents and improve cash flow through converting units to market-rate occupancy. One strategy to increase the turnover of units has been the surveillance of tenants and their apartments with the intention and hope of discovering lease and code violations, and giving legal cause to evict. Indeed, neoliberal policy creates a climate in which public spaces, and communities in general, become mere assets that require careful supervision. Landlords protect the exchange value of their assets in increasingly intrusive ways, cloaking their actions in language about the tenants' best interests and management's desire to maintain order and prevent crime.

Landlord surveillance often takes the form of spying on tenants' finances.[26] The *New York Post* reported on tenant leaders' and residents' anger and outrage over landlords who pry into their financial records by "building tax dossiers on tenants in a massive effort to drive out low-paying families and jack up rents."[27] Landlords justify the "audits" by proclaiming that the problem of tenants abusing rent-stabilization rules is commonplace across New York City, as when tenants leave town and illegally sublet their unit, use their apartment as a non-primary residence or pied-à-terre, or just pass the unit on to ineligible family members—all legitimate landlord concerns.

Tishman-Speyer's crackdown on potential rent-stabilization abuses was extensive, and their investigation into tenants' public tax records and property holdings stretched nationwide, including their hiring of private detectives.[28] According to the *New York Sun*, the company hired Fred Knapp, whom the *New York Times* called the "scourge of illegal tenants" for his persistence and imagination in researching public documents, property deeds, and credit applications in search of residents' use of alternative addresses.[29] The goal was to show that Stuyvesant Town was not a tenant's primary residence, and this effort resulted in numerous eviction and non-renewal notices. Councilman Garodnick encouraged tenants to attend legal clinics to learn about their rights, and he affirmed the tenants' feelings that "these are scary letters to get."[30] A July 2015 email from the tenants association warned that management had resumed the practice of issuing non-renewal notices and evictions to tenants suspected of having another residence. The email stated that tenants are the ones who bear the burden of disputing the accusations: "Tenants may be challenged if they have another address, or show out-of-state car or voter registrations, tax payments, or utility bills. Keycard usage [to get into the building] can also be checked for the requisite number of days."

Affordable housing advocates argue that aggressive eviction tactics overreach and victimize the innocent tenants who adhere to their leases.[31] Our interviews show that stabilized tenants often feel harassed and perceive that they are vulnerable to frivolous housing court suits.

Many non-violators are on a budget and do not have the financial re-sources to hire lawyers to challenge false claims and pay legal fees. For example, Felice Golden, a seventy-four-year-old tenant who entered the Peace Corps while residing in Stuyvesant Town, said that management had once targeted her for eviction:

> They tried to kick me out when I went into the Peace Corps. I went to the office and told the woman at that city department that I was going away for two years, and I was coming back. [I told them] to leave [the apart-ment] as it is. They told me to fill out my information. I was working for the federal government and volunteered to go to Africa, so they kind of believed me. What happened was, the bank put the African address on the rent check, so they never looked in my file. They just started to send me letters. I was never there. I got an eviction notice on my door, and my neighbor saw it and called me while I was in Africa, so I contacted my son. He wrote to them and dealt with them. I was a nervous wreck, though. I didn't want to lose my home. That is my home. When I got back, there were all of these things going on. I went to see them, and there were all these letters from my son. I was told that they were going to evict me, but they never looked into my file. That was Stuyvesant Town and MetLife. They tried to kick me out.

We noted in chapter 2 that a Federal Express employee told a ten-ant that management had asked him to spy on tenants and report any name and address discrepancies that appeared on packages. Stuyvesant Town's grounds workers, housing staff, custodians, and repairmen also have been engaged in spying. In some cases, in exchange for tips about lease violations, management has promised employees $150 American Express gift cards. For instance, back when MetLife owned the prop-erty and prohibited pets, management asked employees to act as "pet detectives" and search for tenants with illegal animals.[32] Underscoring MetLife's intentions, the reward came with stipulations: "Please be aware that this award is contingent upon the success of the legal action . . . If we are not successful, there will be no reward."[33] In a *New York Post* article, Assemblyman Steven Sanders said, "It's appalling. It's creating a kind of totalitarian environment where MetLife is encouraging employ-ees to spy and inform on tenants."[34]

The unauthorized use of temporary pressurized walls is another target of surveillance that makes tenants vulnerable to eviction. Pressurized walls often violate building codes and require Department of Buildings work permits. A high-profile fire in the Bronx in 2005 killed tenants who were unable to escape because of an illegal wall partition. New York tenants have long used these walls, in part because city enforcement of the rules against them has been lax.[35] Though the Department of Buildings does not conduct random audits and inspections, Tishman-Speyer claimed that the Fire Department and Department of Buildings was inspecting Stuyvesant Town buildings, so management must engage in blanket enforcement of city laws.

However, many residents told stories about management *selectively* enforcing the rules against pressurized walls in order to evict longtime residents, while also promoting the use of these walls to incoming student tenants. As brazen as it may seem, it is not uncommon to see in Stuyvesant Town white trucks that say "Manhattan Pressurized Walls, Inc." along with the website "divideyourroom.com." Younger tenants reported that Stuyvesant Town's leasing office actually provided them with information and brochures about companies that install these walls. The leasing office and management also gave tenants verbal permission to install the walls, but later threatened some tenants to either remove them or else face eviction. Tenants perceive these behaviors as part of the larger effort to turn the apartments over to new tenants in order to take full advantage of vacancy increases and raise the rent.

## Partnering with NYU to Pile Up Students

Given that Stuyvesant Town will never be a luxury community by New York City standards, management pursued a strategy that nibbles at the lowest rung of that market by targeting lower Manhattan's burgeoning student population. For instance, on NYU's website, under the heading "Explore the Residence Halls," is a link simply called "Stuyvesant Town." A recent version of the text reads:

> Welcome to the Graduate Student Halls! Comprised of Washington Square Village and Stuyvesant Town, the "Grad Halls" (as we are commonly known) are a diverse community of graduate students at NYU

with approximately 250 residents and 8 Resident Assistants. Located in the village, near Union Square, our halls work together to create a dynamic environment where our graduate students can engage with one another and participate in social, academic, and cultural programming. The "Grad Halls" strive to be a support system and important resource for our residential students. Throughout the year, we collaborate with many campus offices, such as the Office of Graduate Student Life at the Student Resource Center and the Office for International Scholars, to bring you exciting and useful programs. Our staff members are eager to introduce students to the activities and the leadership opportunities found at NYU and in NYC. We look forward to this year with the "Grad Halls"!

In addition, the website for NYU's Graduate School of Arts and Sciences has featured ads for the MacCracken Housing Program (MHP), which provides housing in converted two-bedroom apartments located in Stuyvesant Town. The website warns students against renting elsewhere and showcases the dorm-like features:

When comparing off-campus housing alternatives to MHP housing, please keep in mind that the MHP rates are more affordable than most comparable non-NYU apartments listed at market rates. MHP has many attractive features: utilities are included in the room cost (heat, water and electricity); apartments are furnished; MHP housing is close to campus; laundry facilities are on site; all buildings have elevators; security is maintained by Stuyvesant Town Security; residents are provided with a Stuyvesant Town issued photo identification swipe-card.

As early as 2003, longtime residents began to notice the influx of students, and given their distrust of their landlord and management, many tenants expressed concerns.[36] Some speculated that the shift to a focus on students was management's response to the failure of their luxury upgrades and marketing. In other words, it was obvious to savvy New Yorkers that Stuyvesant Town was not luxurious. The high rents on market-rate units in old buildings with few modern amenities in a low-profile neighborhood caused apartments to remain vacant and rents to drop, thus motivating Stuyvesant Town's management to recruit college students as tenants.[37] At that time, two-bedroom furnished apartments of two different sizes were renting for $10,250 or $11,550 for the academic year.

The tenants association responded to these changes in the following way on its website in 2012:

> Recent publicity has called to front and center the appalling conditions created in both Stuyvesant Town and Peter Cooper Village by Rose Associates' aggressive marketing plans to fill apartments—reconfigured through the use of newly-constructed "pressurized walls"—with college students. Obviously, neither the Tenants Association nor the community at large has anything against college students or, for that matter, college dormitories. However, students and dormitories both have an appropriate setting. A residential community is not such a setting.
>
> What is behind this rental strategy? It seems obvious that it is the patent desire to rapidly fill vacant apartments with the expectation of rapid turnover, thus affording the landlord incremental rent increases under the rent stabilization laws. All of this comes at the expense of straining the facilities in the buildings (laundry, sewage, refuse accumulation, elevator congestion, etc.) and the quality of life of residents interested in long-term stability.
>
> Management needs to hear from tenants how they have been affected by the influx of students in their buildings. All residents who have trouble sleeping, encounter filth in the laundry rooms or in the stairwells, or experience other negative impacts from "overstuffed" apartments are urged to call and share their issues with Rose Associates.

A 2011 blog post featured the following characterization of modern-day Stuyvesant Town:

> I have fond memories of living in Stuyvesant Town before it became dorm/transient accommodation. It was a nice place to live and most of us took pride in living there and respected our neighbors. Unfortunately, it has reached the point where I am ashamed to invite visitors because one is usually met by the sight of leaking, stinking garbage bags dumped outside the recycling area, dog schmears in the halls and elevators and the constant intrusive barking of dogs. Also, I can't remember when I last had a good night's sleep. Having noisy, crowded dorm apartments upstairs

and downstairs from me has made unbroken sleep a nostalgic memory. May the Speyers rot in hell for what they have done.

## How Did Tenants Cope? Strategies for Maintaining Residence in Manhattan

Given the threats to their housing stability, tenants asserted their agency both as individuals and in cooperation with tenants. To reduce housing costs, they conducted individual negotiations or else followed the students' lead and attempted to sublet their apartments. To improve quality of life and enforce norms and community codes, they engaged in acts of informal social control. To express their distrust of management, they began using social media to share information with invested neighbors, whom they deemed to be more credible and trustworthy than Stuyvesant Town's management.

### Making Ends Meet: Negotiating, Downsizing, and Subletting

Individual tenants and their representatives sometimes attempt to negotiate the terms of their leases with management, and a few even succeed. Tenants described their attempts to negotiate lower rents, and several reported better success at haggling over smaller conveniences, such as having their apartment repainted. Of course, negotiation usually implies give *and* take, and even in situations when management made some concessions to tenants' interests, residents still reported that "rent is rent" and that a fresh coat of paint does not help to pay the bills. Thus, many have been forced to scale back on their lifestyles and conveniences in order to meet higher rent obligations. For instance, some tenants have tried to convince their relatives to move in with them in order to defray costs. Many stated that they have been forced to downsize, moving into smaller units within Stuyvesant Town. Of course, others have simply moved farther away from the core of the city to places like Westchester, Brooklyn, Queens, and Jersey City, which are also becoming less affordable.

Another strategy has been subletting. In New York City, tenants sublet their apartments for a variety of reasons. Some are looking to move, but cannot get out of their lease, or else want to make sure they like their new place before giving up their old units (and stabilized rents). Many students who only live in the city part time and tenants who travel for lengths of time or who go on vacations to summer homes often try to rent out their units to cover their rent and generate income while away.

In Stuyvesant Town and other New York City communities, residents seeking to sublease often advertise their apartments on websites like Street Easy, Yelp, Craigslist, or Airbnb, an online sublet service. For instance, a recent Craigslist ad attempted to entice prospective short-term tenants with this offer: "$1500 1BR in 3BR sublet in Stuy Town available 6/3 (East Village)." However, in most cases, sublets are prohibited without the landlord's written consent, and even then, advertising online is risky because landlords seeking to evict tenants routinely scan websites for advertisements about their properties and can recognize photos of apartments by the images of renovations, window views, and layout configurations.

Furthermore, landlords now enforce existing laws in order to crack down on sublet arrangements. In fact, Airbnb, which has been costly to the hotel industry, is generally illegal in New York because it violates laws that prohibit residents from operating a hotel out of an apartment. One thirty-year Stuyvesant Town tenant has been acting as a detective and vigilante by searching the Internet for ads posted by neighbors who illegally rent out their apartments as hotel rooms, some asking for $200 per night.[38] This tenant and others use photos of the apartments and additional information, as well as Facebook, to figure out the identities of the tenants who are renting their apartments to "hotel guests" with luggage on rollers, citing fears about bedbugs, security risks, and noisy parties. The *New York Times* reported a story on "a recent wave of hotel listings" in Stuyvesant Town, saying "one of the illegal hoteliers was reported to have taken vengeance on her neighbors, putting glue in their locks. As a result, some now are afraid to go public with their complaints."[39]

The tenant of record is required to live in a stabilized apartment as their primary residence, but some seek to maintain their lease while also attempting to buy a condo or another property. Many New Yorkers view a stabilized apartment as a great deal and one that they could pass on to family or else sublet. However, if the tenant is not living there, he or she is at risk. Maintenance staff members, neighbors, security cameras, and delivery people may notice an outsider in the apartment and report it to the landlord as a lease violation.

According to New York City's Rent Guidelines Board, a sublet must last for thirty days or more, though many engage in "micro-subletting," in which one rents out a room or apartment for weeks or even days at a time as some do on Airbnb. If the building has four or more units and a lease, tenants are entitled to request permission from their landlord to sublet their apartments and "the owner may not reasonably refuse" such a request. Tenants must then submit a letter of intent to sublet to the landlord at least thirty days in advance, and the letter must state the terms of sublease, the reason for subletting, the name and address of the proposed tenant, written consent of anyone else on the lease or any co-tenants, and it must include copies of the lease and sublease with both the tenant and subtenant acknowledging the terms. Landlords are also permitted to request additional information within ten days of the request and may stall this process by enforcing strict rules that govern the subletting of rent-stabilized apartments. However, if landlords do not respond to the original request or additional information response within thirty days, the inaction is viewed as consent, and the tenant may proceed. Still, the tenant remains liable for all terms of the lease. Some perceive tenants who sublet a unit or room as overcharging for rent. For instance, some tenants charge a hefty fee, but they argue that they are factoring in the use of furniture and other amenities that would not come with a vacant unit. Court dockets are crowded with cases in which landlords have sought to evict tenants because of a sublet and cases where subtenants have overpaid for their unit or have been evicted without warning because tenants did not get approval from a landlord.

One tenant reported that she sublets a room for three months at a time because her business has been struggling. She mentioned that as a single woman with children who are now grown and living on their own, she has found that that having a roommate is both a source of social comfort and financial security. Even so, she seemed confused about the complicated lease rules and reported that she lives in a state of constant worry and paranoia, fearing that she is somehow violating her lease and risking eviction:

I have students renting my [kids' old] bedroom . . . I know I'm on a limb, but every penny that I'm not making I have to cover as rent, and every penny has to go into promotion of trying to keep [my business] afloat. So I've had these students here for a couple years now. When [my children] come home, [they] sleep with me in my bedroom. The girls who come here are lovely . . . It's keeping me sane to have someone here with me, too. Now they're just like surrogate daughters. Yeah, they're lovely . . . 'cause I would never ever advertise on Craigslist. This is my one and only home, so I like to know that I can walk out and feel safe and leave my possessions and my home in their hands. Oh, it's just been a godsend, but I know I could lose my lease and get kicked out of here if management got wind of it. But then again, I've been told—well, I know I'm entitled—I could be entitled—I *am* entitled to have roommates. . . . They said if I were to really move out like they knew other families did and buy a home—*that* is against the rent stabilization lease.

The Rent Guidelines Board stipulates that stabilized tenants are permitted to have only one roommate, and even then, the tenants are required to maintain the residence as their primary home.

Some in Stuyvesant Town empathize with neighbors who seek to sublet their apartments while on vacation or visiting family members, but they also admit that other tenants take these privileges way too far. Beatrice referred to such behavior as "abuses":

Now, there are also abuses. There were people living here who were living in Australia, and they sublet their apartments for the regular price . . . They were gone for many years, and I don't think that was fair, either. But they are a minority now. The ones I know personally are gone. They've married and moved on, but like, I thought that was enough, and I told them so. Like, it was depriving someone else of a home that they wanted here in Stuy Town or in Peter Cooper.

Evelyn also expressed ambivalence about tenants who sublet: "I often understand it. When we first moved here it was a little upsetting, but I had met some neighbors who had actually moved out and sublet their home illegally and they used the income to pay for their mortgage of their home." Leslie Reid, a thirty-nine-year-old rent-stabilized tenant, also recalled a vague example of sublet abuse that she learned about through word-of-mouth: "Actually, I knew one guy. It came out later that one partner at my law firm illegally sublet his [apartment]. He lived in a fancy doorman building in the Upper East Side, or maybe a brownstone even. I don't know. He lived somewhere fancy on the Upper East Side."

Though some people exploit the practice of subletting, other tenants who might otherwise have been forced to move out of Stuyvesant Town have regained some semblance of housing stability from renting out a room in their apartments.

## Informal Social Control

All societies exercise social control over their members, whether formally through police action, for instance, or informally, through social pressure. The concept of informal social control tends to be associated with neighbors' efforts to intervene to reduce violent crime, often in low-income communities. However, in Stuyvesant Town, some tenants have developed a sense of interdependence as a result of their proximity, length of residence, and desire to maintain their affordable housing and quality of life. In this context, informal social control can be observed as residents seek associations with like-minded neighbors, those who want to stay in Stuyvesant Town and those who believe tenants should conform to historical community norms.

To enforce norms in Stuyvesant Town, some tenants have engaged in "neighbor versus neighbor" threats.[40] In an extreme case in 2011, one tenant placed flyers under the doors of fellow tenants warning them that smoking marijuana on the grounds of the property can (and has) resulted in eviction. Specifically, the flyer warned: "If you are smoking pot . . . you will be found and evicted. Other potheads like yourself were evicted from this building." This type of behavior can discredit longtime residents. One tenant who believed he was driven out of the community by longtime tenants blogged about his Stuyvesant Town experience in 2012:

> My older neighbors, particularly the older women in this community, have often been incredibly rude, condescending, arrogant, and nasty. I have witnessed them slam doors in people's faces, yell at nannies, bark at people trying to board empty elevators with them, slip anonymous

passive-aggressive notes under doors, leer at and spy on their neighbors . . . and just generally engage in incredibly childish and boorish behavior . . . Good bye all, and good riddance.

For their part, longtime tenants have reason to resort to their own methods of informal social control. Research on older urban residents shows that length of residence is a major predictor of community social bonds and friendship, and that disorder significantly reduces social cohesion, trust, and informal social control.[41] In general, the residents who are the sources of crime and minor disorder rarely have favorable views of their neighbors who step in and try to reclaim the community. Stuyvesant Town's longtime tenants are older, many have few resources or housing alternatives, and they want to defend their community because they believe it is under attack by disorderly college students, their landlord, and management. In addition, they perceive that they have no recourse, as the people collecting their rent would prefer that the buildings were populated with large numbers of transient market-rate students rather than smaller numbers of rent-stabilized middle-aged and older tenants who refuse to leave.

Tenants who do have the courage to speak out often do so after much hesitation and with much trepidation. In reaction to what some have called "Orwellian tactics," the levels of paranoia in Stuyvesant Town are palpable. Most tenants we interviewed seemed excited to participate in this study so they could help to finally get out the "real story," but only under the protection of pseudonyms. Many have been reluctant to talk to the press, interviewers, and even their own neighbors about the most mundane aspects of their lives, as they believe it could result in eviction.

## Credibility and Trust: Neighboring with Social Media

Perceiving management to be unresponsive to their concerns and often hostile to their requests, residents have turned to social media as a tool to engage with the community, share information, ask for advice, and air grievances. They view the messages they read as informative, and generally, credible and influential. Residents' use of social media to communicate about community matters demonstrates a sense of trust in Stuyvesant Town's neighbors and conveys tenants' good intentions. It also serves as a contrast to their beliefs about landlords, management, and the short-term, less engaged tenants.

Tenants have created several blogs and have started various Facebook groups focusing on a range of topics. For instance, on the official tenants association Facebook page, tenants share positive stories, they post historical artifacts to help build institutional memory, and they mobilize neighbors to get together for fun and good causes, such as food drives for the poor. Those with children have created parenting support networks on meetup.com (e.g., Stuyvesant Town Moms and the Toddler Playgroup).

Of course, management also uses Facebook to further its purposes, such as advertising fee-based services (e.g., Oval Fitness memberships), promoting events, releasing public safety warnings, and encouraging tenants to share photos and stories that will boost efforts to lease apartments to a desirable demographic. As an example of the latter case, management has asked tenants to "send us your best shot on the [basketball] court with an Instagram video." It has also offered to pay tenants up to $2,500 as part of a "lease referral program" meant for tenants who tell their friends about "how much you love your spacious apartment." Also, as part of an effort to combat negative reviews, CWCapital promotes a "community rewards game," offering $10 and $20 gift cards to tenants who promote Stuyvesant Town on social media and earn a sufficient number of points.[42]

Tenants use Facebook to get answers about basic housing problems. For instance, they ask questions about getting their heat restored in frigid temperatures, about ways to deal with neighbor problems, and about the notices on mid-lease rent hikes. One can click on a blog called the "The Stuyvesant Town Report," which purports to tell "the truth about a complex built for veterans and the middle class and how it has evolved through the years to become one of the more interesting and controversial of New York stories." The anonymous blogger claims to be an army veteran, resident, and published author and moderates the comments for inappropriate content, such as name-calling and unfounded or extreme accusations. The site often features photographs capturing landlord and management failures and the younger tenants' bad behaviors. Titles of posts include: "Projects Living at Market Rate

Pricing" and "Welcome to Slum Town! CWCapital's Masterful Reinvention of Stuy Town/Peter Cooper Village into the Projects." The blog also includes informational posts about tenant protests, meetings, and legal issues, updates about the status of the property's sale, ownership, management, and the politics surrounding it, and photos and commentary about neighborhood problems such as management's discriminatory enforcement of wall partition rules, student neighbors urinating in public on the Oval, and problems with dog feces and swarming flies on the grounds.

Residents mainly use the tenants association's Facebook page to urge others toward activism, to share information about management's unfair actions (e.g., the site explains what mid-lease rent increases are in "plain English"), to advise tenants on handling management requests (e.g., maintenance workers entering one's apartment, which could be used to gather evidence for eviction), and to update tenants about the status of legal cases against landlords. In one post titled "Community Not a Commodity Update" readers learned that a documentarian was planning to film the location in front of Stuyvesant Town's leasing office, where tenants had protested to warn prospective renters about mid-lease rent increases and other negative community conditions.

## Tenant Activism and the Right to the City

When sociologist Henri Lefebvre was writing about the "right to the city" in 1968 in Paris, he was concerned about the ways that capitalism manifests in cities, including the erasure of public space, the creation of architecture that neglects human and social needs, and the fact that government pays too much attention to the demands of private business actors. He saw these as threats to citizens' capacities to fully inhabit their own cities.

Forty years later, Lefebvre's ideas remain important and researchers and activists have transferred the right to the city concept to contemporary settings, where it finds new expression. According to geographer and urban planner Edward Soja, entering the phrase "right to the city" into a search engine yielded nine million results, reflecting the globalization of the concept,[43] so it is easy to see that the term remains evocative for groups striving to improve urban residents' living conditions. The renewed focus on the right to the city can be applied to the provision of citizens' basic needs, including access to shelter, food, clean water, health care, and quality education. However, the right to the city also applies to concerns about neoliberal policies and how they take the form of the government retreating from traditional areas of social life, including the provision of public housing and public space. Certainly, the right to the city has found expression in Stuyvesant Town through the tenants association's efforts to act on behalf of residents.

According to its website, residents created the Stuyvesant Town-Peter Cooper Village Tenants Association in 1971 with the goal of "promoting the unity of the tenants . . . and to initiate the programs and collective action which will inure to the benefit of the tenants and their families." The site explains that rent deregulation was the impetus for the group forming:

> Governor Nelson A. Rockefeller pushed a package of bills through the New York State Legislature, commonly referred to as "Vacancy Decontrol." The Legislation enacted full vacancy decontrol for all rent controlled and rent stabilized housing in the state, effective June 30, 1971. Full vacancy decontrol was repealed in 1974 when the Legislature and Governor Malcolm Wilson enacted the Emergency Tenants Protection Act.

In recent years, tenants who have felt tentative or afraid about going it alone against Stuyvesant Town's management, and those who have tried and failed, have increasingly sought to band together for mutual assistance. Tenants association activists aided these efforts as members began to reach out to neighbors when privatization encroached, as well as in the aftermath of the default. One newer tenant explained the timing of the surge in tenant activism:

> It was right after the Tishman-Speyer bankruptcy, like soon after that. There was a big meeting in front of the housing court or something, and the tenants association was going door-to-door to each apartment, trying to get people to sign petitions and things like that . . . Then they have flyers posted in the elevator and in the lobby all the time for like, "Come to Baruch [College] for the meetings," the town hall meetings and stuff. I haven't gone to any of them.

In addition to facilitating information sharing among tenants, the tenants association has provided a collective voice in negotiation and a means to organize tenants. This has helped tenants with two major sets of goals that would have been impossible to reach alone. First, the tenants association has assisted tenants in both their individual and collective actions, including complaints and lawsuits. Second, it has organized tenants to give them a say in the final disposition of the Stuyvesant Town complex in the wake of bankruptcy Ultimately, the tenants association negotiated with the Blackstone Group and the city to ensure that 2015 sale deal would preserve 5,000 units of middle-class housing.

### Greasing the Wheels for Complaints and Lawsuits

Many residents reported that the tenants association is the first resource they seek out when they are having trouble with their apartments. Many also said that they regularly monitor the website to stay aware of their neighbors' concerns and to protect themselves from management's whims. Its leaders share information in plain language, facilitate complaints (e.g., contacting city officials to review charges for major capital improvements), and conduct due diligence on matters of concern to tenants, like rent increases. Important to this story is the fact that the tenants association played an instrumental role in restoring rent stabilization and recovering rent for tenants in the so-called Roberts lawsuit or Stuyvesant Town class action, as mentioned in chapter 1. Councilman Garodnick called the case a "historic win," exceeding $173 million.[44]

Specifically, in January 2007 the tenants association helped file a case against MetLife, Tishman-Speyer, and their associates, also known as the *Roberts v. Tishman-Speyer* class action. A group of tenants sued, claiming that the landlords had overcharged tenants on past and future rent that landlords were not entitled to because they were simultaneously receiving a tax break for providing affordable housing. The case involved almost 22,000 tenants, and was settled in 2012, with class member tenants recovering cash through refunds of overpaid rent and through future rent savings gained from required rent recalculations. In addition, rent stabilization on the case's 4,311 decontrolled units is scheduled to continue until June 2020.[45]

Garodnick, along with tenants association leaders and dozens of residents, went to Albany to try to prevent legislators from repealing the Roberts decision to re-regulate apartments. The association joined with other housing advocacy groups to bring attention to their cause, and tenants organized rallies, including "Unity Day." The following is from the tenants association's November 12, 2009 newsletter:

> Housing advocates and the community's elected representatives have dubbed November 14th Unity Day—a day when tenants and their champions will bring to the attention of legislators, policy makers, potential new landlords, creditors, and the general public the importance of preserving the affordability and unique character of the 62-year-old buildings that have historically been home to many of the city's most essential workers.[46]

The association held informational meetings on the state of the lawsuit and posted the transcripts of the meetings on its website. Active members created and posted "Frequently Asked Questions" documents and canvassed the buildings to encourage tenants to file the complicated paperwork needed to recover their money.[47]

When rent stabilization laws were set to expire on June 15, 2015, the association organized a free air-conditioned bus ride to Albany and implored residents to "get on the bus!" The website asked tenants to "join your neighbors" and stated, "We're busing up to Albany to keep Stuy Town and Peter Cooper Village affordable. Governor Andrew Cuomo and Speaker Carl Heastie have to make this happen." It also listed the reasons tenants should dedicate an entire weekday to the event (with the bus scheduled to leave at 7:15 a.m. and return at 7:30 p.m.): "Will your next rent increase force you to move? Don't want to pay for MCIs forever? Want to keep apartments rent-stabilized? . . . Renewing the laws as they stand is not a victory for tenants. They must be strengthened!" In the aftermath, the association called the state's extension of stabilization until 2019 with only minimal strengthening measures a disappointment, until the city's Rent Guidelines Board stepped in: "Amid hundreds of tenants chanting 'the Governor betrayed us/the RGB [Rent Guidelines Board] will save us,' the RGB made a historic move in freezing rents on one-year leases, something never before done in its history. In another rare move, the board, in a 7 to 2 vote, approved the guidelines proposed by the tenant representatives at a first pass."

## Organizing to Press for Condo Conversion

The tenants association first attempted to play a larger role in the disposition of Stuyvesant Town in 2006, when MetLife announced the sale of the property. As summarized in chapter 1, this bid was ultimately unsuccessful, and the property went to Tishman-Speyer. After the Tishman-Speyer default, tenants began to investigate the feasibility of finding an investment partner to assist them in converting the development to condos or co-ops where current tenants would have the option to either stay as renters or buy at a discounted price.

The two main options under discussion were non-eviction conversion and eviction conversion. The former, which is supported by the tenants association, requires the purchaser to commit to pay for 15 percent of the units, but all of the tenants would be eligible to buy their units, and rent-stabilized tenants who would opt to continue renting would not be allowed to face eviction. In contrast, an eviction conversion would require 51 percent of the tenants to commit to buy their apartments, and all others would be eligible for eviction, but rent-stabilized tenants would have up to three years before eviction; older and disabled tenants who are stabilized would be exempt from eviction.

In September 2010, Condo Recovery LLC was interested in a condo conversion of Stuyvesant Town, speculating that tenants could purchase their units and pay a monthly amount similar to their current rent.[48] In an effort to recoup some of their $3 billion investment, investors Winthrop and Pershing Square wrote a letter to the tenants association offering a major financial stake in the property—as much as 50 percent, according to some—as well as the power to set the price of the apartments and veto important co-op decisions.[49] CWCapital, the lender, reported that it was open to a tenant-based purchase, but later delayed the process, citing legal problems related to setting Stuyvesant Town's rents.[50]

In November 2011, tenants again sought a condo conversion that would allow them to either purchase their units or remain rent-stabilized. Along with Brookfield Asset Management as a partner, the tenants association's board approached the bondholders, hoping they would view conversion as the best way to regain assets.[51] The plan would call for some units to remain permanent rentals, but tenants who

Figure 5.1 Tenants Association Logo. *Source*: Stuyvesant Town-Peter Cooper Village
Tenants Association

wanted to buy would be allowed to do so either at a reduced price with
resale restrictions or at market rate with fewer resale rules.[52] However,
Guterman-Westwood Partners also wanted to place a bid. The company
created a website called "STPCV Facts" and opened a twitter account.
Using harsh language that mocked the tenants association, Guterman-
Westwood Partners claimed to "empower residents" and advocated for
a co-op conversion rather than the condo conversion that the tenants
association was promoting. The website asserted that the co-op conversion plan would take less time than a condo conversion and would be
less costly to tenants.[53]

In the name of "gaining control of our future," the tenants association
embarked on a full campaign for condo conversion. It included a version
of the tenants association logo that features a rendering of the Stuyvesant Town buildings with tenants' hands holding each other in solidar-
ity. This one read "Unite: Focus on Conversion" instead of the usual
tagline: "A Community. Not a Commodity." The association released

informational question and answer videos, referring to the "tenant-led, non-eviction conversion plan." It also organized well attended "house meetings" to stimulate tenant engagement, provide information, handle concerns, and gather feedback.

In May 2012, with many tenants eager for action, the tenants association provided a status update on efforts to reach a deal for a bid with CWCapital and to enact the "TA-Brookfield Condo Conversion Plan." The tenants association even provided a space on its website urging tenants to commit to a "unity pledge." It asked residents to "recognize that the interests of all tenants—those who want to own their apartments and those who don't, those who are long-term rent-stabilized tenants and those who rented more recently at 'the market'—will best be served if we join together and speak with a single voice," and asked them to agree that "I want to stand with my neighbors as one united community."[54] To this end, volunteers from each of the fifty-six buildings went door to door to recruit neighbors to sign this pledge, eventually getting signatures from 7,100 residents.[55] With the Blackstone deal in place, condo conversion is off the table, as the contract stipulates that the landlord will not build new units or attempt a condo conversion.

## When an Economic Transaction Becomes Personal

Stuyvesant Town's social dimension is as important a component of the story of urban rent control as the economic dimensions of supply and demand. As neoliberal development processes continue to dominate the built environment, citizens attempt to subvert or supplant plans to convert affordable housing into market-rate units. Much of this activism occurs through Stuyvesant Town's tenants association, a manifestation of the unique composition of residents who currently reside there. Rather than the poor and disorganized communities who were cleared from the Gas House District to make way for Stuyvesant Town, today's residents are well-educated and informed about the threats to their community. Thus, context matters in debates over affordable housing.[56] In Manhattan's Stuyvesant Town, the vulnerable residents are not the poor and disenfranchised people who are most frequently the subjects of housing research.

Manhattan's extremely low vacancy rate pushes traditional conflicts between landlords and tenants to seemingly perverse limits and provides ample motivation for creativity on both sides. Although neoliberal policies have generally given the upper hand to landlords in recent years, Stuyvesant Town also provides examples, most notably in the Roberts case, of limits to what even large real estate firms can accomplish. Additionally, it illustrates the variety of strategies that middle-class New Yorkers may use to maintain their residence in the city. Still, longtime resident Felice Golden lamented the changes to Stuyvesant Town's sense of place:

> There is still some community, but I think it is going away. They are making a one-bedroom apartment into a two. Can you imagine? They want me to go, too. Only 35 percent of the people pay the market price. The rest are people like us. They are dying. My friend just recently died. My neighbor, he was in his late 80s, and he died. If I had a lot of money I wouldn't move because this is my paradise. I want to die here. I love this place. When I come into my apartment, I am home. I love New York City.

However, the 2015 sale of the property, which has been called "the single biggest deal to preserve affordable housing in the city's history," has also been called a "mixed bag" by tenant activists. First, less than half of the units will be kept affordable, and even those have a time limit. Second, many so-called affordable units will not actually be affordable to middle-income families. Third, tenants whose apartments have already been deregulated will not have their units reinstated as affordable. Finally, the city is giving Blackstone $225 million in benefits through uncollected taxes and a loan, and the city also gave the buyers permission to sell 700,000 square feet of "air rights," which could yield hundreds of millions of dollars, according to real estate industry news sources.

The story of Stuyvesant Town shows that the search for spatial justice or geographical aspects of justice[58] in particular urban settings may well involve very different participants than those traditionally depicted in the struggle for the right to the city. The right to the city movements that gain the most attention are those attempting to aid the urban poor—even in studies that also refer to the displacement of middle-class residents. However, in Stuyvesant Town, the groups seeking rights to inhabit the city do not fit the traditional profile of the dispossessed. Those clamoring to remain in Stuyvesant Town are long-term residents, middle-class families, college students, and young professionals. This tenant coalition is certainly privileged when compared to social movements at the global scale, but they remain engaged in important and efficacious social action that should not be dismissed. Importantly, the localized fight in Stuyvesant Town is consistent with Lefebvre's right to the city framework, which encompasses the protection of urban tenants' civil rights, promotes fewer restrictions on affordable housing (which thereby supports the rent-control or rent-stabilization movement), and argues that renters should be more empowered, as they are entitled to direct participation in decisions that affect their housing. As Edward Soja explained:

> The urban dweller, by the very fact of urban residence itself, has specifically spatial rights: to participate openly and fairly in all the processes producing urban space, to access and make use of the particular advantages of city life, especially in the highly valued center (or centers), to avoid all forms of imposed spatial segregation and confinement, to be provided with public services that meet basic needs in health, education, and welfare.[59]

The next chapter provides an overview of the newer people who have moved into Stuyvesant Town, replacing the long-term residents. It highlights the specific ways that this population transition has affected the community culture, and it introduces the newcomers' perspectives on the importance of creating a sense of place and community in Stuyvesant Town and New York City.

# 6

## The New Kids in (Stuy)Town

*Luxury or Liability?*

Between 2000 and 2010, the size and composition of Stuyvesant Town's population changed dramatically. The number of people living in the community increased by 1,948, as families with children, young singles living with roommates, and groups of college students replaced senior citizen households. This chapter describes Stuyvesant Town's newer tenants, outlining their subgroups and the ways in which they differ from each other and from longtime residents. In general, newer tenants reported that their expectations and priorities seem to differ from those of the long-term residents.

The newer tenants are younger, and some have created their own sense of place and community in Stuyvesant Town. Some newcomers reported that they appreciate the stability and traditional sense of community that longtime tenants bring to the neighborhood. However, others—especially college students—expressed indifference and even resentment toward longer-term neighbors. This is, in part, because many longtime and family tenants have made no secret of the fact that they would prefer that the students move elsewhere. Many newcomers also resent that Stuyvesant Town does not deliver on the luxury branding promise that is attached to its steep price tag. Still, overall, like their longtime resident counterparts, newcomers appreciate the convenience of living near work or college, the spacious apartments, and the access to open space—amenities available to all residents, regardless of the amount of rent that they pay.

The various categories of newer residents expressed their own unique lifestyle expectations, habits, and norms. Families with young children explained that they value the safety and security of Stuyvesant Town, treasuring the green space and playgrounds, and expressing relief that they can live in Manhattan in relatively large apartments. Many of the students who have moved in are relatively unsentimental and detached. They value Stuyvesant Town for two main reasons: it is located near several college campuses including NYU, Parsons (The New School for Design), and Baruch College (City University of New York), as well as other colleges, such as Marymount Manhattan College and Pace University, and they appreciate that they can easily keep costs down by finding roommates and taking advantage of the subdivided apartments that management has specifically marketed to them.

Single professionals are also less sentimental about Stuyvesant Town. Many would prefer to live in the charming, trendy, and interesting neighborhoods for which Manhattan is celebrated, but they know that they are early in their careers, money is tight, and working long hours in a hypercompetitive city leaves them with little time in their homes anyway. Many simply cannot afford to live in comparable apartments in Manhattan's more desirable neighborhoods. Apartment hunters quickly learn that "charming" is often a euphemism for an extremely small, rundown apartment that lacks amenities, such as elevators and air conditioning. Thus, they compromise their residential aspirations in order to live in the modest but comfortable and affordable dorm-like buildings on the far eastern edge of the island. They plan to spend minimal time there, but it makes a convenient home base. Some professionals and many families have embraced the community, getting to know the older neighbors, forming friendships, and helping older residents. However, many view Stuyvesant Town as a temporary housing arrangement, are less invested in the community and its history, and in some cases they are disdainful of longtime residents' concerns.

To some degree, the influx of families has revived Stuyvesant Town's historical image as a place for middle-class people to start families and raise children. The outdoor areas now bustle with neighborhood children who revel in the joy of running free in the safety of their home community. However, Stuyvesant Town has also adopted a new seasonal tradition, less celebrated by longtime residents and families. This is the new tradition of population churning that begins every fall when the atmosphere morphs into what universities call "move-in day," with college students and their parents lining the community's walking paths and streets, using the building's laundry carts to transport their belongings, and unloading U-Hauls filled with old futons, secondhand furniture, and bulk toilet paper from Costco. During spring and summer, the whole process repeats as new batches of students move in for a brief time. As such, mass comings and goings coincide with the start and end of academic terms, along with the ritual of parents picking up and dropping off their adult children en masse. Thus, the student tenants disrupt the traditional dynamics of the community not just by their mere presence, but through their repeated patterns of arriving and then leaving, placing the community in a state of flux for weeks at a time.

## Stuy Town U: Stuyvesant Town Becomes a Dorm

The number of young people aged eighteen to twenty-four living in Stuyvesant Town more than tripled from 2000 to 2010, rising from 3.7 percent to 14.5 percent.[1] Additionally, the number of apartments occupied by two or more roommates (i.e., non-family households with two or more residents) almost doubled, going from 878 in 2000 to 1,539 in 2010.[2] Though these groups comprise a relatively small percentage of Stuyvesant Town's total population, residents perceive that the negative effects of the student presence are significant.

While students are attracted to Stuyvesant Town mainly because of its proximity to many college campuses, it is also located near popular neighborhoods like the Flatiron, East Village, and Union Square; the latter is an especially popular place to meet people, shop, and catch multiple subway lines. Many of NYU's off-campus housing registry listings are located in Stuyvesant Town because the development's brokers advertise the units to students as "no-fee" rentals—meaning lease-signers do not have to pay the traditional broker's fee, which is commonly one month's rent or 15 percent of the annual rent. NYU even offers a campus shuttle bus that stops right in front of Stuyvesant Town, and which Jeremy, an NYU graduate student who lives in Stuyvesant Town with his girlfriend, calls the "Stuy Town-NYU Express." Joanna Asada, a twenty-three-year-old former resident and NYU student, explained the convenience and affordability that she enjoyed after leaving the NYU dorms for Stuyvesant Town during her junior and senior years:

> I chose to live there because I was a student at NYU, and a lot of students
> at NYU choose that because you can walk to class . . . During the winter,

when there is a lot of ice and stuff on the streets, there is a shuttle that takes students back and forth. So, that was a convenient option, and it was cheaper than most places around that area, and that was my relation to the area and why I chose to live there.

Residents' complaints about entitled college students are abundant on the Internet, with bloggers referring to the off-campus housing phenomenon as "Stuy Town U" or a "glorified NYU dorm." On the tenants association Facebook page, one resident is known for sharing photos and commentary that document students' misdeeds in public spaces. One photo posted in July 2013 showed seven students engaged in a drinking game, crowding an older tenant nearby. The seven "sorority girls," as they were called, had open containers, and one was blindfolded with her arms outstretched in search of a target for a kind of "pin the tail on the donkey" game. One tenant commented on the photo this way:

> See, I don't have a problem with college kids having fun—I know I did— and I still got a great education—but I was tucked away on a campus, not tripping over strollers and playgrounds. I just think it's funny that management has no regard for best practices of tenants and also floored that they want to do this when there are kids all around.

Summers in Stuyvesant Town mean that dozens of students in skimpy bikinis lounge in public spaces shared by older residents and small children, evoking anger from residents who resent their immodesty and lack of consideration for families. Conflict between sunbathers and other residents (which media sources have referred to as a battle between "bikini beauties" displaying "side-boob" and "soccer moms") received brief international media attention. However, the tenants we interviewed seemed less reactionary than the few who were quoted in media accounts, and they seemed more concerned about other kinds of quality of life issues. Katie Friedman, a twenty-three-year-old Hofstra graduate, moved to the development in August, and commented, "A body's a body, and they need to get over themselves."[3] Even Ruthie Goldblum, the original tenant described in detail in chapter 3, expressed ambivalence about the bikini controversy: "I don't really mind the people in the Oval, but I heard people complaining they don't like the bikinis, you know? What do I care? I mean, I don't really care."

However, general antipathy toward the influx of students is a frequent topic on the Stuy Town Reporter blog, which includes many nasty exchanges in the comments section between the blogger and an NYU student. In one example, the blogger states: "I think the problem is that universities bring a different culture into Stuy Town, a transient one, that considers this place just a temporary home, and in some cases, an animal house. And packing these kids into apartments is not right either, as the quality of life goes down for everyone." Of course, residents tend to generalize the behaviors of some students to all of them, so students have a bad reputation as a group because of the highly visible behavior of just a subset of them. Many students are defensive about the way they have been labeled. One NYU student responded to the blogger's previous thread this way:

> I understand, and I sympathize with your cause. Previous to moving to Stuy Town, I lived for 20 years in the same apartment, and so I clearly understand the concept of creating a community where you live, and respecting neighbors and property. I just feel that this blog and (much worse) the Lux Living blog [another blog critiquing Stuyvesant Town's living conditions] have been using students as a scapegoat to all the bad things that are happening in the property. Tishman Speyer is to be blamed, not us.

Here, the student urged residents to blame management rather than students for community problems.

Some college students reported that they, too, value the sense of community in Stuyvesant Town that the longtime residents enjoy. Cameron Dillion, a nineteen-year-old NYU student from the Midwest, expressed why he and many other students are drawn to Stuyvesant Town: "A lot of people from NYU actually live in Stuy Town just 'cause it's so convenient for school, and it's nice and homey and friendly and that kind of thing."

Though he had considered other neighborhoods and looked at apartments "in the low 100s on the East Side," an area known as Spanish Harlem, he decided on Stuyvesant Town because of the convenience to campus, stability, and safety, factors that mattered to his parents: "My parents felt a little bit more comfortable in this kind of neighborhood just 'cause it is so established, and there's so many families."

Cameron shares a converted one-bedroom with two roommates, a fellow NYU student and a recent graduate who aspires to be an actor. He takes classes in the summer and works two jobs, so he is hardly ever in his apartment. In fact, when he met his downstairs neighbor in the elevator one day, the neighbor was surprised to learn that Cameron lived just above his apartment and said, "I didn't know that anyone lived there 'cause I can never hear you guys." Cameron went on to describe how, despite the fact that he sees himself as a responsible tenant, he believes that many of his neighbors, and the longtime ones in particular, were unwelcoming to him when he arrived:

When I first moved in, the first time I went to do laundry in the laundry room, I was down there doing my laundry, and a woman was asking me like, "Oh, did you just move in?" And I was like, "Yeah, we just moved in like, a week ago." And she was asking me like, what I did, and I said I was a student at NYU, and she was asking if I was in like, the NYU housing here, which I think NYU has like, a building devoted to graduate students here, and I was like, "No. I'm actually here just on my own. Like, I just live in an apartment here. I just happened to go to NYU, as well." And she went on this really big tirade about how she hates how many students [live here], about how students live here so frequently, and she thinks that we're like, really disrespectful to all the like, families and older people that live here. And she thinks that we try to run the place and own the place, and we just moved in. And I was just really confused because I just moved in like, a week ago. I didn't know what to say. But yeah, it seems like a lot of the people who have lived here for a while have very clear opinions about people like us who move in, which is kind of frustrating because I guess people, students who used to live here must have set a really bad name for students who live here. A lot of my friends who live here, we haven't had any problems. We're never loud, and we've never had noise complaints or anything. But for some reason, even walking around, I sometimes feel like some of the older people like, give me a dirty look, and I'm kind of like, "I pay rent, too." I don't know what to tell you. It just happens to be that I'm a student, but I'm not trying to disrespect your community or your neighborhood or anything. It's just that I thought it was my space to live, too.

The commonly held view among longtime residents is that management fails to enforce regulations with new and younger tenants. However, Cameron believes he is unfairly scrutinized, albeit from residents rather than management. He also stated that he thinks it is discriminatory that residents approve of certain behaviors for children, but not for adult college students:

> Me and my friends were playing Frisbee in the Oval about a week ago, and a Stuy Town security guard told us to stop because apparently no one wants anyone to play Frisbee in Stuy Town. And I was like, "We're not hurting anyone. We're not like, far apart. Like, we're like barely tossing the Frisbee, you know?" Those kinds of things just keep adding up, and it's kind of frustrating to a point that it feels like I'm back in a dorm or a summer camp or something. It doesn't feel like I'm able to actually like, live in an apartment in New York. And next to us this huge group of like, probably eight-year-olds were playing baseball. And they were throwing the baseball and hitting it with the bat and everything. And we were playing this little game of Frisbee, and we were honestly probably standing like, twenty feet from each other. And we were told to stop when they were playing baseball with a heavy ball, which could do much more damage than a little Frisbee. But it's just because we were older, and I guess, much more troublesome.

Despite experiences like this, Cameron enjoys living in Stuyvesant Town, though he is not going to renew his lease because the rent is too high for him. He explained that, contrary to the popular image of student tenants being dependent on their parents, he pays his own rent. Next year, he plans to search for an apartment that is less costly, better accommodates his lifestyle, and provides the freedom that he associates with off-campus life:

> I'm actually moving out of Stuy Town in the fall. And I don't think I'm going to necessarily miss it that much. It felt a little expensive for me because I have to pay rent myself, so it's a little expensive, and my parents aren't able to help out right now. And I feel like sometimes, there's just like, a lot of little rules and stuff, which gets a little bit suffocating. It feels like I went from living in a dorm, which obviously has a lot of rules, to living in a different dorm when I was expecting to have a little bit more freedom.

## Not All Bad: The Young Helping the Old

Students' positive interactions with tenants and pro-social activities in the community fail to receive the same attention as the parties, shirtless fraternity guys, bikini-clad coeds, and Frisbee games on the Oval, and like Cameron, many students believe that they are unfairly viewed as blights on the community. Jeremy was one of the tenants who volunteered to go door to door to check on neighbors after Hurricane Sandy. One student reported that she regularly babysits for neighbors. Another, Joanna, was surprised and disheartened when she discovered the negative comments about college students online. She said that when she and her roommate moved in during their junior year at NYU, residents welcomed them with freshly baked brownies:

> I had such an easy [time] in my building that I didn't know that there were any problems around me. I was completely oblivious to the problems around me until I found the blog that said bad things about students in Stuy Town . . . When somebody showed me the blog, I was just very, very surprised. It was about older residents, newer residents, and all the students with their parties 'til all hours in the night and empty beer bottles on the staircases, and students puking on the staircases—all kinds of disgusting things that didn't happen in my building. There was so much drama and that behavior going on, but I think there was just one or two isolated cases, but they were so outrageous it became a big thing. It was just a trend, but none of the people I know that live there have the same complaints.

Even with their lower social status and seasonal tenures in the community, some college students report their own version of a sense of place in Stuyvesant Town. While different from that of retirees, some students report that they appreciate the fact that their apartments are in a "real" community, and a desirable one at that. For instance, Joanna asserted that she feels a personal sense of community in Stuyvesant Town that college campuses usually do not have. She likes living with a more authentic cross-section of the population, instead of in an environment exclusively for students. Though it may not sound like much, she also appreciates the simple things like exchanging greetings with neighbors, and the atmosphere of friendliness that she believes is hard to find in the average Manhattan neighborhood:

> Over the summer, if you are able to spend time at the Oval you will see what a nice, peaceful community it is. Picnics, kids, older people, everyone says, "Hi." You don't have to necessarily tell each other your life stories, but everyone comes up and says, "Hi" in the morning and evening, whatever, and I think it's good.

Even though some college students pride themselves on being good neighbors, Stuyvesant Town's students have a bad reputation. One longtime resident, Jerry Wasserman, a forty-eight-year-old who lives with his wife and daughter and who is active in the tenants association, admitted that residents' opinions of the students can been seen as a form of "age discrimination." He went on to point out that some tenants incorrectly lump together all of the young, childless residents into the one category of "students." Surely, the changes in Stuyvesant Town combined with the overall increase in young people fuel the perception that students are taking over the community. The next section introduces another growing demographic in Stuyvesant Town that tenants sometimes mistake for students: young professionals.

## Young Professionals: Stuyvesant Town Is Just a Place to Live

For many young professionals, acquiring an affordable residence in Manhattan near work and social activities is a higher priority than experiencing a sense of community. Karen, a thirty-seven-year-old stabilized tenant, explained, "It was just great to live in Manhattan. Did I feel welcome? Yeah, but I wasn't looking for, like, a community, really. I was just glad to be in the city."

Charlie Price, a twenty-seven-year-old single attorney, has lived in Stuyvesant Town with his roommate for a year, and feels unsentimental and detached from the community, viewing it not as a home, but simply as a temporary rental. His lack of community attachment is exacerbated by his strong belief that Stuyvesant Town is a place where a faceless landlord is exploiting him, so he insists that he owes nothing to the community in terms of personal investment:

It's just a building . . . I don't *own* my place, and I'm not gonna—especially here—I'm not gonna set up shop and say, like, this is my *home*, because it's a big corporation that's running this thing. They're only in it for the money, and they're gonna raise [the rent] . . . If the courts didn't stop 'em, they'd already be charging me more than I would be willing to pay.

Charlie also resents the longtime residents, or as he calls them, "lifers," reserving special ire for them because he believes it is unfair that they are rent-stabilized:

I don't really know if I'm politically in favor of all the rent control and sta-bilization, because—not that I'm all in favor of a free market and survival of the fittest—but why do some people get to have those apartments for a lot less when, you know, everyone would like to live in a really nice place in that neighborhood?

Charlie's comment highlights the common perception that those who have an affordable, rent-stabilized apartment in New York are unfairly privileged. Many market-rate tenants reported their desire to stay in Stuyvesant Town, but also feared that the threat of the landlord increas-ing rents would prevent this. Some have eventually been forced to move out because of large rent increases. Market-rate tenants think that the stabilized tenants, though faced with their own sets of problems and concerns, are not burdened with the same degree of uncertainty. Charlie believes that the tenants association focuses too much on stabilized resi-dents' rights, neglecting market-rate tenants' concerns. Charlie's disdain for activist residents who are "really into" Stuyvesant Town and want other residents to get involved was apparent in his reaction to this en-counter with an older neighbor:

There was this one secretary in my office who also lives in Stuy Town, and she's like a lifer there. She's probably got like fifteen or twenty years living there, and she was *really* into it. Every time I saw her in the hall or we shared an elevator, it'd be something like, "Oh, are you going to the rally?" And [I was] like, "What fucking rally? What the hell are you talk-ing about? No, I'm not going to the rally! Who cares?" Of course, I didn't say that, but that was my feeling. Like, she was all like into this whole,

"Oh, Stuy Town is a *community*, and we have to protect our *rights* as low or stabilized-income tenants or whatever," and I could not care less at all.

NYU undergraduate student Joanna, who had a highly positive view of the community, said that she knew about Stuyvesant Town's tenants association, but did not feel welcome to participate. Joanna admitted that the neighbors had given her fliers inviting her, but said, "There is a difference between being invited and being welcomed." She believes that the Stuy Town Reporter blogger, who is highly critical of students, is a prominent member of the tenants association, and therefore, she was uncomfortable attending meetings.

In the early years of the transition to market-rate occupancy, the tenants association struggled with balancing the rights of longtime rent-controlled and rent-stabilized tenants with those of the market-rate newcomers. The fact that many longtime tenants perceive the newer tenants to be a threat, and many newer tenants see rent-regulated tenants as an economic burden on the community, has made it harder for the tenants association to organize and reach its goals. Even though the association strives to highlight tenants' similarities and common interests, and leaders and members recognize that the tenants' power lies in their capacity to unify, their efforts often fall short in making newcomers feel welcome and getting them involved. It is true that many longtime tenants believe newcomers have a sense of entitlement that accompanies their market-rate status. It does not help when they read comments like this one, which a newer tenant posted to the Stuy Town Reporter blog: "Perhaps, it is time for the older residents to move on. I hear Bayside is quite lovely. I am a market-rater, and I pay more, so I don't want to hear your complaints."

## Young Families: Making a Child-Friendly Home in the City

Families with children are a growing demographic in Stuyvesant Town and Peter Cooper Village. Between 2000 and 2010, the percentage of households in Stuyvesant Town with children under the age of eighteen residing with them increased from 31 percent to 38 percent.[4] With the majority of the eighty-acre development closed to car traffic except for the security and maintenance vehicles, Stuyvesant Town is one of the few Manhattan neighborhoods where parents can feel safe allowing their children to freely roller-skate, ride scooters, and bicycle.

Erin, a stay-at-home mother in her thirties, and her husband Brad, who works in finance, are market-raters. Erin highlighted the community feeling on the playground, "I have my whole mommy network of friends, where I can go out to the playground and see, on a good day, like ten people I know." They moved to Stuyvesant Town seven years ago before they had children and considered it to be a compromise between what they wanted and what they could afford, as she explained:

> Brad, my husband, had lived in the Union Square area already, and we knew we liked downtown, and we knew we couldn't afford the West Village [laughs]. We were delusional and actually thought we were going to be able to buy an apartment. We looked around and realized that we could buy a shoebox and not an apartment, so we gave that up. Brad used to come through here on his way to go jogging on the East River Park, and I used to drive into the city and hang out with my friends in the East Village and thought this was the projects [laughs]. So then he's like, "No. It's nice in there," and we came in here, and it was really nice. They were no-fee rentals, which was a big draw, and the apartment was nice, and that's sort of how we did it. It was sort of like, after we gave up on the delusion of owning an apartment, this was almost like settling, but not really. Like, we were happy to be here, but it was more east than we wanted to be.

Many residents, like Erin, chose Stuyvesant Town recognizing that it lacks the convenience and charm of the more central neighborhoods, such as the West Village, but it offers lower rent and a different type of community. As Erin said, "I think you get a lot of families who want to live here because of how pseudo-suburban it is."

Single mothers, some of whom are market-rate and some of whom are rent-stabilized, make up another group of newcomers, comprising nearly 8 percent of all family households in 2010 (up from 6 percent in 2000). Single parents, all of whom were mothers within our sample, reported that they value Stuyvesant Town's short commute times to work and schools, the quality of the neighborhood public school, and the proximity to Manhattan's child-centered social amenities. With so much responsibility on their shoulders, single mothers especially benefit from

Stuyvesant Town's sense of community, social support, and childcare social networks. Judy Hamm, a thirty-four-year-old lawyer and single mother, put it this way:

> I have a friend that lives in the building, and so I moved in because she lived in the same building. Her daughter is fourteen months older than [my son] Mark. So, they know each other, and they're friends. When you're raising a child—I don't have any family in the city—it's good. In an emergency, you know somebody else in the building.

Later, she described her attachment to the community and the 14th Street Y, a community center that is popular with Stuyvesant Town families:

> Mark knows the parents of all of his friends 'cause he sees them, or he knows their sitters. He feels very comfortable talking to them, and they know him, and people at the Y know him. They've known him since he was three months old 'cause they have early childhood stuff, and they have a preschool, and I've just kept him in the same spot because I'd rather he was known, and I'd rather there are people there who are invested in him. I think that's sort of intangible. That feeling of being a part of a community is lost in a lot of parts in the city, and I'm really happy that we have it here.

At the time of our interview, Judy said that she wanted to stay in Stuyvesant Town, but feared that the climate of sudden rent increases and the uncertainty about the property's ownership would result in her moving elsewhere:

> It seems like there are a lot of people who are middle-class who are really happy to have this space and the quiet and things . . . I think everybody in these buildings is feeling a little worried about what's going to happen with the management. It changed hands apparently again . . . I think the reputation right now is that it is very unstable and with an unstable management you don't know what's gonna happen. And because there has been so much change in Stuyvesant Town in the past five or ten years it's not clear whether the positive changes—the upkeep of the Oval, the nonstop landscaping—whether that is going to continue.

Parents feel very reluctant to move from Stuyvesant Town after they have settled on a quality school and have figured out the logistics of transportation and juggling work and family. Manhattan's public schools are notoriously uneven in quality, and private schools are exorbitantly expensive and exclusive. For families with school-aged children who cannot afford the $40,000 private school tuition, a neighborhood's zoned school is often *the* deciding factor in choosing a home. Jennifer Johnson, a rent-stabilized single mother in her late forties, put it this way:

> Where I grew up in the suburbs of Massachusetts, the school process was just so different. I know that my parents didn't have to be concerned. We just went to school in our neighborhood in our town, and that was it. It's very different living in New York City. From $40,000 [for private school] to nothing [for public school]. If you want [to pay] nothing, then your zone is very important.

Stuyvesant Town parents also explained that their children serve as a generational connection to the older neighbors. Brad, the husband of Erin (mentioned above), values his close relationships with the older neighbors and delights in the cheer his children seem to bring to them. Here, he described his fondness for an older neighbor whom his family sees on a regular basis:

> She's great. Really nice, very friendly. She's kinda experienced our kids growing up and everything, which I think it's kinda cool for her a little bit. 'Cause literally, we moved in here, and there were no kids, and now, we've got one that's almost five [years old] and the other's two and a half [years old] and another one on the way. So she's sort of seen our whole family throughout, which I think created a little bit of a bond with her. If we were just a married couple or whatever, we would be a little less sociable. She's a great neighbor, and we have another neighbor on the floor who's very friendly. She has a cat and the kids love the cat, so she let the cat out into the hallway . . . She's really friendly. Having kids always enhances communication with the neighbors because everyone always pays attention to the kids, and the kids pay attention to them, and so you get to know each other a little bit better.

However, relations between families with children and the older tenants are not always so harmonious. Elisa Garza is a thirty-six-year-old mother of a seven-year-old daughter who has lived in Stuyvesant Town for six years. She described an encounter with her downstairs neighbor, whom she characterized as a curmudgeon: "The lady downstairs has been awful. She called security at 3:00 on Friday afternoon. They came and said the kids can't run around. I was like, 'They're kids. What are they supposed to do?'" In order to try and help ease the tension with her neighbor, Elisa gave her their phone number to call in case they were being too loud, hoping to informally resolve any problems. The neighbor later reported to a mutual friend, "Can you believe she had the nerve to give me her number? I don't call my neighbors. I call security." Many residents would prefer to personally handle neighbor disputes, but high population turnover can prevent neighbors from forming the necessary social bonds for collective efficacy (i.e., mutual trust combined with a willingness to intervene to maintain order). Also, management discourages informal confrontations, so some residents have begun to comply with the policy to call security about even the most minor border skirmishes.

Still, Stuyvesant Town remains a magnet for families. Some tenants who have moved in within the past ten years or so are not newcomers at all, but rather they grew up in Stuyvesant Town, then left for a time, and finally "boomeranged" back years later. These returnees are a testament to Stuyvesant Town's draw as a community. Carrie Evans, a forty-two-year-old tenant, grew up in Stuyvesant Town and returned to the community with her husband in 2005. Now, a single mother with two children, Carrie lives in the same apartment that she shared with her siblings, and her mother lives in Stuyvesant Town, as well. Carrie's two children spend time with their grandmother after school when Carrie is still at work:

> The neighborhood is great for the most part. I mean, it's like a small town in a big city. It has a real community feel. I always liked the way it's set off from the rest of the surroundings—the fact that the streets don't go straight through, and there is a lot of, sort of enclosed, safe space inside. A lot of times you tend to forget that you're in the middle of the city because there are a lot of trees, and they really take care of the landscaping. I mean, it's just nice. It feels removed from the city at large, and I always

enjoyed that as a kid, and I really enjoy it as an adult, too. I also had such a great experience growing up here as a kid. It always felt like such a safe place. Stuyvesant Town had its own security, and [is] set off from the streets. I was allowed to go out and play by myself or with my siblings at a really young age. I wanted my kids to experience that kind of freedom. It's not a typical thing for city kids to have the ability to run free like they can here, because it is enclosed and you know you don't have to worry about your kid venturing into the street. You know, I always knew when I was younger, when I was outside playing that if something happened to me there'd be any number of parents around the playground who would recognize me, and they would know which building to head to, to find my mother or whatever. I wanted my kids to experience some of that. . . . I always knew that I wanted to come back here when I had kids.

## Nobody's Fool: Newcomers' Criticisms of the Luxury Brand

Like the old-timers, newcomers appreciate some of the upgrades and amenities Stuyvesant Town's management has implemented, but they are not fooled by the luxury label. They can see that Stuyvesant Town does not meet the Manhattan standard of upscale housing. A common complaint from newer residents is that the development lacks door-men. Doormen are the most widely recognized symbol of luxury, as they personally screen any visitors, accept packages and deliveries, and conveniently and promptly provide spare keys to residents who have mistakenly forgotten theirs, all at no charge. In Stuyvesant Town, management charges a "lock-out fee" of $75 (recently raised from $50) to tenants who forget their keys. Charlie put it this way:

> I'm not familiar with luxury buildings, but here are some thoughts. There is no doorman. The amenities you have to pay extra for . . . Really, the nicest part about the whole thing is the outdoor facilities—the basketball courts, the hockey rink. I don't even have to live there to use that, so I wouldn't consider it luxury. No.

As Charlie noted, the outdoor spaces are open to outsiders and management has added signs warning that they are for tenants and guests only, but staff rarely enforce it. Stuyvesant Town also offers a concierge service for an extra fee. Alternatively, residents can have packages delivered during the day to a central location, but the tenant has to pick them up or pay a fee to have staff deliver them later. Even though this is an amenity that some residents use, it is not the same level of service one would receive in upscale apartment buildings. Carlo Mancini, a thirty-eight-year-old married father of two, had this to say:

> The model apartments are in this building that we're in, so I'm constantly seeing the type of people who are looking to rent here. And I've heard it once, I've heard it a dozen times: "So, wait a minute, there's no doorman?" Ha ha ha! You know people expect that. You know they see the way this place is marketed, and that's what they expect, and that's what they're expecting for that rent. It's funny. I mean, no, there isn't [a doorman]. They *try* to do a concierge as another amenity, but it's not the same as a doorman. That's what they think they're paying for.

As discussed in chapter 5, this observation points to a view shared by many New Yorkers that the markers of luxury rentals are largely absent in Stuyvesant Town.

An additional important indicator of an upscale building is a clean, modern, inviting, and attractive common area and lobby with sitting areas, flower arrangements, and art, where tenants can comfortably receive guests. Amy Duran, a forty-four-year-old single tenant, complained about the embarrassing condition of her building's hallway, which has a musty cigarette odor, a worn, stained gray carpet, and scuffed walls:

> I think it's so obvious that it's not luxury, and if you're stupid enough to come here because they say it is . . . You look around, and you would see it right away that this is not. Look at the hallway. It's disgusting! When you walk in this building, it's not pretty. But if you go into another building [not in Stuyvesant Town]? Like, I have friends that have a couch and chairs and a table and flowers and the whole thing. That's luxury.

A luxury building located close to Stuyvesant Town is similar to the one in which Amy's friends live. A concierge service picks up the tenants' laundry and dry cleaning in the morning and delivers it in the evening after work. Refrigerated storage is available, so tenants can have their groceries delivered when they are not home. Tall, elaborate bouquets of fresh flowers line the reception desk every day. Two large sitting areas feature elegant couches, upholstered chairs, and shiny coffee tables, and pieces of tasteful modern art flank the gleaming reception desk. A large common area on the fifth floor offers views of the Empire State Building through floor to ceiling windows and from a patio that is the size of an average Stuyvesant Town bedroom. Every morning, tenants enjoy complimentary coffee, bagels, and pastries. The landscaped roof offers a panoramic view of Manhattan, complete with chaise lounges where tenants sunbathe and picnic. Clearly, with friends living in buildings like this, Stuyvesant Town's younger tenants resent the high rent and luxury label being applied to their decaying domicile.

## Great Dividers

As discussed in earlier chapters, management has been capitalizing on the relatively large square footage of the individual apartments by subdividing one-bedroom apartments into two-bedrooms using temporary pressurized walls, which creates a small, windowless common area in the converted apartments. The layout of the approved subdivision is much more attractive to younger people sharing apartments with unrelated adults than it is to families, most of whom would prefer to keep a larger, windowed common space and then add a smaller, child-sized room. The topic of temporary walls is important to this chapter as it has caused conflict between two subgroups of newcomers: young adults with roommates and families with children.

In recent years, management has created floor plans that encourage unrelated roommates to share apartments and has proceeded to subdivide more and more units. In some cases, a two-bedroom apartment has been subdivided into a four-bedroom or even a five-bedroom apartment. One tenant reported that eight unrelated adults were cohabiting on her floor, generating noise, trash, and traffic that angered nearby neighbors. Elisa described her student neighbors' disorderly behaviors:

> Stuy Town makes these arrangements where they divide living rooms and bedrooms and put a lot of the kids in each apartment . . . You see the jani-

Figure 6.1 A two-bedroom apartment converted into a five-bedroom apartment with windowless common space, as advertised on Craigslist in April 2013.

tor going floor to floor every morning picking up the garbage that the kids [college students] leave outside, like bottles of beer and boxes of pizza. I mean, we recycle. We don't leave it outside. This is not a hotel or a dorm.

## Dog Days of Stuyvesant Town

A final group of newcomers to Stuyvesant Town is of the non-human variety. In 2008, management lifted a sixty-year-long ban on dogs, in an effort to market the complex to dog owners, who are often willing (or forced) to pay higher rents and fees. With the influx of dogs came an ever-changing litany of rules limiting the weight, size, and breeds, delineating the places where dogs can and cannot go, and requiring a special registration and licensing system, including special tags for all dogs. Pit bulls and pit bull mixes have been prohibited, but residents report that they can be found on the grounds wearing official Stuyvesant Town registration tags.

Many newcomers were excited to register their animals (a rule that public safety officers enforce as people walk their dogs around the Oval, and a practice that some owners view as harassment), especially "secret" dog owners who previously went to great lengths to hide their pets from management and neighbors. Longtime residents tend to perceive the presence of dogs (and the remains of their defecation throughout the property) as emblematic of management excessively loosening standards to attract and accommodate the tastes of younger newcomers in order to increase cash flow. Many resent that the pets put more pressure on services and infrastructure, and inevitably create more noise and disorder in close quarters. Ellen Carol, a sixty-two-year-old longtime tenant, is typical in her complaint:

> I hear the dogs at 1:00 in the morning, and that's not a happy thing. When we didn't have air conditioning in Stuyvesant Town, our windows were wide open, so we'd get some air, and I would hear babies crying, but I didn't have to pick them up so I didn't mind that. But when dogs are barking at one in the morning . . . I wanna go to sleep, and they are keeping me from going to sleep, and that's not a happy thing. I know a lot of the original people, or ten-year people—people who have been here for ten years or so—who are not happy about the dog situation, but I guess, they are trying very hard to get people to come here. They are offering $500 to the person trying to get the apartment [and] $500 to the person who recommends the person to the apartment.

Residents like Carrie, a single mother of two and market-rate resident who grew up in Stuyvesant Town, views the poor community values of the dog owners as the real problem contributing to decline:

> I don't love the fact that they have a lot of dogs in here now because I think a lot of the dog owners, again, are not very respectful of the fact that other people have to use the sidewalks. I do think that's a problem . . . I don't really know how they handled it, but I think that they needed to establish guidelines a little more firmly before they started letting hundreds of people wander around with their dogs. Probably about half of those people don't clean up after them, and it seems really a shame that you have to watch your children run down the street so they don't step in anything.

Some tenants are dismissive of residents' complaints about dogs and their owners, asserting that those who disapprove are unreasonable, "out of control," and "on the attack," and that complainers are the type of residents who stubbornly resist any form of change. Roger Simmons, a sixty-four-year-old longtime resident, explained:

There are a lot of dogs here now. People are complaining they used to walk with their heads up, but now they have to walk with their heads down so they don't step in the dog poop. Some people don't like any change. I find most of the dog owners are considerate; they walk around and pick up the droppings. We've had dogs here for two or three years, but every year people complain about the dogs and their owners.

The various groups now sharing Stuyvesant Town are united by their attachment, to varying degrees, to Manhattan and its institutions, schools, hospitals, cultural amenities, and by their broader sense of community. Many are striving to stay in the city near their support networks, such as family and friends. Others are aspiring to establish themselves in the city. For some, leaving the city or even moving to outer boroughs would mean long commutes to work and less time with their families. They share the common goal of maintaining a good and affordable quality of life in a city where this is becoming less attainable for the middle class.

This chapter shows that the form and pace of the transitions in Stuyvesant Town have been challenging and divisive at times. Quality of life means different things to different people, and these definitions have increasingly been coming into conflict. Even so, some newcomers, such as families with children, have effectively joined the community, and some of the more transient members have actually come to appreciate Stuyvesant Town's stability and sense of place. Many others are detached and some are even resentful. They believe that they are overpaying for housing that has not met their expectations, and they feel duped by their landlord. Exacerbating the problem is the lack of unity they feel with stabilized residents, whom they believe to be judgmental and prejudiced against younger people and their lifestyles. Aside from investors, landlords, and management, many Stuyvesant Town residents believe the greatest threat to their way of life is the college students. The next chapter presents a vignette about a college student resident named Kara, highlighting her perspective on the desirability of Stuyvesant Town for younger people and the downside of living in a place designed for older, more permanent residents.

7

# The Kids Are All Right?

*Kara's Story*

This chapter tells the story of Kara, a twenty-one-year-old NYU student starting her second year as a Stuyvesant Town resident. Told from her perspective, Kara provides insights into the way young people view Stuyvesant Town, but also highlights how student lifestyles differ from more long-term residents, lead to neighbor conflict, and contribute to perceptions that the community is experiencing a decline in quality of life. The growing population of college students has a brief and fleeting connection to Stuyvesant Town as a community. As temporary residents with their own college-based social networks and dorm-living mentalities, these newcomers attract antagonism from longtime residents and other more stable newcomer subgroups. Students have become a major presence in Stuyvesant Town and surrounding neighborhoods, and many New Yorkers demonize them for their debauchery and their negative effects on the community and the city as a whole. This chapter gives a voice to this group of tenants. It concludes by highlighting the consequences that Stuyvesant Town's new student population has for community conflict and quality of life.

\* \* \*

On the day she told this story, Kara Lenart, a tall, outgoing young woman, appeared in pink running shorts and neon orange sneakers. Kara was preparing to embark on her senior year as a musical theater major, and she let us know that she "loves it" in Stuyvesant Town. For the past year, she has shared her 755-square-foot apartment with her best friend and fellow student, Julia. Originally a one-bedroom apartment, they converted it into a two-bedroom with a legal, temporary pressurized wall, making it a "flex" two-bedroom. This wall divides the living

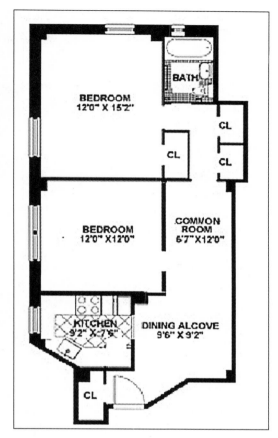

Figure 7.1 Floor plan of a typical Stuyvesant Town one-bedroom apartment converted into a two-bedroom apartment with a pressurized wall, as advertised on Craigslist in April 2012.

room into two rooms: a smaller room for Julia and a tiny, windowless common area. Kara had the privilege of sleeping in the master bedroom.

Their newly renovated market-rate apartment rented for $3,200 a month, which Kara and Julia had split evenly. Some may find it surprising to learn that college students live in a Manhattan apartment outfitted with stainless steel appliances, new lighting fixtures, hardwood floors, and spacious closets like those advertised by custom-closet design companies, such as California Closets. The apartment is also desirable in that it is located in a prime section of Stuyvesant Town, close to First Avenue, a relatively lively street with lots of shopping and dining choices. It is also near the "L" subway stop at 14th Street, a feature that Kara especially prizes. She rides the L every single day, as it stops at NYU and her favorite grocery store, Trader Joe's.

## Why Stuyvesant Town? And How?

Though younger families are slowly outnumbering the older and long-time residents with high school and college-aged children, Stuyvesant Town's walking paths are now populated with throngs of young people wearing collegiate logos and backpacks as they head to class. The location near major universities is an obvious draw, as is the fact that Stuyvesant Town's organization, private security staff, on-site maintenance workers, infrastructure, and institutional architecture bear a striking resemblance to dorms, offering a seemingly easy transition from actual dormitory life to apartment living.

By any account, Kara has led a privileged life as a New York City college student. During her freshman year she lived in a dorm located on Washington Square Park with a view of the Empire State Building. As a sophomore, she lived in a brand new dorm in the posh Gramercy neighborhood. Among the many reasons that students live in dorms is that doing so provides an easy way to make friends and build community on campus. Kara explained that she had originally met Julia in the dorms. In addition, the dorms are ideal because most students have limited experience taking care of themselves and acting as independent responsible citizens of a larger residential community. Kara liked the standard dorm facilities such as laundry, theater practice space, and workout equipment. Not surprisingly, her parents valued the security of NYU's official dorms and their predictable and contained costs compared to the expensive and fluctuating costs of apartments. However, Kara did not want to "dorm" for a third year. Though she said that dorming was an overall positive experience, she was frustrated with the lifestyle restrictions imposed on students. Kara disliked the high level of security, the limitations on visitors, and the strict rules that she found to be excessive. Even though she is young, she wanted more freedom and wanted to have the familiar, homey comforts that independent adults have in their apartments and houses:

> Signing people in and out of the dorms . . . They're so strict about it! Like, if my sister was coming in [to the city] for something, which she likes to do. She likes to come and visit since she lives in Philadelphia. She would take the train a lot, and you have, to like, get a guest pass, like, three days in advance. I have heard stories where they won't let people in that are relatives of someone. One of my friends' sisters surprised her, and they wouldn't let her in the dorm. They wouldn't let her stay in the dorms. It's just crazy to me. They're really strict about a lot of things, like having a toaster in your dorm or just noise.

For students, Stuyvesant Town mainly represents the freedom to have visitors stay over and to live more like an adult. On the day of this interview, Kara apologized and said that her apartment would not be an appropriate meeting spot. She explained that she had several people visiting for the weekend, and it was "crazy" at her place. To some extent, this situation validates other tenants' complaints that students often have frequent visitors, they are loud, and they are frequently disruptive to the other tenants. Indeed, college students who look forward to escaping the dorm and university rules so that they may enjoy a more relaxed lifestyle are often surprised to learn that Stuyvesant Town has a long list of restrictions, and the neighbors are more than willing to help enforce them.

Kara knew students who lived in apartments off-campus and wanted to see what else was out there. She went to the Stuyvesant Town leasing office, took their tour of the property, and then met with one of the leasing agents. Like many student residents, Kara then compared the Stuyvesant Town cost of living to dorm life, and decided to sign a lease:

> It was just so perfect. I was telling my mom about the prices, and she did all the math because she was very skeptical . . . It ended up being cheaper than what we paid for dorming, so that was a big thing. And also, it's nicer, and we had a lot of stuff, so we didn't really need to pay to furnish the place. We just kind of got a truck and moved a lot of stuff that we had from home. Yeah, it just worked out really nicely.

Unlike the older tenants, Kara's parents were paying, so they were the ones who needed to make the ultimate decision that the housing costs would be lower than the dorms and within their means. Kara tried to convince them that Stuyvesant Town was the perfect destination for a college student seeking the comforts of home, complete with convenience to campus, and amenities like elevators, air conditioning, and a newly renovated apartment.

Her family ultimately acquiesced to their daughter's preference to live outside of the dorms. After all, NYU was the nation's most expensive college in 2013. Kara, like many college students, but especially those who choose to attend pricey New York City colleges, relies on her parents to fund not only her education, but also her housing and lifestyle preferences. For instance, in Stuyvesant Town, as in most Manhattan apartment buildings, management requires tenants who fail to meet the minimum income requirement to obtain a guarantor or co-signer who takes full responsibility for the lease terms. The guarantor is often required to earn double the salary required of the lessee. Manhattan landlords tend to require that tenants have a minimum combined salary that is equal to forty times the monthly rent. A guarantor would have to have a salary twice that or eighty times the monthly rent. For example, an apartment that rents for $3,200 per month would require a combined salary of $128,000 for the tenants or $256,000 for a guarantor.

The minimum guarantor income required in Stuyvesant Town is lower than the standard criteria for the average Manhattan apartment, another feature that draws in students and their parents. Stuyvesant Town only requires that lessees make thirty times the monthly rent (as opposed to forty), and it only requires that guarantors earn fifty times the monthly rent (as opposed to eighty). In Kara's case, for a $3,200 apartment, the guarantor would only have to earn $160,000, not $256,000, clearly making Stuyvesant Town a more attractive and feasible option for students and their families.

As longtime tenants have asserted, Stuyvesant Town's management is notorious for pressuring tenants to sign a lease, and students are especially vulnerable. Kara reported that her leasing agent warned her that if she did not sign right away, someone else would surely snap up such a well-located apartment. Though the reported Stuyvesant Town vacancy rate is quite low, the large number of units and high turnover mean that some apartments are usually available to rent, even if they are not in an ideal location.

In Kara's case, the leasing representative was effective in pressuring her to move quickly on the apartment:

> The woman that was helping us out called me and said—like after we did the tour—she called me and said, "There's a place on 16th Street and First Avenue, and it's right by the L, and it's this much." The price was right, and she was like, "It's going to sell really quickly." You know, that kind of thing. So I was just kind of like, "Okay, we want it."

Kara did not visit any other apartments before deciding on Stuyvesant Town. She intended to, but once she saw Stuyvesant Town, reviewed the costs with her mother, and received the leasing agent's high-pressure call about the available apartment in the prime location, she ended her search. For Kara, living for two years in NYU dorms and visiting the off-campus apartments of fellow students taught her all that she needed to know about other student housing options. She said that Stuyvesant Town compares favorably in terms of size and amenities: "I've seen a lot of my friends' places, and I haven't seen a place nicer than mine. It's just spacious." Clearly, one aspect of New York residential life that Kara does share with longtime Stuyvesant Town residents is that she signed a lease for her new home, sight unseen.

## Spreading the Word

The increase in Stuyvesant Town's student population is not the result of a natural spillover effect, nor is it a surprise to the landlord and staff. Stuyvesant Town's management has been aggressively and directly marketing apartments to students in ways that some residents believe misrepresents both the property and the existing residents. Advertisements that target college students can be found on subways, buses, and the Internet, with youthful language exclaiming how "awesome" it is to live there. One student we interviewed said that he had learned about Stuyvesant Town from a flier that someone had slipped under his dorm room door. Management also recruits students and recent graduates by sponsoring events that appeal to young people, such as a summer concert series.

The most formal recruitment strategy is the deal between NYU and Stuyvesant Town to provide dorms to graduate students. According to some residents, the leasing office even offers a roommate-matching service to students who want to live there but who cannot find friends who are interested and also able to afford the rent. The word has spread fast that Stuyvesant Town is a college student destination. Kara found out about Stuyvesant Town the same way that many of the longtime residents did: through their peers' word of mouth.

Current residents are bombarded with advertisements for referral bonuses. Rent statements are thick with glossy inserts offering cash rewards for referrals. Residents who have signed up to receive email announcements of upcoming community events automatically receive referral bonus offers in their inboxes. A recent promotion offered residents $500 for the first referral, $1,000 for the second, and $2,500 for the third. In fact, Kara now has three other friends who live in Stuyvesant Town, all based on her referrals:

> I have friends that were kind of skeptical about it when they were looking for apartments, but they were having nightmares with looking at apartments. They were so small, and they were just more expensive and walk-ups with no elevator. They were having such a horrible time looking, and then they came and looked at my apartment, and they were like, "Oh, this is so nice," and so, they ended up getting a place across the street. And then I had like, three other friends that came and looked at my apartment, and then decided to go with Stuy Town. So they're all in Stuy Town, as well.

According to Kara, Stuyvesant Town's suburban features and outdoor amenities do not exist on NYU's campus. She provided the example of her apartment's proximity to the nearby East River bike path, where she often goes running: "Another thing that I love about Stuy Town is being so close to the river. I love running and being close to the river and just walking outside and being able to go for a run right there. I love it. Like, I love that. That's one of my favorite things." Kara also mentioned that she likes the free concerts on the lawn, as well as other organized events.

However, she admitted that she rarely plans far enough ahead to attend these, but has stopped by on occasion when she has stumbled upon an event in progress:

> I love the Oval. Last summer, that was one of my favorite things. I loved just coming back from a run, and everyone is just in the grass, and sometimes, there are free concerts, and that's just so nice. Last year, they did that silent dance party or something. It was so funny. You, like, put on headphones, and there was a DJ, and everyone was just dancing under this tent, but to music that was in the headphones. So, if you were just walking by, all these people were just dancing to no music, which was really funny.

Kara recently renewed her Stuyvesant Town lease for a second year, but Julia moved out the day before our interview. Kara was emphatic that the typical college roommate problems were not to blame for Julia's departure; rather, it was the $150-per-person rent hike. She characterized the increased rent as only a "tiny bit," but Julia clearly disagreed. Even with her roommate leaving and the rent increase, Kara decided to stay because she believes the New York City moving costs would offset any savings that might result from a less expensive apartment. Student demand for Stuyvesant Town had been high enough for her to know that she could find another college-aged roommate quickly.

All off-campus housing options are attractive to students who seek the freedom to live a more carefree, unmonitored lifestyle. However, many of New York City's affordable apartments lack the amenities to which today's students have grown accustomed, such as elevators and air conditioning. Kara shared what she knew about Julia's post–Stuyvesant Town apartment hunt. Julia had a wish list that included "exposed brick and the real New York City." Authenticity is becoming a highly prized feature of urban life, as described by urban sociologist Sharon Zukin.[1] However, this is how Kara unfavorably described Julia's new place:

> She moved to a place on 13th Street and First Avenue. She just moved yesterday. We had dinner last night, and she was, like, crying to me because she was like, "They said it has air conditioning. It doesn't have air conditioning." And like, "It's not that much cheaper, and I thought it was

going to be okay, but now, like, I'm living with someone I don't know." So she's definitely regretting it. I kind of had a feeling she was going to realize this. I wish she realized it earlier because we were so great as roommates. It's really sad. But I hope everything works out. But she'll probably still be over all the time. She was already over yesterday. She walked into the apartment and was like, "It's so cold in here. It's so nice."

Julia's story illustrates how difficult it is for New Yorkers to find an apartment that meets their desired housing needs, is affordable, has an authentic look or charming style, and is as the landlord has promised. She also learned that sometimes, the real New York City includes unscrupulous landlords and bait-and-switch apartment deals.

## Easing into Adulthood: Stuyvesant Town as a Manageable, Familiar Transition

Though Kara is satisfied with Stuyvesant Town, she said that some of her peers refuse to live there. For some, it is far too expensive, but for others, the isolation and institutional design of the community conflict with their desire to experience an "authentic" New York:

For some reason, there's kind of this like, negative feeling on Stuy Town. Like, with some people, they think it's not, like, real New York. It's not a real New York apartment. I guess, I'm just thinking of people like my friend that is moving out. She signed a two-year lease, but she's moving out after one year, because she just doesn't like the feel of it. She just has this very specific view of New York and what it is to live in a New York City apartment, and this feels too much like a dorm to her, and too much like, I don't know, just like a college campus, I guess. I mean, it is weird. On my floor there are people that go to NYU in my grade [third year], but that's kind of what I like about it. I like that it has a sense of community. I can understand, but I just don't feel the same way. Because a lot of [my friends] come into my apartment, and they're like, "Oh my gosh! Like, I love it." And then they're looking for a place. Well, then [when I ask], "Why don't you want to live in Stuy Town?" That's, like, the reason that they give. They would even prefer to live in Brooklyn to have the New

York City life. I don't know. I think I'm living the New York City life, but maybe not. I don't know.

When Kara first moved to New York City, she had difficulty leaving her family and friends, knew very few people, and felt overwhelmed by the city. She described the difficulties she faced during her freshman year as she tried to fit in with the people in her performing arts major:

> I feel like probably every single person in my major was the star of their high school, and then you go to NYU, and everyone's so talented. Every. Single. Person. It's like, small fish/big pond, and we're all kind of not used to that, and it's nice being surrounded by people that are really talented and really motivated just like you are, and I love that. I love that about NYU, but at first, it was kind of overwhelming and a little bit scary, and you know, being away from your family and away from your friends. 'Cause I have a really great family and great friends at home. So, I think I was a little homesick, but I wouldn't really let myself admit it because I was so excited and so eager to start my new life.

Kara believes she is a good neighbor and that getting settled in Stuyvesant Town helped her to recover from her homesickness: "Now that I look back, I can definitely see that I'm so much happier now. I love it here. I don't want to move."

Those who dislike the large presence of students often complain that they seem unattached to the community. Kara confirmed that she does not plan to remain in Stuyvesant Town for more than one more year. Therefore, she pays little attention to the tenants association's agenda or residents' concerns about preserving affordability. However, Kara does not fit the characterization of students as completely detached from the community. For instance, she interacts with nonstudent residents by babysitting for several families: "That's another thing I love about Stuy Town is that I have jobs through it. A bunch of the families that I babysit for are through Stuy Town. So that's great." Though she does this work to earn spending money, her contact with "older" tenants creates non-student social ties within the community. She also frequents the local shops and has developed a sense of loyalty to some of the family-run businesses: "I always buy from the food cart across the street from me. I am faithful to the guy that owns the liquor store across the street. If I'm buying, like, wine or anything, I will only buy from him because he's so sweet, and he's always there working. I don't know. I just feel like he's a really sweet guy."

Admittedly, her closest friends in the community are a group of NYU students who live on her floor, but she says that she has developed relationships with other neighbors, as well:

> I have a neighbor in the corner, who as soon as I moved in, she brought over a bottle of Champagne. She's so nice. She's really nice. She's an actress, and she has lived in Stuy Town in the same apartment for thirty years. And so she's rent-control, I guess. She pays like nothing. She's a character. She's really funny. She's really nice. During [Hurricane] Sandy, she brought over chicken noodle soup. She's really sweet. I have neighbors across the hall that are also going to be seniors at NYU. They're three guys, and they're so sweet, and now we hang out like all the time. They're really, really cool. We, like, have been talking about collaborating on something [a creative endeavor], which is cool. Just having somebody, like my neighbors, I don't know, want to work together. I don't know. It's kind of cool. Another one of my neighbors owns Bell House. I think it's like, Asian food. They're really, really nice, and they give us a discount if we go there. I would have never gone to this place if it weren't for them. We ran into them in the elevator the first day we moved in, and they were like, "Yeah, come to Bell House, and we'll get you stuff for free." And we're like, "Okay."

Despite the very real tensions between college students and the longer-term Stuyvesant Town residents, Kara says that she felt welcomed when she arrived. By her account, she has made friends, or at least acquaintances, with her neighbors. Her description of her relationships with her neighbors is largely asymmetrical in that she is the recipient of some benefit or form of support. Despite probing, she did not share any stories where she reciprocated by doing something helpful or thoughtful for her neighbors. Though babysitting is helpful, she noted that the neighbors she sits for allowed her to set the schedule and that she is compensated. It seems that Kara benefits greatly from this situation by having a flexible, convenient source of additional income and a high demand for her services from large numbers of working families.

## Honeymoon Over?

In contrast to Kara's report of positive relations with her neighbors, the growing number of students living in Stuyvesant Town is a major source of tension for many longtime tenants and families. Tenants perceive students' lifestyles as threatening to the quality of life of families and older people, and conflict often arises over nuisance disputes and the highly transient nature of student populations. As with other students, Kara's short tenure in Stuyvesant Town is tied to the uncertainty of her schooling and future career:

> I was debating so much if I should sign a one-year lease or a two-year lease because I don't know what's going to happen with my, like, career . . . Maybe I get a [theater] tour or something, or something that puts me somewhere else. And as much as I'd love to stay here, I would also be really open to, like, a tour or maybe working on a cruise line. Anything. I'm like, just excited to start working, and so I don't think it would be smart for me to sign a two-year lease. 'Cause I don't know what's gonna happen.

Notably, Kara does not even mention the financial aspect of signing a lease, possibly because she is not planning to support herself in the next few years as she begins a career in the arts in the city. Uncertainty about the future is reasonable at this life-cycle stage, and is the very reason that students make a poor fit in a community that has long valued length of residence, investment in the neighborhood, and forming meaningful relationships with neighbors.

Kara's case illustrates that Stuyvesant Town's population churning is the result of both student lifestyles and management practices. When Kara and her roommate received their renewal lease at the end of their first year, they were shocked to see a rent increase of 20 percent, $600 per month more than the first year. In Kara's case, her mother stepped in and fought back. After finding out that the leasing office was listing comparable apartments to new tenants at lower rates than Kara's renewal price, her mother called the leasing office and negotiated a smaller increase of 5 percent or $150. Arguably, college students are less informed and skilled about handling such matters, and many have parents that pay the rent anyway, so they respond to rent increases by asking their parents for the extra money or else they move.

However, the more stable tenants who want to stay in Stuyvesant Town have suffered financial hardship in their efforts to cover rent increases associated with lease renewal, and many others have been forced out by the new costs. Tenants generally assume that management encourages high tenant turnover because a rise in vacancies translates into raising the maximum allowable rent, as decided in the Roberts case. To most, management has not been concerned about the negative effects of transiency on the community, and has been single-mindedly concentrated on extracting the most profit possible from each apartment.

## Studentification and Disorder

There is no doubt that the number of college students in the United States is growing; between 1990 and 2000 the number of students enrolled in degree programs increased by 11 percent. In the following decade, it increased 37 percent, from 15.3 million to 21 million.[2] Students bring with them different lifestyles, hours, interests, and habits, which has resulted in a growing debate over the impact of the increasing number of college students on existing communities located near colleges. The trend, termed "studentification,"[3] is characterized by an increasing presence of students in previously stable communities, often accompanied by social and environmental changes, such as more noise, traffic, garbage, disorderly behavior, and frequent visitors coming and going at all hours. In places where studentification is occurring, landlords convert living spaces into units with extra rooms in order to accommodate the growing student demand for housing and to maximize the amount of rent they can charge for an apartment. These changes often create social conflict for residents who stay or else drive out families and displace long-term residents. The effects of studentification are worsened by the lack of policy and planning related to student housing and the assumption that the unregulated private rental sector and associated developers will simply absorb the demand.[4] As a result, student housing becomes increasingly concentrated in residential neighborhoods, desta-bilizing established communities.[5]

Though unexpected in a city like New York, the increasing presence of students in Stuyvesant Town fits this model of studentification. Residents assert that students are inconsiderate neighbors who are regularly noisy, host loud parties and gatherings with frequent visitors, and engage in other nuisance behaviors that show that they have little understanding (or concern) about how to live in close quarters in a non-student residential community. At times, Kara seemed oblivious to the impact that her own behaviors have had on her neighbors, and at other times, she seemed to suggest that her neighbors should simply be less uptight. Kara explained that she has a loud speaking voice and that as a musical theater major, she needs to spend a lot of time singing and dancing in her apartment. Though she knows that she and her friends annoy the neighbors, Kara thinks that they should understand that it is just part of her oversized personality. She seemed heartened by the fact that her neighbors have not directly complained to her, interpreting this to mean that her impact on them is negligible: "I'm really loud with singing. I'm always singing in my apartment at night or practicing dance or something. I probably really annoy my neighbors, but they don't say anything."

She went on to describe her apartment as *the* gathering place for her friends. Kara then conceded that, in fact, her neighbors have called security officers to intervene because of the loud noise coming from her apartment:

> The Stuy Town police have come to my apartment one time. I wasn't having, like, a party, but my friends were just really loud because we're musical theater majors, so we're just a loud bunch. So, they came one time, but they were just like, really nice about it. And I was like, "I'm sorry." But they were really nice about it.

Kara minimized this incident, interpreting the security guards' polite attitude as validation that her behaviors are not really considered a meaningful nuisance. Even if her interpretation is correct in this case, many residents argue that security staff members tend to downplay or dismiss nuisance neighbors. Tenants report that they find it difficult to convince security to intervene, and they complain that the procedure for handling such matters is rather elaborate. First, a tenant has to call security, which could take a half hour or more to arrive. Then, the guard must actually hear the noise or witness the problem; otherwise, no official record of a nuisance behavior is recorded, and the inquiry is terminated. This is problematic because tenants often wait for a period of time before calling security, allowing for a drop in the noise level or a winding down of the festivities. When a security guard does hear a disturbance, it must be deemed excessively loud. Only then does the guard knock on the neighbor's door to request that the tenant quiet the guests. As Kara reported, this is a rather gentle warning, and it is up to the tenant to comply. Unlike college dorms, which have quiet hours, resident assistants who can "write someone up," and institutional penalties for noise violations, Stuyvesant Town residents have little recourse.

Tenants who reported repeated problems with loud neighbors expressed a sense of powerlessness about their situation. They indicated that security did not help, calling 311 [New York City's non-emergency police number] was pointless, and said that local police have stated that they are too busy to respond to noise complaints in Stuyvesant Town. As mentioned in earlier chapters, tenants reported that management has discouraged them from directly addressing problems with their neighbors to avoid potential conflict. However, tenants also suspect that this policy and security's lax enforcement are management's efforts to prevent the profitable population of students and younger market-rate residents from feeling harassed and spreading the word that the community is not friendly to young people. Some longtime tenants admitted that they feel uncomfortable knocking on neighbors' doors to complain, especially young tenants whom they do not know and who appear to be intoxicated. A safer route for voicing complaints, and one that longtime tenants seem inclined toward, is social media. For instance, one tenant posted about a conflict that was resolved in a friendly fashion on the day before a Super Bowl party, when loud neighbors left a letter and flowers, apologized in advance for the noise, and provided an invitation to stop by their apartment and join the party. Though frowned upon by management, residents believe that this type of personal contact could go a long way toward easing tension between neighbors.

College students have legitimate needs and interests that they are entitled to pursue that include socializing and keeping different or irregular hours, but these nonetheless conflict with community norms and neighbors' perceptions of order. When diverse groups of people with different priorities, interests, and schedules live in close proximity, there is a heightened need for established community norms and enforcement of basic guidelines about mutual respect. The new residents are inexperienced with adult responsibilities even as they crave freedom from the strict codes imposed by their parents, families, hometown communities, and universities. Their short-term tenancy also means they fail to develop strong ties with neighbors, rendering informal social controls less effective. Kara's experiences in Stuyvesant Town highlight the importance of voluntary compliance with rules and courtesies in order to create a harmonious community environment. As she explained, she and her friends view the city as their playground and her apartment is an extension of that:

> The first day that I moved in, the first thing I did was, I went to the roof. You can get up there. But you're not supposed to. And so I went up there, and I was just like, "This is amazing!" 'Cause I just like roofs. I just like rooftops. 'Cause I think it's cool. So, I went up there, and my friends and I were just kind of like, hanging out up there. We were running around taking pictures and 'cause it's such a beautiful view. And it's nice. It's huge.

A tenant reported them, and security guards arrived to the scene:

> The Stuy Town police came up and were like, "We are supposed to fine you like $500, but it's okay." At first, they were pretending to be really, really mean about it, and we were like, "Oh, my gosh. Are we going to get arrested?" But then they were sweet. And so it was fine, but I don't like that. I wish that we could go on the roof, because then we wouldn't have to be so loud in my room all the time. We could just go on the roof.

Kara fully understood that Stuyvesant Town prohibits tenants from being on the roof. She even reported that the roof door features a sign stating, "Do not enter," but she disregarded it and invited her friends to join her: "We just put like, an umbrella or something in the door, and then we looked to see if there were any cameras or anything, and there weren't. So we were like, 'Yay!'" Kara's unabashed candor in conveying this story, her confession that she is often loud, and her admission that she suspects that her neighbors dislike her behavior, all convey immaturity and disrespect for community norms. This incident, along with her story about the security officers visiting her apartment for noise problems, also illustrates the lax enforcement of noise rules in Stuyvesant Town.

Kara went on to reveal that this incident was not her only rooftop excursion. She had gone to the roof before, and having escaped the watchful eyes of tenants and security, she felt more brazen about returning with her friends. This blatant disregard for community rules is an example of student behavior that tenants believe is becoming widespread. In general, Kara seemed to think some nuisance behavior is acceptable, as long as no one complains, no one catches her in the act, and management leaves her alone. To long-term tenants, this attitude is indicative of a way of life that is, at the minimum, unneighborly, and worse, a sign of community decline that contributes to tension between neighbors.

Of course, students and youth are certainly not the only residents who disrespect neighbors and community rules. However, they are an easy target for angry residents who feel victimized by landlords and management. Kara acknowledged that she has detected hostility from older neighbors, though she seemed unsure whether it was specifically directed at her or whether she is just a symbol of college students in general. Although she seemed unable to make the connection between her behaviors and her neighbors' attitudes, she did acknowledge that the negative sentiment about quality of life issues has spread across the community and has worsened as more students have moved to Stuyvesant Town:

> I noticed in the beginning, when I first moved in, I was like, "Everyone is so nice in Stuy Town." People would just be smiling and like, saying "hi" on the street, and maybe it was because it was summer. Maybe that will start to happen again, but people started to get less nice as the year went on. That's definitely something I noticed.

\* \* \*

This chapter tells Kara's story because it is illustrative of the experiences of many Stuyvesant Town students, and it highlights the complexity of how changing demographics affect quality of life. Her experience as a privileged college student contrasts sharply with the longtime residents we have met in this book, such as Ruthie Goldblum, who moved to Stuyvesant Town in 1948 because it was her only option during the postwar housing crisis, and who has lived there ever since and is desperate to stay. Kara's narrative also gives voice to students, a group of residents who are much discussed but seldom heard. Of course, many tenants would argue that students are heard all too often, which is exactly the problem. In the next and concluding chapter, we summarize the effects of the changes in Stuyvesant Town on its residents, discuss the path forward, and suggest theoretical and policy implications regarding the right to city, affordable housing, and achieving a sense a place and community in the city.

# Conclusion

## Community and Commodity

Stuy Town, when it opened in 1947 provided our city with
11,250 affordable apartments . . . a community where trees and
parks, and shops dotted a landscape from which residents
could actually see the sky. We're bringing that same kind of
scale—and a real sense of urgency—to Sunnyside Yards . . .
and setting the same exact goal of 11,250 affordable units, as
part of a neighborhood that anyone would be proud to call
home. And in contrast to the recent history of Stuy Town,
we're going to make sure that affordable housing at Sunnyside
Yards stays that way.
—Mayor de Blasio's 2015 State of the City address

This book explains how Stuyvesant Town has become increasingly unaffordable to the kinds of people for whom it was originally intended. We
argue that the loss of New York City's middle-class housing cannot be dismissed as solely the result of an inevitable or passive tide of neighborhood
change. Nor can it be seen as a simple by-product of the weakening of rent
regulations. Rather, the loss of affordable housing stems from the interaction of these factors. The aging of Stuyvesant Town's tenant population
coincided with the emergence of policies aimed at liberalizing the housing market. Landlords and investors ran with the business opportunities
that opened up and attempted to exploit and accelerate Stuyvesant Town's
demographic change in ways that would be financially advantageous
for them. We showed how the aging of a large cohort of residents raised
the prospect of mass apartment turnover in Stuyvesant Town. We also
explained how the economic and political actors used the aging tenants as
a base from which to engineer an even more radical change in community
population composition. With the goal of maximizing profit and incen-
tivized by vacancy decontrol policies rewarding rapid tenant turnover,

Stuyvesant Town's owners and management effectively forced a growing portion of apartments into a continuous cycle, churning residents in and out of the community. Freed from the stability of its historical mission as a haven for middle-class families, Stuyvesant Town now seeks residents who wish to move there not for the promise of community, but rather for the development's convenience as a foothold to begin an ambitious life in New York City, or as a stepping stone on the way to an aspirational, higher-status residence. This case study illustrates how demographic factors interact with contemporary urban policy to destabilize existing communities. The question remains, what can be done to maintain quality of life and a sense of community when a growing number of residents only stay for a year or two, and when real estate actors engage in behaviors that threaten longtime tenants' housing security?

Stuyvesant Town is, in some ways, a highly unusual community. It is middle-class, yet everyone rents. Corporate entities have controlled Stuyvesant Town, but their authority has shifted over time. It has been subject to rent-stabilization laws and policies, but landlords have sought to circumvent them. Indeed, Stuyvesant Town defies easy categorization, and in some ways, it appears to be so unique that its lessons for other urban neighborhoods may appear to be limited. Yet the story of Stuyvesant Town also points to several important and specific trends in urban middle-class housing. For instance, it reveals the paucity of urban housing options for middle-class families and the threat to their ability to live in and have access to the city. It also highlights the complications that ensue when a large cohort ages in place to form a naturally occurring retirement community. Moreover, Stuyvesant Town illuminates the difficulties of creating multiple complementary senses of place when a growing cohort of young, childless urban professionals and college students move into in a community built for families. Finally, Stuyvesant Town's story also introduces the growing issue of "studentification" or increasing populations of itinerant students who enter stable adult communities, a phenomenon that results in part from increased college enrollments that outstrip existing university housing stocks and also from landlords' marketing strategies that target students. Student housing shortages are unlikely to decline in the near future. Total undergraduate enrollment in degree-granting postsecondary institutions increased by 48 percent from 1990 to 2012 and is projected to continue rising through

2023.[1] All of these phenomena have both structural and cultural implications for community change in a broad range of urban settings, far beyond the borders of Stuyvesant Town and New York City.

## Implications of Neoliberal Ideology for Urban Middle-Class Housing

We have shown how the neoliberal ideology of deregulation, privatization, and small government commodifies communities. At its core, the intellectual foundation of neoliberal urban policy asserts that over time, self-interested real estate actors will use their collective wisdom to provide more effective solutions to housing problems. This implies that market-based decisions are superior to those enacted by federal, state, and local government planners, which in theory are largely based on projections of housing needs and constituents' interests and preferences. Whether or not this is true on a macro level has been, and no doubt will continue to be, the subject of much debate. From the slum clearance policies of the 1930s and 1940s to more recent government efforts to use tax incentives and creative zoning laws to entice development, one observation that rings true is that solving one type of housing problem often creates others. Hence, both government-based and market-based approaches are likely to present unintended side effects. Indeed, the genesis of Stuyvesant Town was public and private interests intervening to respond to the post–World War II housing shortage, which also displaced the residents of an existing neighborhood.

As such, Stuyvesant Town has been both praised and reviled by experts on cities. Urbanists tend to have the highest regard for Jane Jacobs. In her book, *The Death and Life of Great American Cities*, she refers to the "ballet" of urban streets, and she attacks the kinds of large-scale housing complexes that Robert Moses built. Accordingly, many view Robert Moses as a villain who schemed and used his power and public money to bulldoze entire neighborhoods in order to build highways and create ugly, anonymous projects that fail to serve the citizens. Strangely, though it is not popular to suggest this, Moses' focus on high-density affordable housing, whether it was intended or not, did much to preserve middle-class community in Manhattan throughout the latter part of the twentieth century, despite Jane Jacobs's criticism of it.

One reason that critics of large-scale urban renewal projects are skeptical of their benefits to the city landscape is the often undemocratic political process that speeds them from the conceptual rendering stage to the ribbon cutting ceremony. Although the many years of negotiation that precede development projects can make "speed" seem like an absurd descriptor, once developers initiate urban development plans and gain political allies, their impact on neighborhoods can be both rapid and profound. Stuyvesant Town provides an opportunity to examine more closely how the aggressive push for a neoliberal approach to housing creates problems for communities that government regulations have sustained. Other examples of rapid change promoted by such government-backed neoliberal approaches to development are abundant.

Amanda Burden, the former City Planning Commissioner who worked under Mayor Bloomberg for twelve years, considers herself to be pro-development,[2] and has called gentrification the "improvement of neighborhoods." She is especially proud of the High Line development on the West Side of Manhattan, which features a walking trail flanked by expensive condos, and serves as a destination for locals and tourists.[3] This project was a massive undertaking that nonetheless went from concept to near completion in about ten years. The High Line project exemplifies a broader neoliberal trend toward rezoning. Indeed, during her tenure with the Bloomberg administration, Ms. Burden oversaw an unprecedented level of rezoning—40 percent of New York.[4] This neoliberal approach to development did not end with the election of a more populist mayor. For instance, the de Blasio administration has embraced Bloomberg's favored policy of inclusionary zoning, which requires that private developers reserve a specific share of new housing construction for tenants who will pay rent that is below market rate. The October 2015 sale agreement to the Blackstone Group included this type of provision. In exchange, the government allows greater zoning capacity for such buildings and provides tax credits to subsidize the affordability mandates. Such policy changes have set the stage for a flurry of development activity that continues to remake many of New York City's communities and to increase gentrification. Such strategies exemplify how neoliberal approaches to development can create rapid community change, but they also demonstrate that projects that attract developers and wealthy residents can sometimes provide benefits to the general public.

In fact, some would argue that some aspects of the Stuyvesant Town transformation has actually addressed some of New York City's housing market shortages. Its green and common spaces, separation from the surrounding city, and the large number of units that landlords can subdivide to accommodate more tenants position the housing complex to meet demand for student housing and make it a desirable starting point for young, well-paid professionals who are just embarking on their work lives in the city. On the other hand, one could argue that students and young singles do not need Stuyvesant Town as much as families and older people do; they admit that have no need for playgrounds, are not in search of community, are rarely at home, and already have access to dorms and less family-oriented apartment buildings. In addition, the use of Stuyvesant Town to solve a housing shortage for market-rate students and young singles creates new problems. For instance, the introduction of a large number of houses filled with partying students would be an unwelcome presence in almost any neighborhood, and Stuyvesant Town's current configuration of piles of students and temporary residents living cheek-by-jowl with retirees and families who desire stability creates conflict and reduces satisfaction for all groups.

Housing insecurity has been perceived as the most serious threat to Stuyvesant Town's middle-class households and is a side effect of neoliberal policies and the financialization of housing that reduces people's homes to impersonal tradable commodities. This process involves speculative investing (often by actors who are far removed from the physical property), targeted demolitions and disinvestment, and the encouragement of home ownership over renting.  Historically, admission to Stuyvesant Town meant that a family had attained reliable, permanent, affordable residency in Manhattan. This base, in turn, contributed to New York's mid-tier workforce and created a stable, safe residential community in the city. Our interviews, specifically those with middle-class families, reveal a near-universal concern that this permanency will be lost, and with it, the hope of a long and flourishing career in the city will be diminished. One possible rhetorical response from a neoliberal perspective might be to assert that industries that require such a workforce do not belong in Manhattan unless they can justify salaries commensurate with market-rate rents. Yet viewed from a rights-based perspective, in which community affordability, stability, and cohesion are seen as necessary components of vital cities, Manhattan's real estate market should not be completely overtaken by the drive to furnish intermittently occupied apartments to the world's wealthiest citizens. Doing so might easily result in overshooting the target to the point of destroying the very fabric that draws such individuals to New York in the first place.

Certainly, a large part of Stuyvesant Town's value lies in its very stability and strength of community. The problem with allowing the market to sort this out on its own, free from government influence, or with government authority favoring capital over community, is that while capital is mobile, labor is much less so. This is precisely the point of Lefebvre's generational cry that asserts a "right to the city." According to him, though "the Olympians of the new Bourgeois" can escape the material conditions of the city, the same luxury is not available to the majority of citizens who lack a voice to contest the shape of urban change. Just as industries such as manufacturing are limited in their ability to rebound when the economic winds change, extinguishing Manhattan's few remaining middle-class refuges might have lasting effects even after the real estate markets change. It is necessary to look past the short- and medium-term rents that landlords might attain and to focus on the city's longer-term health. A market-fueled exodus of middle-class and working-class people leads to class-based homogenization. Many are already finding themselves missing the very characteristics that make New York City what it is (or was), and without intervention, there may be no easy way to get it back.

As mayor, Michael Bloomberg proposed one solution to the affordable housing crisis: cramming people into even smaller spaces. The city is constructing a tower of fifty-five micro-apartments near Stuyvesant Town.[5] The units, which are sized between 250 and 370 square feet, are considered "single-adult housing" and are slated to be available for occupancy in 2016.[6] Forty percent of them will be affordable to middle-class residents, with some costing as little as $939 a month for single tenants earning a maximum of $48,100; for those earning up to $93,210, rent will be capped at $1,873 a month.[7] The rent for studio apartments in new buildings is usually between $2,400 and $2,900 a month in New York City, and they are required to be at least 400 square feet in order to meet city code.[8] Single people living in mini-spaces may be the wave of the future, but residents are unlikely to want to spend much time in tiny apartments found in high-density construction projects. It seems more likely that such places would house urban workaholics who use them exclusively as sleeping "crash pads" and for partying rather than as long-term homes in which to spend time and foster community relationships.[9]

The future of Manhattan's middle-class housing looks bleak, but New York is not alone. In large cities with high levels of income inequality and significant numbers of affluent residents, middle-class communities are becoming a smaller share of all neighborhoods and income segregation is on the rise.[10] A significant loss of middle-class neighborhoods has already been documented in Baltimore, Chicago, Indianapolis, Los Angeles, Philadelphia, San Francisco, and Washington, DC.[11] Stuyvesant Town offers a cautionary tale, but at present, it also remains an opportunity to preserve an increasingly scarce commodity, a community specifically for middle-class families in the urban core of a large city.

## Contributions to Urban Theories about the Social and Economic Value of Community Stability

Established models of neighborhood change tend to draw heavily on the ideas and language of the invasion-succession model, which focuses on populations competing for housing, and coming into conflict, which ultimately ends when one of the groups withdraws as the other overtakes the community. Another prominent approach is the neighborhood life-cycle model, also a demographic paradigm that focuses on the fact that both populations and housing age, transition, and renew.[12] In addition, as scholars have questioned the passive tone of these kinds of ecological models that tend to downplay the roles of actors' agency and institutional influences, political economy approaches to urban change have argued for a greater appreciation of the larger forces affecting communities, such as economic-political linkages and connections between business and housing.[13] For instance, regardless of residents' desires and actions, research shows that institutional forces outside of neighborhoods allocate resources to communities, and real estate actors representing financial institutions engage in discriminatory lending, steering, blockbusting, and redlining, all of which shape the composition, stability, and vitality of urban spaces.[14] Though larger community life-cycle factors triggered some of Stuyvesant Town's changes, it would be difficult to overstate the degree to which political economy issues, such as the deregulation of rents, triggered an invasion of newcomers, an escalation of population churning, and a rise in social conflict. Thus, integrating these theoretical orientations to neighborhood change provides a more inclusive understanding of the factors that contribute to or detract from urban community-building.

In essence, life-cycle explanations and political economy approaches interact. In some places, life-cycle factors are less important, such as when many stable homeowners reside within a community that has significant demographic variety across age cohorts. In such a situation, and especially in one where homeowners are sufficiently homogeneous and powerful to politically counterweight any move for change, political economy factors may have less opportunity to remake a community. When life-cycle factors become more important, as in Stuyvesant Town or any community where a large group of residents reaches a natural point of outmigration within a short period of time, the opportunity for policy to remake a community may increase unless residents are replaced by similar kinds of people. For instance, some high-status suburban communities in aging metropolitan areas are facing large property turnover rates as residents die, but the people who are buying the homes match the community's general demographic profile. In some cases, the so-called newcomers might have been community members as children and are returning to raise a family.

Stuyvesant Town's case also adds to the literature on community social disorganization, caused by population change, policy change, and resulting cultural change. Much of the research on neighborhood disorder leaves the impression that communities that are largely white and nonpoor have few struggles worth studying. However, our findings challenge this view and reveal strong divisions within this largely white, middle-class community. The fact that stabilized residents are not poor and, in some ways, are protected by rent regulation, pits them against other constituencies. This leads to a broader conversation on community that scholars, residents, landlords, and governments continue to debate: What is disorder?

Theories of disorder focus on the importance of residents and landlords for setting norms that signify to others that the community is a place where order and safety reign. Neighbors who are invested in the community are expected to monitor it, maintain it, and act on behalf of residents to prevent small problems from escalating into serious nuisances and crime. However, the elements that allow order to thrive are fading in Stuyvesant Town. Disorder tends to be lower in neighborhoods with long-term residents and higher population stability. Stability increases the chances that residents have spent enough time over the years to build meaningful social ties and to foster a sense of trust, to feel sentimentally attached and socially invested, and to possess a willingness to intervene when community problems arise. Though Stuyvesant Town has always been a rental community, tenants who rent their apartments have the capacity to be invested in the future of their homes. To families, aging retirees, and some professionals in Stuyvesant Town, disorder is defined as residents who are loud, fail to clean up after themselves, and damage the facilities. For a smaller subset, such as some of the older residents and single professionals, the sounds of children running and playing in their apartments and causing noise to pound through the ceilings constitutes disorder. To residents with the longest tenure, disorder also can be found in any change to traditions or rules, including nannies occupying too many washing machines, families and professionals with unruly, yappy pets that defecate on the lawn, or fast-moving cyclists that nearly knock them down as they walk the grounds. Most recently, it has involved student behaviors, as residents share fewer commonalities.

Students and other short-term residents represent a contingent of tenants who are more likely to engage in disorderly behavior, are less responsive to interventions, and are less concerned about the outlook in years to come. The social and physical incivilities that are sometimes called "broken windows" are unlikely to be a priority in their lives. In this context, Stuyvesant Town's management seems to have favored policing the visible forms of disorder that may dissuade future tenants from moving there, such as physical disorder (e.g., trash, vandalism, noise, and deterioration), while relaxing rules about social disorder that interfere with youthful lifestyles.

The conflicting views of disorder suggest that today's Stuyvesant Town residents have multiple definitions of community, whether they are seniors, families with younger children, or students who are seeking independence from dorm life. This calls for a reordering and negotiation of what some residents consider to be disorder, a value system that is being contested among antagonistic groups. Middle-class citizens who wish to live in the city may need to further lower their expectations of what it means to live in a quality neighborhood. However, the notion of an ideal community is, in part, mythical. Residents often have diverse experiences of the same place, based on their social positions and backgrounds. Thus, in order to achieve community in the city, the heterogeneous groups who inhabit the same space must establish strong relationships and unify politically in pursuit of their best interests.

## What Is Next for Stuyvesant Town?

Urban environments are dynamic and the story of Stuyvesant Town will continue to evolve. Although the settlement of the Roberts case in 2012 included $68.75 million in reimbursements for tenants who had been overcharged on their rents since 2003, the suit did not fundamentally alter the complex dynamics involved in Stuyvesant Town's rental landscape. For instance, the settlement set new maximums for stabilized rents that are either at or above the market rate for many apartments; this cannot preserve community stability in Stuyvesant Town.

Upon announcement of the settlement, Councilman Garodnick said he would "reserve judgment" about the decision because it could—and ultimately did—result in increased rents for many tenants, forcing many to move with as little as one-month's warning. Even though the settlement resolved some uncertainty for some tenants, unpredictability remained until October 20, 2015, when Mayor de Blasio, Councilman Garodnick, and representatives from the Blackstone Group gathered to announce the $5.3 billion sale of Stuyvesant Town. Media reports in the immediate aftermath were enthusiastic, deeming the sale a victory for housing affordability in New York. However, the reality is far more sobering.

Under the sale conditions, only 5,000 of the 11,241 units will be rent-regulated. Of these, 4,500 are to be reserved for households making less than $121,000 per year, and 500 units will be for households making less than $64,000 per year. In contrast to the founding intentions of Stuyvesant Town, the rest are to be listed as market-rate rentals, placing them far outside of the reach of New Yorkers of moderate means. At the same time, a sunset clause was imposed on the affordable units: in twenty years, or eighty-eight years after the complex first opened, it is likely that no rent-stabilized housing will remain in Stuyvesant Town.

Looking ahead, one possible future for New Yorkers is a kind of permanent state of transition—an "up or out" model. In this scenario, escalating market rates coupled with rent deregulation would force most New York City newcomers to live in difficult circumstances, such as in apartments that are too small for their families, housing that is too far from work, or in the city but financially house-poor, meaning spending so much on housing that citizens have little money left for expenses and discretionary items. Still, many New Yorkers might hold out hope that they could "make it there" within a certain time frame, at the end of which they would plan to settle down in one place, better able to live a more comfortable life. Of course, some percentage would succeed, but many more would continue to struggle in subpar conditions, and a significant number would leave for outer boroughs, New York suburbs, or cities and suburbs in other states. Hence, residents would come to the city as young and ambitious, and parallel to the professional careers to which many aspire, they would eventually move either up or out of the city.

A second possible outlook considers Stuyvesant Town to be insufficient for forming a community. Similar to the distinction found in the white flight literature that depicts aging seniors who have been "left behind," these marooned urbanites live in deteriorating neighborhoods because they are economically stranded and have insufficient resources to leave. Though research suggests that this metaphor may be overused,[15] a model in which residents are involuntarily left behind would posit that rent stabilization's market inefficiency, combined with the planned churning of market-rate units, are twin forces that conspire to trap long-term residents as their neighborhood becomes increasingly unrecognizable. The key to this scenario is management policy that focuses on market-rate tenants who will form the majority of residents. With their sights on the twenty-year rent-regulated window closing, the landlord and property managers will likely view remaining stabilized tenants as a burden. This would result in a neighborhood in which management increasingly customizes amenities to suit transient tenants, and over time, the community becomes divided along class lines, between the market-rate tenants who take advantage of an increasingly specialized slate of add-ons and stabilized tenants who must fend for themselves as a sizable yet increasingly marginalized class. A two-class model of housing in which regulated and stabilized tenants co-reside might seem to offer the best of both worlds, but it is often divisive, as evidenced by our observations of Stuyvesant Town as well as the public outrage about New York buildings with "poor doors." The stabilized tenants would be forced to deal with the social disorder wrought by the new transient class, often with the tacit approval of civic authorities such as Stuyvesant Town's management. In addition to the demographic heterogeneity, contractual differences would work against the sense of community, with market-rate and stabilized tenants living side by side and market-raters questioning why they should be invested in protecting the stabilized tenants' rights, given that this form of housing is becoming even more marginalized in Stuyvesant Town.

An unlikely protection for these tenants is the strengthening and broadening of a rent-regulation paradigm. The Rent Act of 2015, which extends rent regulation and includes some minor measures in favor of tenants' rights, may signal the persistence of regulation for years to come. On the other hand, tenants have not been successful in their push to reintroduce rent-control and rent-stabilization programs in Boston and parts of Maryland and New Jersey.[16] Although seemingly unfeasible under the neoliberal regime of the luxury city, it is hypothetically possible that some future administration would introduce new rent regulation to the city or region that would apply to a broad range of units, including those in Stuyvesant Town. However, the Blackstone Group deal seems to close the door on any future regulation that would apply only to Stuyvesant Town.

Another potential outcome now evaporated is homeownership. Condo or co-op conversion was frequently discussed between 2010 and 2015, and represented the most traditional path to stability for middle-class neighborhoods, although many cities also have stable rental communities. Equity stakes in Stuyvesant Town would have shifted the conversation and might have given middle-class families the formal voice they have lacked in recent years. Yet this path is far from a panacea. One does not have to look far to find examples of conflict between apartment owners in New York City, and the sheer scale of such an undertaking in Stuyvesant Town raised many questions, ranging from how such a deal would be structured to its viability in terms of post-deal governance.

Could the property be built up or broken into smaller parcels and sold? The Blackstone deal requires that the physical layout of the complex remain intact for the foreseeable future. Indeed, a key element of the sale was the way in which Blackstone leveraged the site's low density. Stuyvesant Town's site, with its large green spaces between buildings, contains development rights (or "air rights" used to circumvent zoning restrictions) that could be worth hundreds of millions of dollars. Thus, in an ironic twist of fate, Stuyvesant Town's park-like setting that Jane Jacobs once criticized is now a commodity that Blackstone can sell, leading to much taller buildings with higher densities elsewhere in Manhattan. Still, the sale of air rights helps to maintain Stuyvesant Town's footprint, as any future attempt to break up the parcel for dense construction would presumably require the reacquisition of development rights. For now, one thing that will be protected by the proposed sale of Stuyvesant Town is the green space. The physical character of the development will be maintained even as its mission to house the middle class continues to erode.

One could imagine that some day a developer will have designs on Stuyvesant Town's enormous parcel of land to create a brand new super-housing development with a phased demolition. A real estate developer could then use the land intensively and efficiently, constructing modern, energy-saving buildings that are easier to maintain, while also maximizing density and minimizing green space. In this scenario, "through streets" might be reintroduced to make the area more attractive for mixed-use development and retail. One barrier to such a plan could be the historical significance of the community. Tenants launched a 2008 campaign to designate Stuyvesant Town as a New York City landmark, with the hope of adding a layer of protection to their fight for affordability.[17] The *New York Times* referred to this effort as an attempt to preserve a "shrine to the ordinary."[18] However, the landscape of Manhattan changes every day. Stuyvesant Town is an important symbol of postwar construction efforts, but it seems unlikely that non-tenant historic preservationists would be successful even if they chose to spend the time and money to protest; after all, the buildings are not in the best condition, and they are far from architecturally unique.

Perhaps in the more distant future, Stuyvesant Town will become a college campus. Just as Columbia University has expanded into Harlem using eminent domain, displacing residents and disrupting the lives of local residents, NYU has drawn a great deal of controversy from Greenwich Village community members and preservationists for its aggressive development projects that have encroached on local communities. For instance, in 2014 NYU was permitted to go forward with a $6 billion expansion plan that Michael Bloomberg approved. Judges had blocked the plan in part because it would involve "implied park land," but an appeals court overturned the ruling. Now, the university will remove several community gardens and add shadowy high-rise towers and other architecture inconsistent with the historic low-rise community. Perhaps, Stuyvesant Town will serve not just NYU, but colleges and universities around the city and state as a master housing complex. If so, it could follow the model of Cornell University, located more than 200 miles away from the city in Ithaca, New York, which now has a new "tech" campus on Manhattan's Roosevelt Island using land that the city leases.

Regardless of what happens, the options outlined here are tightly circumscribed around the operating conditions of late capitalism. A final possibility is far less likely, but would involve what David Harvey has termed "spaces of hope," in which capitalist forms of land ownership are discarded in favor of a more utopian, anti-capitalist form of urbanism.[19] Without at least considering that radical form of urbanism, Stuyvesant Town's residents and decision-makers are likely to exacerbate the problems of social change presently facing the community. Urban change is uncertain, and landowners and residents will continuously adapt spaces as they reuse them. Recall that the Gas House District persisted for a long period of time, but nothing is eternal, especially residential structures designed with relatively short life expectancies.

## Final Thoughts

We have demonstrated that neoliberal policies, such as deregulating apartment rents, can subject communities to changes that transform their character. Stuyvesant Town's longtime tenants and families have lost a stable community and live in fear of rent increases that threaten to force them out of their homes and sever ties to neighbors, schools, and local businesses. Newcomers have few reasons to become attached to the neighborhood given their arrival during a hostile and tumultuous time period characterized by mid-lease rent increases, surprise apartment inspections, population churning, and high levels of uncertainty about rents. Stuyvesant Town was intended to house a fairly homogenous population of residents and families of average means. Though the brick buildings and playgrounds remain in plain view, the profile of residents has changed and the costs that they are forced to bear are hidden from the public.

Stuyvesant Town highlights the causes and effects of neighborhood change. We are convinced that federal, state, and local government officials can take a more active and protective role in helping the city's workers, families, and retirees live affordably in the city. Urban policy has shifted away from the concerns of average people, toward a focus on the wealthy and the extremely poor. Urban problems such as poor housing and slums, poverty, and social conflict can be documented, dating back to the founding of the United States, and we have come to realize that it is necessary for the federal government to intervene by allocating funds and providing aid to local jurisdictions, and by taking action to protect vulnerable populations. Though plagued by negative and sometimes unintended consequences, policies such as public housing, urban renewal, and the creation of the Department of Housing and Urban Development are examples of such interventions. Compared to the past, state and local governments have more discretion in how they use federal money, including block grants and other forms of funding. In public-private partnerships and with pro-business policies, market-driven calculations fail to take into account the costs to *all* urban residents, who are a valuable resource and want to be able to afford to remain with their families in their residential and social communities. Research describing gentrification and urban renewal suggests that many middle-class families desire urban residency, whether for convenience to work, access to amenities, or an affinity for cultures and lifestyles more easily found in cities. The fate of these desires may well depend upon the negotiation of the dual nature of neighborhoods as both communities and commodities.

Though businesses, politicians, and citizens use the word "community" in a wide array of contexts today, the story of Stuyvesant Town demonstrates that the place-based meaning of community remains significant. Even in a neoliberal city where interest-based communities are ubiquitous, residents continue to search for a tangible and meaningful sense of place. It remains a fundamental and common interest that citizens share. What is made clear in this book is that the catalyst for creating Stuyvesant Town in the 1940s remains present today: a need for middle-class families to have access to affordable housing in the city. But Stuyvesant Town flourished and became far more than a place to house large numbers of middle-class families; it became a community in every sense of the word, a reflection of the efforts of the residents who have lived there. Today, Stuy Town continues to represent the very real struggle of ordinary families who refuse to surrender their city and who insist that they have a right to stay put and hold on to their community even as they are being priced out of it.

# NOTES

## INTRODUCTION

1 Most of the names of people in this book are pseudonyms.

2 See Bagli (2010a).

3 In addition to informal conversations, field observations, and archival research, we interviewed a total of forty-nine informants between the ages of nineteen and ninety-two; forty-five were recorded and transcribed between January 2009 and May 2013. The sample includes twenty-three "newcomers," defined as residents who moved in as market-rate tenants after the waiting list for stabilized apartments closed in 2001. Twenty-six informants who moved in before the original transition to market-rate are considered "long-term" tenants. Among the long-term tenants, nine were between the ages of nineteen and twenty-nine, ten were between the ages of thirty and thirty-nine, nine were between the ages of forty and forty-nine, six were in their fifties, seven were in their sixties, five were in their seventies, and four were original tenants in their eighties and nineties.

4 This is the title of an ongoing post on Curbed NY, a blog about New York real estate and neighborhoods.

5 Mollot (2014).

6 Craig and Kaplan (2015) and Kaplan and McKinley (2015).

7 Estis and Turkel (2015).

8 Ibid.

9 Satow (2015).

10 Hackworth (2007).

11 Wolf-Powers (2005).

## CHAPTER 1. HISTORY

1 See Lewis (1980).

2 Schwartz (1993).

3 Gratz (2010).

4 New York City Housing Authority (1937: 8).

5 This quotation is from Morris (1987: 162).

6 Bloom (2008).

7 This quotation is from Reeve (1907: 334). For another perspective on New York's historic neighborhoods, see Burrows and Wallace (1998).

8 Schwartz (2007: 132).

9 See Schwartz (1993).

10 A large body of scholarship examines the use of public-private partnerships as mechanisms to redevelop neighborhoods that have fallen below their optimal use values. See Harvey (1985) for a classic overview of the private sector's intrusion into the "public city." See also Smith (1996) for an evaluation of gentrification and public-private partnerships in New York's Lower East Side.

11 See Ballon and Jackson (2007).

12 See Schwartz (1993).

13 Moses (1943a).

14 Schwartz (1993).

15 Capeci (1978).

16 Ibid., 293.

17 Biondi (2003: 121).

18 Moses (1943b).

19 Garrett (1961).

20 Plunz (1990: 256).

21 Ballon and Jackson (2007).

22 Moses (1948).

23 Krinsky (1988).

24 Mumford (1948a, 1948b). Mumford's original critique of Stuyvesant Town, "Prefabricated Blight," appeared in the October 30 issue of the *New Yorker*. His answer to Robert Moses' rebuttal appeared as "Stuyvesant Town Revisited" in the November 27 issue.

25 Mumford (1948b: 65).

26 Ibid., 68.

27 Mumford (1948a).

28 Zipp (2010).

29 See Krinsky (2007). See also Vitullo-Martin (2006).

30 Mumford (1948b).

31 Ibid., 64.

32 Mumford (1948a).

33 Fullilove (2004).

34 Zipp (2010: 92).

35 Ibid., 93.

36 Moses (1948).

37 Caro (1974).

38 Moses (1970).

39 Bagli (2013); Roberts (1946); Schwartz (1993).

40 Schwartz (1993); Bagli (2013); Schwartz (1993).

41 Schwartz (1993).

42 Zipp (2010).

43 Ibid.

**44** These figures are from 1950 decennial tract data from the U.S. Census, and Beveridge (2006).

**45** These data are from the 1950 U.S. Census tract information on foreign-born population. Presumably, many of these residents relocated to the United States after the war. It is possible that veterans from allied forces and Jewish immigrants were given preference to live in Stuyvesant Town.

**46** Moses (1970: 432–433).

**47** Fox (2006).

**48** Martin (2000).

**49** These figures are from 1960 tract data.

**50** These figures are from 1970 tract data.

**51** Demas (2002).

**52** These figures are from 1960 tract data.

**53** Smith (1996).

**54** Kennedy (1991).

**55** The Rent Act of 2015 raised vacancy deregulation to $2,700.

**56** Oser (2001).

**57** Bagli (2006).

**58** Demas (2006).

**59** U.S. Census Bureau, 2011 American Community Survey Population Division—New York City Department of City Planning (2012).

**60** Bagli (2013: 83).

**61** Brash (2011).

**62** Bloomberg in Bagli (2013: 170).

**63** Bagli (2013: 111).

**64** Finn (2006).

**65** See Brescia (2010).

**66** Fernandez (2009).

**67** See Pattillo (2013) for a review of the literature on the negative outcomes stemming from the commodification of housing and the reemergence of conceptual and theoretical frameworks that conceive of housing as a right.

**68** Ibid.; Brenner, Marcuse, and Mayer (2011).

**69** Weber (2002).

**70** Brescia (2010).

## CHAPTER 2. STAYERS THEN AND NOW

**1** This quotation is from Demas (2002: 6–7).

**2** Bayor and Meagher (1997).

**3** Zeitz (2007).

**4** Ibid.

**5** Ibid.

**6** Ibid.

**7** Ibid.

8 Margolick (2014).

9 Yancy (2008).

10 See Sabaugh, Van Arsdol, and Butler (1969).

11 New York City Department for the Aging (2012).

12 Abbott, Carman, Carman, and Scarfo (2009).

13 Mooney (2006).

14 MacLaren, Landsberg, and Schwartz (2007).

15 Stuyvesant Town-Peter Cooper Village Tenants Association (2014).

16 DeGood (2011).

17 Kocieniewski (2008).

18 Dwoskin (2010).

## CHAPTER 3 AGING IN PLACE IN THE CITY

1 Jackson (1985).

2 Ibid.

3 Garodnick (2014).

## CHAPTER 4 NEOLIBERALISM, DEREGULATION, AND THE CHALLENGES TO MIDDLE-CLASS HOUSING

1 Elliman (2015).

2 Gopal (2014).

3 Elliman (2015).

4 See Squires (1996).

5 Hackworth (2007).

6 Harvey (1989); MacLeod (2002).

7 MacLeod (2011); Young and Keil (2010).

8 Rankin and Delaney (2011).

9 Robinson (2011).

10 Leitner, Peck, and Sheppard (2006).

11 Mallach (1986).

12 Jones, White, and Dunse (2012).

13 See Friedman and Stigler's (1946) anti-rent control manifesto pamphlet, *Roofs or Ceilings,* for an early example of neoliberal housing scholarship. It was published by the Foundation for Economic Development, a libertarian think tank that states that its mission is "to inspire, educate and connect future leaders with the economic, ethical and legal principles of a free society."

14 See Brenner and Theodore (2002) and Mele (2015).

15 Brenner and Theodore (2002).

16 Gotham, Shefner, and Brumley (2001).

17 Furman Center for Real Estate and Urban Policy (2006).

18 See Berenyi (1989), Furman Center for Real Estate and Urban Policy (2006), and Schwartz (1999).

19 Waters and Bach (2014).

**20** Waters and Bach (2013).

**21** Nolan (2008).

**22** Furman Center for Real Estate and Urban Policy (2011).

**23** Levitt (2013).

**24** See Podair (2002); and Starr (1985).

**25** New York State Homes and Community Renewal (2015).

**26** See Buckley (2010) and Furman Center for Real Estate and Urban Policy (2011).

**27** Susman (2011).

**28** Furman Center for Real Estate and Urban Policy (2006).

**29** Salama, Schill, and Roberts (2003).

**30** Furman Center for Real Estate and Urban Policy (2006).

**31** Ibid.

**32** Oser (1990).

**33** City of New York (2001).

**34** Ibid.

**35** Ibid.

**36** City of New York (2014).

**37** City of New York (2001) and Schill (2001).

**38** City of New York (2001).

**39** Michael Schill, email message to authors, February, 2014.

**40** Jerry J. Salama, telephone conversation with authors, February 18, 2014.

**41** Toy (2008).

**42** Ibid.

**43** Ibid. See also Brash (2011) for an analysis of Bloomberg's use of neoliberal principles to create housing policy and address the affordability crisis in ways that favored wealthy investors and residents.

**44** Ellen, Schill, Schwartz, and Voicu (2003).

**45** Salama et al. (2003).

**46** City of New York (2004).

**47** Ibid.

**48** de Blasio (2013).

**49** Velsey (2015).

**50** Waters and Bach (2014).

**51** Ibid.

**52** Katz, Turner, Brown, Cunningham, and Sawyer (2003).

**53** Ibid.

**54** Collins (2014).

**55** Ibid.

**56** Ibid.

**57** New York State Division of Housing and Community Renewal (1993).

**58** Ibid.

**59** New York State Homes and Community Renewal (2012).

**60** Gaumer and West (2015).

61 Bratt, Stone, and Hartman (2006).

62 Phillips-Fein (2013).

63 Ibid.

64 Harvey (2005: 48).

65 New York State Homes and Community Renewal (2012).

66 Ibid.

67 Ibid.

68 Ibid.

69 Ibid.

70 Nolan (2008).

71 Ibid.

72 Ibid.

73 For a full chronology of the New York City rent regulation system, see Gurian (2004).

74 Firestone (1997).

75 Gurian (2004).

76 Ibid.

77 Ibid.

78 Ibid.

79 Gaumer and West (2015). The 2011 data are from the Furman Center for Real Estate and Urban Policy (2012) and Lee (2012).

80 Pereira and Cuevas (2015).

81 Green and Wachter (2005: 98–99).

82 Immergluck (2009: 92).

83 Fabozzi (2005: 29).

84 Aalbers (2009: 283).

85 Kiplinger.com (2014).

86 Gaumer and West (2015). These data are from selected and preliminary New York City Housing Vacancy Survey data from 2014. The data are collected every three years. The 2014 data are scheduled for a public release date of June 1, 2015, after the time of this writing. In addition, the Rent Guidelines Board cautions against comparing the released 2014 data to past years because of changes in calculations and coding.

87 Gaumer and West (2015).

88 Ibid.

89 Ibid.

90 Ibid.

91 Miller (2014).

92 Gaumer and West (2015).

93 Miller (2012).

94 Goldman and Levitt (2013).

95 See Liu (2012) and Waters and Bach (2013).

96 Elliman (2013).

97 Miller (2014).

98 See Elliman (2013) and Lee (2013).

99 See Been et al. (2005); Furman Center for Real Estate and Urban Policy (2011); and Glaeser, Kolko, and Saiz (2001).

100 Brash (2011).

101 Pesce (2014).

102 New York City Council (2013).

103 Sampson (2012).

104 Aristotle (1928).

105 Lefebvre (1968); Purcell (2002).

106 Harvey (2008: 36–37).

107 Soja (2003).

108 Harvey (2012: 20).

109 Bowles, Kotkin, and Giles (2009).

110 Ibid.

111 See Putnam (2000) and Woldoff (2002; 2011).

112 O'Leary (2013).

113 Galster, Cutsinger, and Booza (2006).

114 Reardon and Bischoff (2011).

CHAPTER 5 LANDLORDS' AND TENANTS' STRATEGIES FOR COPING WITH THE NEW YORK CITY RENTAL HOUSING MARKET.

1 Lee (2009).

2 Toy (2012).

3 Ibid.

4 Barrionuevo (2012).

5 Satow (2012).

6 Ibid.

7 Ibid.

8 Fine (1980).

9 Barbanel (2006).

10 Handschuh and Cohen (1974).

11 State of New York Office of Attorney General (2008).

12 Barbanel (2006).

13 Fung (2012).

14 Barbanel (2006).

15 Kusisto (2014).

16 See Fine (1980) and Handschuh and Cohen (1974).

17 City of Los Angeles Housing Department (2009).

18 Vitullo-Martin (2006).

19 Some of the details and caveats about vacancy increases have changed under the Rent Law of 2015.

20 Steinhardt (2003).

21 Flynn (2006).

22 Ibid.

23 Ibid.

24 Mollot (2013).

25 Ibid.

26 Liddy (2007).

27 Ibid.

28 Brown (2007).

29 See Finder (1988).

30 Liddy (2007).

31 Brown (2007).

32 Lovett (2004).

33 Ibid.

34 Ibid.

35 Santora (2010).

36 Steinhardt (2003).

37 Ibid.

38 Leland (2012).

39 Ibid.

40 Arak (2011).

41 Oh (2003).

42 Budin (2015).

43 Soja (2010: 106).

44 Garodnick (2013).

45 Stuyvesant Town-Peter Cooper Village Tenants Association (2012).

46 Stuyvesant Town-Peter Cooper Village Tenants Association (2009).

47 Durkin (2013).

48 Jonas (2010).

49 Bagli (2010b).

50 Bagli (2011).

51 Ibid.

52 Ibid.

53 Polsky (2012).

54 Stuyvesant Town-Peter Cooper Village Tenants Association (2015).

55 Bagli (2013).

56 See Glass, Woldoff, and Morrison (2014).

57 Kusisto and Brown (2014).

58 Soja (2010).

59 Soja (2010: 99).

## CHAPTER 6. THE NEW KIDS IN (STUY)TOWN: LUXURY OR LIABILITY?

1 These data are from the 2000 and 2010 Decennial U.S. Census.

2 Authors' calculations based on U.S. Census data.

3 Briquelet (2013).

4 Authors' calculations based on U.S. Census data.

CHAPTER 7. THE KIDS ARE ALL RIGHT?

1 Zukin (2010).

2 Snyder and Dillow (2012).

3 Smith (2008).

4 Ibid.

5 Ibid.

CONCLUSION

1 National Center for Education Statistics (2014).

2 Satow (2012).

3 Ibid.

4 Ibid.

5 Seifman (2013).

6 Ibid.

7 Ibid.; Wong (2013).

8 Seifman (2013).

9 Wildermuth (2012).

10 Booza, Cutsinger, and Galster (2006).

11 Ibid.

12 Schwirian (1983).

13 See, for example, Castells (1983) and Harvey (1985).

14 Galster (1990).

15 Woldoff (2011).

16 Apartment and Office Building Association of Metropolitan Washington (2008); Meacham (2003); Renda (2014).

17 Morrone (2008).

18 Kinetz (2001).

19 See Harvey (2012).

# REFERENCES

Aalbers, Manuel B. 2009. "The Sociology and Geography of Mortgage Markets: Reflections on the Financial Crisis." *International Journal of Urban and Regional Research* 33(2): 281–290.

Abbott, Pauline S., Nancy Carman, Jack Carman, and Bob Scarfo, eds. 2009. *Re-creating Neighborhoods for Successful Aging.* Baltimore, MD: Health Professions Press.

Apartment and Office Building Association of Metropolitan Washington. 2008. "Some Implications of the Re-imposition of Rent Control on Montgomery County, Maryland." https://www.aoba-metro.org/uploads/docs/2014/UM_2008_Rent_Control_Report_FINAL.pdf.

Arak, Joey. 2011. "Stuy Town Toker Told to Go to Rehab or Face Eviction." *CurbedNY*, March 4. Retrieved March 1, 2015, http://ny.curbed.com/archives/2011/03/04/stuy_town_toker_told_to_go_to_rehab_or_face_eviction.php.

Aristotle. 1928. *A Treatise on Government.* Translated from *The Greek Of Aristotle* by William Ellis, A.M. New York: E. P. Dutton & Co.

Bagli, Charles V. 2006. "Megadeal: Inside a New York Real Estate Coup." *New York Times,* December 31.

Bagli, Charles V. 2010a. "N.Y. Housing Complex Is Turned Over to Creditors." *New York Times,* January 25.

Bagli, Charles V. 2010b. "Stuyvesant Town Tenants Are Offered Co-op Plan." *New York Times,* September 13.

Bagli, Charles V. 2011. "Stuy Town and Peter Cooper Tenants Hope to Buy Apartments." *New York Times,* November 29. http://www.nytimes.com/2011/11/30/nyregion/stuyvesant-town-and-peter-cooper-tenants-hope-to-buy-apartments.html.

Bagli, Charles V. 2013. *Other People's Money: Inside the Housing Crisis and the Demise of the Greatest Real Estate Deal Ever Made.* New York: Penguin Group.

Ballon, Hilary and Kenneth Jackson. 2007. *Robert Moses and the Modern City: The Transformation of New York.* New York: W.W. Norton.

Barbanel, Josh. 2006. "80 Tenants Face Eviction for a Teardown in Midtown." *New York Times,* May 19. http://www.nytimes.com/2006/05/19/nyregion/19condo.html?pagewanted=print&_r=0.

Barrionuevo, Alexei. 2012. "Rising Tower in Manhattan Takes on Sheen as Billionaire's Haven." *New York Times,* September 18.

Bayor, Ronald H. and Timothy J. Meagher. 1997. *The New York Irish.* Baltimore, MD: Johns Hopkins University Press.

Been, Vicki, Caroline K. Bhalla, Ingrid Gould Ellen, Solomon J. Greene, Andrew E. Schinzel, and Ioan Voicu. 2005. "State of New York City's Housing and Neighborhoods." *The Furman Center for Real Estate and Urban Policy*. Retrieved December 22, 2014, http://wagner.nyu.edu/files/news/furmanreport.pdf.

Berenyi, Eileen B. 1989. *"Locally Funded Housing Programs in the United States: A Survey of the Fifty-One Most Populated Cities."* New York: *New School for Social Research*.

Beveridge, Andrew. 2006. "Stuyvesant Town and Peter Cooper Village, Then and Now." *Gotham Gazette*, September 14. Retrieved December 22, 2014, http://www.gothamgazette.com/index.php/demographics/3362-stuyvesant-town-and-peter-cooper-village-then-and-now.

Biondi, Martha. 2003. *To Stand and To Fight: The Struggle for Civil Rights in Postwar New York City*. Cambridge, MA: Harvard University Press.

Bloom, Nicholas Dagen. 2008. *Public Housing that Worked: New York in the Twentieth Century*. Philadelphia: University of Pennsylvania Press.

Booza, Jason, Jackie Cutsinger, and George Galster. 2006. *Where Did They Go? The Decline of Middle-Income Neighborhoods in Metropolitan America*. Washington, DC: Brookings Institution. Retrieved December 22, 2014, http://www.brookings.edu/research/reports/2006/06/poverty-booza)http://www.brookings.edu/research/reports/2006/06/poverty-booza.

Bowles, Jonathan, Joel Kotkin, and David Giles. 2009. "Reviving the City of Aspiration: A Study of the Challenges Facing New York City's Middle Class." Center for an Urban Future. Retrieved December 22, 2014, http://nycfuture.org/pdf/Reviving_the_Middle_Class_Dream_in_NYC.pdf.

Brash, Julian. 2011. *Bloomberg's New York: Class and Governance in the Luxury City*. Athens: University of Georgia Press.

Bratt, Rachel G., Michael E. Stone, and Chester Hartman. 2006. "Why a Right to Housing Is Needed and Makes Sense: Editors' Introduction." Pp. 1–19 in *A Right to Housing: Foundation for a New Social Agenda*, edited by R. Bratt, M. E. Stone, and C. Hartman. Philadelphia, PA: Temple University Press.

Brenner, Neil, Peter Marcuse, and Margi Mayer, eds. 2011. *Cities for People, Not for Profit: Critical Urban Theory and the Right to the City*. New York: Routledge.

Brenner, Neil and Nik Theodore. 2002. "Cities and the Geographies of 'Actually Existing Neoliberalism.'" *Antipode* 34(3): 349–379.

Brescia, Raymond H. 2010. "Line in the Sand: Progressive Lawyering, "Master Communities," and a Battle for Affordable Housing in New York City." *Albany Law Review* 73(3): 715–763.

Briquelet, Kate. 2013. "Stuy Town Tenants Fume Over Bikini Beauties Sunbathing in Children's Playground." *New York Post,*, May 12.

Brown, Eliot. 2007. "Tishman Speyer May Become Residential Giant." *New York Sun*, May 30.

Buckley, Cara. 2010. "Albany Sides with Independence Plaza in TriBeCa Rent Suit." *New York Times*, March 10.

Budin, Jeremiah. 2015. "Stuy Town Rewards Renters for Leaving Nice Yelp Reviews." *Curbed NY,* May 27. Retrieved August 1, 2015, http://ny.curbed.com/archives/2015/05/27/stuy_town_rewards_renters_for_leaving_nice_yelp_reviews.php

Burrows, Edwin G. and Mike Wallace. 1998. *Gotham: A History of New York City to 1898.* New York: Oxford University Press.

Capeci, Dominic J., Jr. 1978. "Fiorello H. La Guardia and the Stuyvesant Town Controversy of 1948." *New York Historical Society Quarterly,* October.

Caro, Robert. 1974. *The Power Broker: Robert Moses and the Fall of New York.* New York: Alfred A. Knopf.

Castells, Manuel. 1983. *The City and the Grassroots: A Cross-Cultural Theory of Urban Social Movements.* Berkeley: University of California Press.

City of Los Angeles Housing Department. 2009. "Economic Study of the Rent Stabilization Ordinance and the Los Angeles Housing Market." Retrieved December 23, 2014, https://lahd.lacity.org/lahdinternet/Portals/0/Rent/RSO_Study_Exec_Summary_wCover.pdf.

City of New York. 2001. "Mayor Giuliani Announces New York City's Financial Plan for Fiscal Years 2001–2005." Retrieved December 23, 2014, http://www.nyc.gov/html/om/html/2001a/pr021–01.html.

City of New York. 2004. "The New Housing Marketplace: Creating Housing for the Next Generation." Retrieved December 24, 2014, http://www.nyc.gov/html/hpd/downloads/pdf/10yearHMplan.pdf.

City of New York. 2014. "ANCHOR." Retrieved December 23, 2014, http://www.nyc.gov/html/hpd/html/developers/anchor.shtml.

Collins, Timothy L. 2014. "An Introduction to the New York City Rent Guidelines Board and the Rent Stabilization System." New York City Rent Guidelines Board. Retrieved December 23, 2014, http://www.nycrgb.org/html/about/intro%20PDF/full%20pdf/intro_2014.pdf.

Craig, Suzanne and Thomas Kaplan. 2015. "New York Rent Regulation Laws Expire Amid Last-Minute Talks." New York Times, June 16.

de Blasio, Bill. 2013. "One New York, Rising Together." Retrieved February 27, 2015, http://dnwssx4l7gl7s.cloudfront.net/deblasio/default/page/-/One%20New%20York,%20Rising%20Together.pdf.

de Blasio, Bill. 2015. "State of the City Address." *New York Times,* February 3.

DeGood, Kevin. 2011. "Aging in Place, Stuck without Options: Fixing the Mobility Crisis Threatening the Baby Boom Generation." *Transportation for America.* Retrieved December 23, 2014, http://t4america.org/docs/SeniorsMobilityCrisis.pdf.

Demas, Corinne. 2002. *Eleven Stories High: Growing Up in Stuyvesant Town, 1948–1968.* New York: SUNY Press.

Demas, Corinne. 2006. "Our town." *New York Times,* September 3. http://www.nytimes.com/2006/09/03/opinion/nyregionopinions/03CIdemas.html?pagewanted=print.

Durkin, Erin. 2013. "Stuyvesant Town Tenants Could Lose Millions Won in Legal Settlement." *New York Daily News,* May 6.

Dwoskin, Elizabeth. 2010. "New York's Ten Worst Landlords, Part 1." *Village Voice*, March 16.

Ellen, Ingrid Gould, Michael H. Schill, Amy Ellen Schwartz, and Ioan Voicu. 2003. "The External Effects of Place Based Subsidized Housing." Working Paper 05–02. Furman Center for Real Estate and Urban Policy, New York. http://furmancenter. org/files/publications/hsg_extern_paper_ssrn_rv7.pdf

Elliman, Douglas. 2013. *New York Real Estate Market Reports*. Douglas Elliman Real Estate: New York. Retrieved December 23, 2014, http://www.elliman.com/ reports-and-guides/reports/new-york-city/1q-2013-manhattan-sales/1–408.

Elliman, Douglas. 2015. "The Elliman Report: May 2015." Douglas Elliman Real Estate: New York. Retrieved July 14, 2015, http://www.elliman.com/pdf/ f2e3f5d6f1cae97433b2b8ea27da3bc95f1d7e5b.

Estis, Warren A. and Jeffrey Turkel. 2015. "Noteworthy Changes En-acted by the Rent Act of 2015." *New York Law Journal*, July 1. Retrieved July 21, 2015, http://www.newyorklawjournal.com/id=1202730988580/ Noteworthy-Changes-Enacted-by-the-Rent-Act-of-2015?slreturn=20150609130326.

Fabozzi, Frank J. 2005. *The Handbook of Fixed Income Securities*. New York: McGraw-Hill.

Fernandez, Manny. 2009. "At Independence Plaza North in TriBeCa, a Dispute Over Tax Breaks and Rents." *New York Times,* November 4.

Finder, Alan. 1988. "Fred Knapp, Private Eye, Scourge of Illegal Tenants." *New York Times*, May 9.

Fine, David A. 1980. "The Condominium Conversion Problem: Causes and Solutions." *Duke Law Journal* 306: 306–335.

Finn, Daniel R. 2006. "25,000 Constituents, Their Destiny on the Line." *New York Times*, September 22.

Firestone, David. 1997. "Rent Regulations Firmly Supported in New York City." *New York Times*, June 11.

Flynn, Gerard. 2006. "Metlife: Tenants 'Not Qualified' to Buy Stuy Town." *Villager*, September 20.

Fox, Amy. 2006. "Battle in Black and White." *New York Times*, March 26.

Friedman, Milton and George Stigler. 1946. *Roofs or Ceilings? The Current Housing Problem*. Irvington-on-Hudson, NY: Foundation for Economic Education.

Fullilove, Mindy. 2004. *Root Shock: How Tearing Up City Neighborhoods Hurts America, and What We Can Do about It*. New York: One World/Ballantine Books.

Fung, Amanda. 2012. "For Apartment Landlords, 2011 Was Grand Indeed." *Crain's New York Business*, January 12.

Furman Center for Real Estate and Urban Policy. 2006. "State of the City's Housing and Neighborhoods." New York University. Retrieved December 23, 2014, http:// furmancenter.org/research/sonychan/.

Furman Center for Real Estate and Urban Policy. 2011. "State of the City's Housing and Neighborhoods." Retrieved December 23, 2014, http://furmancenter.org/research/ sonychan/.

Furman Center for Real Estate and Urban Policy. 2012. "Rent Stabilization in New York City." Fact Brief. New York: New York University. Retrieved December 23, 2014, http://furmancenter.org/files/publications/HVS_Rent_Stabilization_fact_sheet_FINAL_4.pdf.

Galster, George C. 1990. "Neighborhood Racial Change, Segregationist Sentiments, and Affirmative Marketing Policies." *Journal of Urban Economics* 27(3): 344–361.

Galster, George C., Jackie Cutsinger, and Jason C. Booza. 2006. "Where Did They Go? The Decline of Middle-Income Neighborhoods in Metropolitan America." Living Cities Census Series. June. Washington, DC: Brookings Institution.

Garodnick, Dan. 2013. "About." Retrieved December 21, 2014, http://www.dangarodnick.com/about.

Garodnick, Daniel R. 2014. "CW: Look into Heating Issues." *Town and Village*, Letter to the Editor, February 6.

Garrett, Charles. 1961. *The La Guardia Years: Machine and Reform Politics in New York City*. New Brunswick, NJ: Rutgers University Press.

Gaumer, Elyzabeth and Sheree West. 2015. "Selected Initial Findings of the 2014 New York City Housing and Vacancy Survey." New York City Department of Housing Preservation and Development, February 9. Retrieved March 1, 2015, http://www1.nyc.gov/assets/hpd/downloads/pdf/2014-HVS-initial-Findings.pdf.

Glaeser, Edward L., Jed Kolko, and Albert Saiz. 2001. "Consumer City." *Journal of Economic Geography* 1(1): 27–50.

Glass, Michael, Rachael A. Woldoff, and Lisa M. Morrison. 2014. "Does the Middle Class Have Rights to the City? Contingent Rights and the Struggle to Inhabit Stuyvesant Town, New York." *International Journal of Housing Policy* 14(3): 214–235.

Goldman, Henry and David M. Levitt. 2013. "NYC Council Unable to Reach Agreement on Midtown Rezoning." *Bloomberg Business*. November 12. Retrieved February 27, 2015, http://www.bloomberg.com/news/articles/2013-11-12/nyc-council-unable-to-reach-agreement-on-midtown-rezoning; http://old.gothamgazette.com/print/3095.

Gopal, Prashant. 2014. "Brooklyn Worst in US for Home Affordability." *Bloomberg Business*, December 4.

Gotham, Kevin Fox, Jon Shefner, and Krista Brumley. 2001. "Abstract Space, Social Space, and the Redevelopment of Public Housing." Pp. 313–335 in *Critical Perspectives on Urban Redevelopment* (Research in Urban Sociology, Volume 6), edited by K. F. Gotham. Bingley, UK: Emerald Group Publishing Limited.

Gratz, Roberta Brandes. 2010. *The Battle for Gotham: New York in the Shadow of Robert Moses and Jane Jacobs*. New York: Nation Books.

Green, Richard K. and Susan M. Wachter. 2005. "The American Mortgage in Historical and International Context." *Journal of Economic Perspectives* 19(4): 93–114.

Gurian, Craig. 2004. "Let Them Rent Cake: George Pataki, Market Ideology, and the Attempt to Dismantle Rent Regulation in New York." *Fordham Urban Law Journal* 31(2): 339–411.

Hackworth, Jason. 2007. *The Neoliberal City: Governance, Ideology, and Development in American Urbanism*. Ithaca, NY: Cornell University Press.

Handschuh, Gregory and Victor Cohen. 1974. "Tenant Protection in Condominium Conversions: The New York Experience." *St. John's Law Review* 48(4): 17.

Harvey, David. 1985. *The Urbanization of Capital: Studies in the History and Theory of Capitalist Urbanization*. Baltimore, MD: Johns Hopkins University Press.

Harvey, David. 1989. "From Managerialism to Entrepreneurialism: The Transformation in Urban Governance in Late Capitalism." *Geografiska Annaler*. Series B, Human Geography 71(1): 3–17.

Harvey, David. 2005. *A Brief History of Neoliberalism*. New York: Oxford University Press.

Harvey, David. 2008. "The Right to the City." *New Left Review* 53 (September–October): 23–40.

Harvey, David. 2012. *Rebel Cities: From the Right to the City to the Urban Revolution*. Brooklyn, NY: Verso.

Immergluck, Dan. 2009. *Foreclosed: High-Risk Lending, Deregulation, and the Undermining of America's Mortgage Market*. Ithaca, NY: Cornell University Press.

Jackson Kenneth T. 1985. *Crabgrass Frontier: The Suburbanization of the United States*. New York: Oxford University Press.

Jonas, Illaina. 2010. "Condo Conversion Veteran Eyes NY Apartment Complex." *Reuters*, September 15, http://www.reuters.com/article/2010/09/15/stuyvesanttown-condorecovery-idUSN1520134520100915.

Jones, Colin, Michael White, and Neil Dunse. 2012. *Challenges of the Housing Economy: An International Perspective*. Hoboken, NJ: Wiley-Blackwell.

Kaplan, Thomas and Jesse McKinley. 2015. "Tentative Deal in Albany Would Extend Rent Laws; Key Issues Are Unresolved." *New York Times*, June 23.

Katz, Bruce, Margery Austin Turner, Karen Destorel Brown, Mary Cunningham, and Noah Sawyer. 2003. "Rethinking Local Affordable Housing Strategies: Lessons from 70 Years of Policy and Practice." Discussion Paper. Washington, DC: Brookings Institution.

Kennedy, Shawn G. 1991. "Taking the Sizzle Out of Summer in Stuyvesant Town." *New York Times*, September 22.

Kinetz, Erika. 2001. "Neighborhood Report: East Side; Preserving Stuyvesant Town as a Shrine to the Ordinary." *New York Times*, November 8.

Kiplinger.com. 2014. "Most Expensive U.S. Cities to Live In." May. Retrieved December 25, 2014, http://www.kiplinger.com/slideshow/real-estate/T006-S001-most-expensive-u-s-cities-to-live-in/index.html.

Kocieniewski, David. 2008. "For Rangel, Rent-stabilized Apartments." *New York Times*, July 11.

Krinsky, Carol Herselle. 1988. "Architecture in New York City." Pp. 89–122 in *New York: Culture Capital of the World, 1940–1965*, edited by L. Wallock. New York: Rizzoli International.

Krinsky, Carol Hershelle. 2007. "View from a Tower in the Park: At Home in Peter Cooper Village." *Sitelines* 3(1): 15–16.

Kusisto, Laura. 2014. "A 'Poor Door' on a Planned New York Apartment Tower with Affordable Housing Gets a Makeover." *New York Times*, August 28.

Kusisto, Laura and Eliot Brown. 2014. "Delay for New York City on Stuyvesant Town." *Wall Street Journal*, June 12.

Lee, Moon Wha. 2009. "Selected Initial Findings of the 2008 New York City Housing and Vacancy Survey." New York City Department of Housing Preservation and Development, February 10. Retrieved March 1, 2015, http://nycrgb.org/downloads/research/hvs08/08summary.pdf.

Lee, Moon Wha. 2012. "Selected Initial Findings of the 2011 New York City Housing and Vacancy Survey," City of New York Department of Housing Preservation and Development November. Retrieved December 20, 2014, http://www.nyc.gov/html/hpd/downloads/pdf/HPD-2011-HVS-Selected-Findings-Tables.pdf.

Lee, Moon Wha. 2013. "Housing New York City 2011." City of New York Department of Housing Preservation and Development, November. Retrieved December 20, 2014, http://www.nyc.gov/html/hpd/html/pr/vacancy.shtml.

Lefebvre, Henri. 1968. *Le Droit a la Ville*. Paris: Anthropos.

Leitner, Helga, Jamie Peck, and Eric Sheppard. 2006. *Contesting Neoliberalism: Urban Frontiers*. New York: Guilford Press.

Leland, John. 2012. "They Can List, but They Can't Hide." *New York Times*, July 21.

Levitt, David M. 2013. "Related Hudson Yards Approved for $328 Million Tax Break." *Bloomberg Business*, October 15. Retrieved February 27, 2015, www.bloomberg.com/news/articles/2013-10-15/related-hudson-yards-gets-approval-for-328-million-tax-subsidy.

Lewis, Eugene. 1980. *Public Entrepreneurship: Toward a Theory of Bureaucratic Political Power*. Bloomington: Indiana University Press.

Liddy, Tom. 2007. "Tenants Blast Stuy Town 'Spying.'" *New York Post*, May 29.

Liu, John C. 2012. "Income Inequality in New York City." New York City Comptroller's Office. Retrieved December 24, 2014, http://comptroller.nyc.gov/wp-content/uploads/documents/NYC_IncomeInequality_v17.pdf.

Lovett, Kenneth. 2004. "Pet Detectives—Apt. Complex out to Evict Animals." *New York Post*, February 25.

MacLaren, Catherine, Gerald Landsberg, and Harry Schwartz. 2007. "History, Accomplishments, Issues, and Prospects of Supportive Service Programs in Naturally Occurring Retirement Communities in New York State: Lessons Learned." *Journal of Gerontological Social Work* 49(1–2): 127–144.

MacLeod, Gordon. 2002. "From Urban Entrepreneurialism to a 'Revanchist City'? On the Spatial Injustices of Glasgow's Renaissance." *Antipode* 34(3): 602–624.

MacLeod, Gordon. 2011. "Urban Politics Reconsidered: Growth Machine to Postdemocratic City?" *Urban Studies* 48(12): 2629–2660.

Mallach, Alan. 1986. "The Fallacy of Laissez-Faire: Land Use Deregulation, Housing Affordability, and the Poor." *Washington University Journal of Urban and Contemporary Law* 30(1/4): 35–72.

Margolick, David. 2014. "Lee Lorch, Desegregation Activist Who Led Stuyvesant Town Effort, Dies at 98." *New York Times*, March 1.

Martin, Douglas. 2000. "Community; Stuyvesant Town: Urban Dream at Midlife." *New York Times*, March 8.

Meacham, Steve. 2003. "Will Rent Control Make a Comeback in Boston?" *Dollars and Sense*. Retrieved January 18, 2015, http://www.dollarsandsense.org/archives/2003/0703meacham.html.

Mele, Christopher. 2015. "Contemporary Urban Development and Compounded Exclusion." Pp. 75–89 in *Race, Space, and Exclusion: Segregation and Beyond in Metropolitan America*, edited by R. Adelman and C. Mele. New York: Routledge.

Miller, Jonathan. 2012. "Change Is the Constant in a Century of New York Real Estate." Miller Samuel Inc. Retrieved January 4, 2015, http://www.millersamuel.com/files/2012/10/DE100yearsNYC.pdf.

Miller, Jonathan. 2014. "The Elliman Report, November 2014." *Monthly Survey of Manhattan, Brooklyn and Queens Rentals*. Douglas Elliman Real Estate: New York. Retrieved December 25, 2014, http://www.elliman.com/pdf/97d89d917e4b7860d09 dbe570e23458d310d9927.

Miller, Jonathan. 2015. "Elliman Report, January 2015." *Monthly Survey of Manhattan, Brooklyn and Queens Rentals*. Douglas Elliman Real Estate: New York. Retrieved February 28, 2015, http://www.millersamuel.com/files/2015/02/Rental_0115.pdf.

Mollot, Sabina. 2013. "Stuy Town Residents Get Video Intercom MCI." *Town & Village Blog*, October 17, 2014. Retrieved December 24, 2014, http://town-village.com/2013/10/17/stuy-town-residents-get-video-intercom-mci/.

Mollot, Sabina. 2014. "Roberts' Attorney Responds to Tenants' Concerns on Checks." *Town & Village Blog*, June 27, 2014. Retrieved July 26, 2015, http://town-village.com/2014/06/27/roberts-attorney-responds-to-tenants-concerns-on-checks/.

Mooney, Jake. 2006. "Counting Graying Heads." *New York Times*, January 1.

Morris, Jan. 1987. *Manhattan '45*. New York: Oxford University Press.

Morrone, Francis. 2008. "Preserving Stuyvesant Town." *New York Sun*, May 22.

Moses, Robert. 1943a. "Letter to the Editor: Stuyvesant Town Defended." *New York Times*, June 3.

Moses, Robert. 1943b. Memo, Conference with Harry Allen Overstreet. *Robert Moses Papers*, Rare Book and Manuscript Division, Box 134, August 30, New York Public Library.

Moses, Robert. 1948. "The Sky Line: Stuyvesant Town Revisited." *New Yorker*, November 27, pp. 65–68.

Moses, Robert. 1970. *Public Works: A Dangerous Trade*. New York: McGraw-Hill.

Mumford, Lewis. 1948a. "The Sky Line: Prefabricated Blight." *New Yorker*, October 30, pp. 49–55.

Mumford, Lewis. 1948b. "The Sky Line: Stuyvesant Town Revisited." *New Yorker*, November 27, pp. 66–72.

National Center for Education Statistics. 2014. "The Condition of Education: Undergraduate Enrollment." Retrieved January 26, 2015, http://nces.ed.gov/programs/coe/indicator_cha.asp.

New York City Council. 2013. "The Middle-Class Squeeze: A Report on the State of the City's Middle Class." Retrieved December 24, 2014,http://council.nyc.gov/html/action/acpdfs/middle_Class_squeeze.pdf.

New York City Department for the Aging. 2012. "Census 2010: Changes in the Elderly Population of New York City 2000 to 2010." Retrieved February 27, 2015, http://www.nyc.gov/html/dfta/downloads/pdf/demographic/elderly_population_070912.pdf.

New York City Housing Authority. 1937. *Toward the End to Be Achieved: The New York City Housing Authority, Its History in Outline.* New York: New York City Housing Authority.

New York State Division of Housing and Community Renewal. 1993. "History of Rent Regulation: New York State 1943–1993." Retrieved December 24, 2014, http://www.tenant.net/Oversight/50yrRentReg/history.html.

New York State Homes and Community Renewal. 2012. "2012 Annual Review/Office of Rent Administration." Retrieved December 24, 2014, http://www.nyshcr.org/Rent/2012AnnualReview.pdf.

New York State Homes and Community Renewal. 2015. "Mitchell-Lama Housing Program." Retrieved July 8, 2015, http://www.nyshcr.org/Programs/Mitchell-Lama/

Nolan, Kelly. 2008. "Stuy Town Blues." *BER Business Times,* December 8. Retrieved December 24, 2014, http://journalism.nyu.edu/publishing/archives/ber/2008/12/08/stuy-town-blues/.

Oh, Joong-Hwan. 2003. "Assessing the Social Bonds of Elderly Neighbors: The Roles of Length of Residence, Crime Victimization, and Perceived Disorder." *Sociological Inquiry* 73(4): 490–510.

O'Leary, Amy. 2013. "What Is Middle Class in Manhattan?" *New York Times,* January 18.

Oser, Alan S. 1990. "Perspectives: The 10-Year Housing Plan; Issues for the 90's: Management and Costs." *New York Times,* January 7.

Oser, Alan S. 2001. "The Upscaling of Stuyvesant Town." *New York Times,* January 28.

Pattillo, Mary. 2013. "Housing: Commodity versus Right." *Annual Review of Sociology* 39: 509–531.

Pereira, Ivan and Karina Cuevas. 2015. "NYC Rent-stabilized Units Increasing, But Housing Advocates Call for More Protection Laws." *AM New York,* June 3, http://www.amny.com/real-estate/nyc-rent-stabilized-units-increasing-but-housing-advocates-call-for-more-protection-laws-1.10501152.

Pesce, Nicole Lyn. 2014. "Taylor Swift's Global Welcome Ambassador Gig Questioned by New Yorkers Dee Snider, Jill Zarin and Pat Kiernan." *New York Daily News,* October 27. Retrieved March 1, 2015, http://www.nydailynews.com/entertainment/new-yorkers-question-taylor-swift-global-ambassador-gig-article-1.1989231.

Phillips-Fein, Kim. 2013. "The Legacy of the 1970s Fiscal Crisis." *Nation,* May 6.

Plunz, Richard. 1990. *A History of Housing in New York City: Dwelling Type and Social Change in the American Metropolis.* New York: Columbia University Press.

Podair, Jerald E. 2002. *The Strike that Changed New York: Blacks, Whites, and the Ocean Hill-Brownsville Crisis*. New Haven, CT: Yale University Press.

Polsky, Sara. 2012. "Stuy Town Hopefuls Take Conversion Battle to the Web." *Curbed NY*, January 26. Retrieved December 24, 2014, http://ny.curbed.com/archives/2012/01/26/stuy_town_hopefuls_take_conversion_battle_to_the_web.php.

Purcell, Mark. 2002. "Excavating Lefebvre: The Right to the City and Its Urban Politics of the Inhabitant." *GeoJournal* 58: 99–108.

Putnam, Robert D. 2000. *Bowling Alone: The Collapse and Revival of American Community*. New York: Simon & Schuster.

Rankin, Katherine Neilson and Jim Delaney. 2011. "Community BIAs as Practices of Assemblage: Contingent Politics in the Neoliberal City." *Environment and Planning A* 43:1363–1380.

Reardon, Sean F. and Kendra Bischoff. 2011. "Growth in the Residential Segregation of Families by Income, 1970–2009." (US2010 Research Brief). New York: Russell Sage Foundation. Retrieved December 24, 2014, http://www.s4.brown.edu/us2010/Data/Report/report111111.pdf.

Reeve, Arthur B. 1907. "Seeing New York in a Horse-Car." *Outlook*, June 15, pp. 331–335.

Renda, Christopher. 2014. "Bloomfield Council to Introduce Rent Control Ordinance." North Jersey.com. August 28. Retrieved January 18, 2015, http://www.northjersey.com/news/rent-control-ordinance-up-for-introduction-on-sept-2-1.1077011.

Roberts, Rosalind G. 1946. *3000 Families Move to Make Way for Stuyvesant Town: A Story of Tenant Relocation Bureau, Inc*. New York: Tenant Relocation Bureau.

Robinson, Jennifer. 2011. "2010 Urban Geography Plenary Lecture—The Travels of Urban Neoliberalism: Taking Stock of the Internationalization of Urban Theory." *Urban Geography* 32: 1087–109.

Sabaugh, Georges, Maurice D. Van Arsdol, and Edgar W. Butler. 1969. "Some Determinants of Intrametropolitan Residential Mobility: Conceptual Consideration." *Social Forces* 48: 88–98.

Salama, Jerry J., Michael H. Schill, and Richard T. Roberts. 2003. "This Works: Expanding Urban Housing." *Civic Bulletin* 35 (February). Manhattan Institute for Policy Research. Retrieved December 24, 2014, http://www.manhattan-institute.org/html/cb_35.htm.

Sampson, Robert J. 2012. *Great American City: Chicago and the Enduring Neighborhood Effect*. Chicago: University of Chicago Press.

Santora, Marc. 2010. "The Fall of Temporary Apartment Walls." *New York Times*, July 16.

Satow, Julie. 2012. "A Rental Market Surge in Brooklyn." *New York Times*, May 29.

Satow, Julie. 2015. "Why the Doorman Is Lonely: New York City's Emptiest Co-ops and Condos." *New York Times*, January 9.

Schill, Michael H. 2001. "Housing Issues and Options for New York City." *Gotham Gazette*. Retrieved February 27, 2015, http://www.gothamgazette.com/commentary/78.schill.shtml.

Schwartz, Alex. 1999. "New York City and Subsidized Housing: Impacts and Lessons of the City's $5 Billion Capital Budget Housing Plan." *Housing Policy Debate* 10(4): 839–77.

Schwartz, Joel. 1993. *The New York Approach: Robert Moses, Urban Liberals, and the Redevelopment of the Inner City.* Columbus: Ohio State University Press.

Schwartz, Joel. 2007. "Robert Moses and City Planning." Pp. 130–133 in *Robert Moses and the Modern City: The Transformation of New York,* edited by Hilary Ballon and Kenneth T. Jackson. New York: W.W. Norton.

Schwirian, Kent P. 1983. "Models of Neighborhood Change." *Annual Review of Sociology* 9: 83–102.

Seifman, David. 2013. "B'klyn Team Wins City's Bid for Kips Bay Micro-units." *New York Post,* January 22.

Smith, Darren. 2008. "The Politics of Studentification and '(Un)balanced' Urban Populations: Lessons for Gentrification and Sustainable Communities?" *Urban Studies* 45(12): 2541–2564.

Smith, Neil. 1996. *The New Urban Frontier: Gentrification and the Revanchist City.* New York: Routledge.

Snyder, Thomas D. and Sally A. Dillow. 2012. "Digest of Education Statistics, 2011." National Center for Education Statistics. Washington, DC: U.S. Department of Education.

Soja, Edward W. 2003. *Postmodern Geographies: The Reassertion of Space in Critical Social Theory.* New York: Verso.

Soja, Edward W. 2010. *Seeking Spatial Justice.* Minneapolis: University of Minnesota Press.

Squires, Gregory D. 1996. "Partnership and the Pursuit of the Private City." Pp. 266–290 in *Readings in Urban Theory,* edited by S. Campbell and S. Fainstein. Malden, MA: Blackwell.

Starr, Roger. 1985. *The Rise and Fall of New York City.* New York: Basic Books.

State of New York Office of the Attorney General. 2008. "State of New York Cooperative and Condominium Conversion Handbook 2008." Retrieved December 24, 2014, http://www.ag.ny.gov/sites/default/files/pdfs/publications/COOP%20 CONDO%20Conversion%20Handbook.pdf.

Steinhardt, Syd. 2003. "Stuy Town Tenants Wary of N.Y.U. Influx." *Villager,* November 11, 73(27).

Stuyvesant Town-Peter Cooper Village Tenants Association. 2009. "Unity Day Rally." November 12. Retrieved January 7, 2015, https://www.stpcvta.org/post/ unity_day_rally.

Stuyvesant Town-Peter Cooper Village Tenants Association. 2012. "At Last, the Roberts Litigation Is Settled." November 29. Retrieved December 24, 2014, http://www. stpcvta.org/ta/post/roberts-is-settled1.

Stuyvesant Town-Peter Cooper Village Tenants Association. 2014. "Stuy Town Peter Cooper Village Tenants Assc. Wins Rent Reduction for Sandy-Affected

Tenants." January 30. Retrieved December 24, 2014, http://stpcvta.org/ta/post/stuyvesant-town-peter-cooper-village-tenants-rent-reduction.

Stuyvesant Town-Peter Cooper Village Tenants Association. 2015. "Unity Pledge." Retrieved January 7, 2015, http://www.stpcvta.org/unity-pledge.

Susman, Sue. 2011. "18,000 Mitchell-Lama Apartments Saved from 'Unique or Peculiar' Increases." (September) Metropolitan Council Housing. Retrieved December 24, 2014, http://metcouncilonhousing.org/news_and_issues/tenant_newspaper/2011/september/18000-mitchell-lama-apartments-saved-%E2%80%9Cunique-or-peculiar%E2%80%9D-increases.

Toy, Vivian. 2008. "Winning That One in a Million." *New York Times*, March 2.

Toy, Vivian. 2012. "For Rentals, No Ceiling in Sight." *New York Times*, February 10.

U.S. Census Bureau, 2011 American Community Survey Population Division—New York City Department of City Planning. 2012. "Selected Economic Characteristics New York City and Boroughs." Retrieved December 23, 2014, http://www.nyc.gov/html/dcp/pdf/census/boro_econ_2011_acs.pdf.

Velsey, Kim. 2015. "De Blasio Heralds Sunnyside Yards as Next Stuy-Town, Unveils Other Housing Details." *New York Observer*, February 3. Retrieved March 1, 2015, http://observer.com/2015/02/de-blasio-heralds-sunnyside-yards-as-next-stuy-town-unveils-housing-plan-details/.

Vitullo-Martin, Julia. 2006. "A Surprise Look at Stuyvesant Town." *New York Sun*, July 6.

Waters, Thomas J. and Victor Bach. 2013, April. "Good Place to Work Hard Place to Live: The Housing Challenge for New York City's Next Mayor." Report published by the Community Service Society of New York. Retrieved December 24, 2014, http://www.cssny.org/publications/entry/good-place-to-work-hard-place-to-live.

Waters, Thomas J. and Victor Bach. 2014. "What New Yorkers Want from the Mayor: An Affordable Place to Live." January. Report published by the Community Service Society of New York. Retrieved December 24, 2014, http://b.3cdn.net/nycss/27ccd4d075e4ff7b10_fwm6b9i60.pdf.

Weber, Rachel. 2002. "Extracting Value from the City: Neoliberalism and Urban Redevelopment." *Antipode* 24(3): 519–540.

Wildermuth, John. 2012. "'Micro-apartment' Plan May Face Limits." *San Francisco Gate*, November 14. Retrieved January 28, 2015, http://www.sfgate.com/bayarea/article/Micro-apartment-plan-may-face-limits-4038467.php.

Woldoff, Rachael A. 2002. "The Effects of Local Stressors on Neighborhood Attachment." *Social Forces* 81(1): 87–116.

Woldoff, Rachael A. 2011. *White Flight/ Black Flight: The Dynamics of Racial Change in an American Neighborhood*. Ithaca, NY: Cornell University Press.

Wolf-Powers, Laura. 2005. "Up-Zoning New York City's Mixed-Use Neighborhoods: Property-Led Economic Development and the Anatomy of a Planning Dilemma." *Journal of Planning Education and Research* 24: 379–393.

Wong, Venessa. 2013. "Will the Middle Class Want Micro-Apartments?" *Bloomberg Businessweek*, January 23. Retrieved December 24, 2014, http://mobile.bsuiness-week.com/articles/2013-01-23/will-the-middle-class-want-micro-apartments.

Yancy, George. 2008. *Black Bodies, White Gazes: The Continuing Significance of Race.* Lanham, MD: Rowman and Littlefield.

Young, Douglas and Robert Keil. 2010. "Reconnecting the Disconnected: The Politics of Infrastructure in the In-between City." *Cities* 27(2): 87–95.

Zeitz, Joshua M. 2007. *White Ethnic New York: Jews, Catholics, and the Shaping of Post-war Politics.* Chapel Hill: University of North Carolina Press.

Zipp, Samuel. 2010. *Manhattan Projects: The Rise and Fall of Urban Renewal in Cold War New York.* New York: Oxford University Press.

Zukin, Sharon. 2010. *Naked City: The Death and Life of Authentic Urban Places.* New York: Oxford University Press.

# INDEX

Mumford, Lewis: on apartment practicality, 23; on security guards, 23; Stuy Town criticism by, 22, 30, 31; tenants condescension, 23–24

National Association for the Advancement of Colored People (NAACP), 41
National Jewish Welfare Board survey, of Jewish residents, 41–42
Naturally Occurring Retirement Communities (NORC), 52, 53, 88
Nehemiah Program, 98
neighborhood life-cycle model, 189
neoliberal housing policies, 6–14, 92, 113; community types created from, 9; deregulation and, 185; development corporations, 93; flipping neighborhoods and, 6–7, 105; government-based and market-based side effects, 185, 186; land-use consumption, 93; long-term residences influenced by, 7; place-marketing, 93; privatization, 8, 16, 20, 185; public-private partnerships, 18, 26, 93, 96; results of, 28; urban middle-class housing and, 185–89
neoliberal policies, in New York: free-market solutions favored in, 93, 106; tax abatements, tax incentives, low-interest loans to private investments, 92
New Homes Program, 98
New Housing Opportunities Program, 98
New Law Tenement House Act, of 1901, 100
New York City (NYC): Bloomberg on luxury city of, 108; decontrol of apartments in, 37, 100–103, 119, 135, 136, 183–84; first comprehensive zoning ordinances, 93; first public housing project, 93; first tenement laws, 93; fiscal crisis of 1970s, 101–2; free-market solutions in, 93, 106; gentrification of East Side, 9, 31; housing facts, 106; housing market shortage, 187; low-income renter

households, 93–94; as luxury city, 105–9; public-private partnership for development construction, 26; reasons for rent control, 26–27; rent regulation, 91–92, 106, 183; rezoning of, 186; Ten-Year Plans, 96–98; tight housing market, 91, 94
New York City East Village, 31, 60
New York City Housing and Vacancy Survey, 103
New York City Housing Authority (NYCHA), 16
New York City Rent Stabilization Law, 101
New Yorker, 22, 23
New York global investment networks, 9, 12, 92
New York government: deregulation law, 32, 135; housing subsidy, 7, 9, 12, 18, 92, 93; rent controls, 38, 91, 100; rent regulations, 7–9, 12, 18
New York Post, 122
New York Times, 19; on hotel listings in Stuy Town, 128; on Knapp, 122; on long-time residents, of Stuy Town, 54; on racial discrimination, in Stuy Town, 29; on rent regulation elimination, 103; on Stuy Town as landmark, 195
New York University (NYU): "Archives of Irish America," 40; Bloomberg approval of expansion plan for, 196; MHP ads, 125; Stuy Town close proximity to, 145–46; Stuy Town dorms for graduate students, 170
New York University students: Asada as, 145–46, 150, 153; Lenart as, 164–81; Stuy Town listed as residence hall for, 125–26; Stuy Town's partnering for, 124–27
NORC. See Naturally Occurring Retirement Communities
NORC Supportive Services Center, Inc., 53
Notice of Application by Owner for MCI Increase, 120

Soja, Edward, 134, 142

Spitzer, Eliot, 95–96

Stacom, Darcy, 34–35

Stellar Management, tax exemption violation, 37

Stigler, George, 202n13

studentification, disorder and, 176–81, 184

Stuypocalypse Now phase: Tishman-Speyer 2006 purchase during, 5, 33–37, 105, 138; Tishman-Speyer Properties 2010 mortgage default, 5, 10, 12, 47, 138

Stuy Town. *See* Stuyvesant Town

Stuy Town Reporter blog, on college students, 147, 153

Stuyvesant Tenants League, 19

Stuyvesant Town (Stuy Town): African Americans planned discrimination by, 20–21, 28, 41; apartment cost, 3, 71; community life-cycle factors and, 189–90; community mix, 2, 3; co-signers for, 86, 168; de Blasio on, 99; demographics comparing 1950 and 2000, 33; deregulation in, 6, 8–9, 11–12, 32, 36–37, 103; flipping neighborhoods in, 6–7, 105; foreign-born residents, 201n45; future uncertainty on status of, 5, 36, 46, 117, 152, 155, 192, 196–97; hotel listings for, 128; luxury market-rate apartments, 3, 60–61, 112, 118, 158–60; mortgage market bubble impact on, 105; Mumford's criticism of, 22, 30, 31; as NORC, 52; population composition changes, 54–57, 143, 183; preschool program, 75, 76; reasons for exiting, 74; rent increases, 175–76; working mothers in, 79

Stuyvesant Town, 2006 sale of, 5, 37, 105; Bloomberg administration on, 35; Garodnick on, 34; Gruen on, 36; international investors, 35; MetLife's reasons for, 33–34; property evaluation, 34; Stacom transaction handling,

34–35; tenant-led group for purchase of, 34–35, 138

Stuyvesant Town, building of, 22–27; Board of Estimates plan approval of, 20–21; criticism of, 22–23; design, 21–22; MetLife's public spaces regulations, 23; population expectations, 21–22

Stuyvesant Town, future options, 14, 34, 38, 58, 90, 136, 139, 184, 188–89, 191, 192–96; anti-capitalist form of urbanism, 196; college campus, 196; developers' sale of buildings in phases, 195; homeownership, 194–95; left behind aging seniors, 193–94; permanent state of transition, up or out model, 193; rent-regulation paradigm, 194; sale to Blackstone Group, 186, 192–95; super-housing development with phased demolition, 195

Stuyvesant Town Corporation, residents relocation assistance, 19

Stuyvesant Town landlord strategies, for rental housing market: aggressive monitoring of stabilized apartments, 121–24; capital improvements to raise rents, 118–21; NYU partnering for students, 124–27

Stuyvesant Town-Peter Cooper Tenants Association (Tenants Association), 47, 153; activism, 135–36; on college student recruitment, 126; on CW mid-lease rent increase, 5, 121; on eviction targeting, 122; impetus for, 135; logo, 139; market-rate tenants concerns neglected, 152–53; non-eviction condo conversion support, 138–40; NORC consultants work with, 53; PAR assistance, 120–21; on rent stabilization, 137; on *Roberts v. Tishman-Speyer* decision repeal, 136–37; social media and, 133, 134, 146

"The Stuyvesant Town Report" blog, 133

# ABOUT THE AUTHORS

Rachael A. Woldoff is Associate Professor of Sociology at West Virginia University. Her most recent book is *White Flight/Black Flight: The Dynamics of Racial Change in an American Neighborhood*, winner of the 2013 Best Book Award from the Urban Affairs Association. She is also a coauthor of the book *High Stakes: Big Time Sports and Downtown Redevelopment*.

Lisa M. Morrison is a Senior Economic Affairs Officer at the United Nations Department of Economic and Social Affairs in New York City and a contributing author to several UN reports including the *Report on the World Social Situation* (*RWSS*), a series that identifies social trends of international concern and provides in-depth analysis of major development issues.

Michael Glass is a Lecturer in Urban Studies at the University of Pittsburgh. Trained as an urban geographer in New Zealand and the United States, his research examines processes of urban change, including the inter-urban transfer of development policies and how regional planning processes affect urban identities.